MODERN ITALIAN PAINTING

GUIDO BALLO

Modern Italian Painting

From Futurism to the present day

WITH 155 PLATES IN COLOUR

FREDERICK A. PRAEGER · NEW YORK

Translated from the Italian by Barbara Wall

BOOKS THAT MATTER

PUBLISHED IN THE UNITED STATES OF AMERICA
IN 1958 BY FREDERICK A. PRAEGER INC.
PUBLISHERS, 15 WEST 47 STREET
NEW YORK 36, N.Y.
ALL RIGHTS RESERVED
LIBRARY OF CONGRESS CATALOG CARD NUMBER: 58-8186
COLOR PLATES PRINTED IN ITALY
TEXT PRINTED IN GREAT BRITAIN BY JARROLD AND SONS LTD NORWICH
THIS BOOK IS PUBLISHED IN ITALY BY EDIZIONI MEDITERRANEE

CONTENTS

List of Illustrations

68 F. DE PISIS—Still Life, oil on wood, 26×9 in. (65×22 cm.), A. Mazzotta Collection.

69 F. DE PISIS—Flowers, oil on cardboard, 14×20½ in. (35×51 cm.), A. Mazzotta Collection.

70 F. DE PISIS—Still Life with Bread, oil, 27×21 in. (67×52 cm.), P. Natale Collection, Rome.

71 F. DE PISIS—Street in Paris, oil, 17×21½ in. (43×53 cm.), A. Giovanardi Collection.

72 M. MACCARI—Women, oil, 20×16 in. (50×40 cm.), De Luca Collection, Rome.

74 O. ROSAI—Still Life, oil, 11½×11½ in. (29×29 cm.), Private Collection.

75 O. ROSAI—Little Concert, oil, 17½×27 in. (44×68 cm.), E. Vallecchi Collection.

76 O. ROSAI—Evening Card Game, oil, E. Vallecchi Collection.

77 O. ROSAI—Tuscan Village, oil, 40×28 in. (100×70 cm.), A. Mazzotta Collection.

78 L. VIANI—Woman of Paris, cardboard, 26½×38½ in. (66×96 cm.), De Luca Collection.

79 F. CASORATI—Seated Nude, oil, 22×29 in. (55×72 cm.), G. Palazzolo Collection, Milan.

80 F. CASORATI—Reclining Nude, oil, G. Bergamini Collection.

82 P. SEMEGHINI—Landscape, oil, 12½×8 in. (31×20 cm.), A. Giovanardi Collection.

83 P. SEMEGHINI—Figure, oil, 20×25 in. (50×62 cm.), G. Bergamini Collection.

84 V. GUIDI—Figures in Space, oil, 24×20 in. (60×50 cm.), Private Collection.

85 V. GUIDI—Figure, oil, 28×35½ in. (70×89 cm.), E. Hintermann Collection, Milan.

87 R. MELLI—Smiling Woman, oil, 16×20 in. (40×50 cm.), De Luca Collection.

89 SCIPIONE—The Prophet in Sight of Jerusalem, oil, 19×16½ in. (47×42 cm.), De Luca Collection.

90 M. MAFAI—Self-Portrait, oil, 21×25 in. (52×63 cm.), in the Artist's possession.

91 RAPHAEL—Walk on the Palatine, oil, E. Jesi Collection, Milan.

93 SCIPIONE—The Roman Prostitute, oil, 16½×19½ in. (41×49 cm.), G. Mattioli Collection.

94 SCIPIONE—Piazza Navona, sketch, oil, 16½×13½ in. (41×34 cm.), G. Bottai Collection, Rome.

95 SCIPIONE—The Pony, oil, 20½×16½ in. (51×41 cm.), G. Mattioli Collection.

97 M. MAFAI—Ponte Sisto, oil, 18×13 in. (45×32 cm.), De Luca Collection.

98 M. MAFAI—Boy with Ball, oil, 17½×52½ in. (44×131 cm.), in the Artist's possession.

99 M. MAFAI—Flowers, oil, 12½×19 in. (31×48 cm.), P. Natale Collection.

102 F. PIRANDELLO—Trees at Grottaferrata, oil, 30×28 in. (75×70 cm.), in the Artist's possession.

103 F. PIRANDELLO—Nudes, oil, 28×40 in. (70×100 cm.), in the Artist's possession.

104 F. PIRANDELLO—Still Life, oil, 16½×24 in. (41×60 cm.), Laudisa Collection, Rome.

105 G. OMICCIOLI—Suburb, oil, 17½×14½ in. (44×36 cm.), De Luca Collection.

106 O. TAMBURI—Houses at Neuilly, oil, 18½×15 in. (46×38 cm.), in the Artist's possession.

107 O. TAMBURI—Garden, oil, 24½×20 in. (61×50 cm.), in the Artist's possession.

109 F. MENZIO—Figure, oil, La Bussola Collection Turin.

110 E. PAULUCCI—Still Life, oil, 24×16 in. (60×40 cm.), Gallery of Modern Art, Turin.

111 L. SPAZZAPAN—The Hermit, tempera, 21×30 in. (53×75 cm.), La Bussola Collection.

112 E. PAULUCCI—Castle, oil, 22×19 in. (55×47 cm.), Private Collection.

114 E. MORLOTTI—Woman Washing Herself, oil, Usuelli Collection, Milan.

115 A. CARPI—Self-Portrait, oil on wood, in the Artist's possession.

116 A. SASSU—The Cyclists, 1931, in the Artist's possession.

118 A. DEL BON—Still Life, oil, 24½×15 in. (61×38 cm.), Private Collection.

119 A. DEL BON—Nude on Rocks, oil, 27×40 in. (67×100 cm.), B. Grossetti Collection, Milan.

120 U. LILLONI—The Wood, oil, 9½×6½ in. (24×16 cm.), Private Collection.

121 A. DEL BON—The Island of San Giorgio, oil, 25×28 in. (62×70 cm.), B. Grossetti Collection.

122 C. BREVEGLIERI—The Races at San Siro, oil on canvas, 34½×16½ in. (86×41 cm.), A. Mazzotta Collection.

123 C. BREVEGLIERI—The Hunter at Lambrate, oil on cardboard, 22×18 in. (55×45 cm.), E. Hintermann Collection.

124 C. BREVEGLIERI—Terrace at Ischia, oil on canvas, 28×24 in. (70×60 cm.), Private Collection.

125 G. BRANCACCIO—Composition with Figure, tempera, Private Collection.

126 B. SAETTI—Landscape with the Sun, oil, 29×20½ in. (73×51 cm.), Luraghi Collection, Rome.

127 E. MORELLI—Beside the Lake, oil, 20×16 in. (50×40 cm.), Private Collection.

128 F. TOMEA—Wild Flowers, oil, 17×22½ in. (42×56 cm.), in the Artist's possession.

129 D. CANTATORE—Girl in Grey, oil, 16×20 in. (40×50 cm.), Luraghi Collection, Rome.

130 E. MORELLI—Summer at Garda, oil, 20×16 in. (50×40 cm.), in the Artist's possession.

130 D. CANTATORE—Still Life, oil on board, 29×17 in. (72×43 cm.), Private Collection.

131 D. CANTATORE—Woman Indoors, oil, 10½×11 in. (26×28 cm.), Private Collection.

132 E. PRAMPOLINI—Geological Metamorphosis, 29×24 in. (72×60 cm.), Benedetta Collection, Rome.

133 E. PRAMPOLINI—Concrete Anatomies, 28×36 in. (70×90 cm.), Cassuto Collection, Milan.

134 A. SOLDATI—Interior with Red Bust, oil, 18½×22 in. (46×55 cm.), Cassuto Collection.

135 O. LICINI—The Dragon, oil, 11×8 in. (28×20 cm.), R. Jucker Collection.

136 O. LICINI—Amalasunta, oil, 40×32 in. (100×80 cm.), Lucio Fontana Collection, Milan.

137 A. MAGNELLI—Composition, oil, 18½×15 in. (46×38 cm.), Cassuto Collection.

139 A. MAGNELLI—Composition No. 6, oil, 18½×22 in. (46×55 cm.), Private Collection.

140 B. MUNARI—Negative-Positive, 32×32 in. (80×80 cm.), in the Artist's possession.

141 A. SOLDATI—Horizontal Image, oil, 58½×32½ in. (146×81 cm.), A. Cavellini Collection, Brescia.

142 M. REGGIANI–Composition No. 9, oil, 21½×26 in. (54×65 cm.), in the Artist's possession.

143 L. VERONESI–Composition, oil, 72×48 in. (180×120 cm.), Private Collection.

144 P. BORRA–Composition, oil, 16×20 in. (40×50 cm.), in the Artist's possession.

145 G. CAPOGROSSI–Composition, 24×29 in. (60×73 cm.), G. C. Argan Collection.

146 M. RADICE–Composition, watercolour on thin cardboard, 10½×7 in. (26×18 cm.), Private Collection.

147 P. BORRA–Composition with Figures, oil, 24×18 in. (60×45 cm.), in the Artist's possession.

148 R. BIROLLI–San Zeno the Fisherman, oil, 30×60 in. (75×150 cm.), in the Artist's possession.

149 A. SASSU–Horses at Fontemara, oil, 28×20 in. (70×50 cm.), in the Artist's possession.

151 A. SASSU–Concert, oil, 23×26½ in. (57×66 cm.), Private Collection.

152 B. CASSINARI–Green Landscape, oil, 24×20 in. (60×50 cm.), Private Collection.

153 I. VALENTI–The Island of Little Girls, oil, D. Del Bo Collection.

154 A. BADODI–The Circus, oil, 36×28 in. (90×70 cm.), F. Schettini Collection.

155 G. MIGNECO–The Lepers' Ditch, oil, 32×32 in. (80×80 cm.), Achrafian Collection, Milan.

156 G. MIGNECO–Boy Removing a Thorn, oil, 26½×20½ in. (66×51 cm.), in the Artist's possession.

157 I. VALENTI–Flying Fish, oil, Cugnasca Collection.

158 I. VALENTI–At the Gardens, oil, 18½×15 in. (46×38 cm.), Private Collection.

161 R. GUTTUSO–Crucifixion, oil, 80×80 in. (200×200 cm.), A. Della Ragione Collection.

162 R. GUTTUSO–The Sleeping Fisherman, paper on canvas, L. Mezzacane Collection, Rome.

163 R. GUTTUSO–Interior with Figure, oil, 17½×24 in. (44×60 cm.), A. Mazzotta Collection.

165 G. MIGNECO–Preparing Maize, oils, Ceccucci Collection, Milan.

167 F. FRANCESE–Boy with Calf, oil, 34½×47 in. (86×117 cm.), Private Collection.

168 M. MORENI–Return at Night, oil, 48×38 in. (120×95 cm.), Private Collection.

169 G. TURCATO–Public Meeting, oil, 46½×36 in. (116×90 cm.), P. Natale Collection.

171 R. BIROLLI–Composition in Red and Purple, oil, 52×32 in. (130×80 cm.), E. A. Beltrami Collection.

172 R. BIROLLI–Agricultural Machine, oil, 40×44 in. (100×110 cm.), in the Artist's possession.

173 R. BIROLLI–Hill in Summer, oil, 43×49 in. (107×123 cm.), in the Artist's possession.

174 B. CASSINARI–Still Life, oil, 24×15 in. (60×37 cm.), Private Collection.

175 B. CASSINARI–Motherhood, oil, 40×56 in. (100×140 cm.), F. Schettini Collection.

176 B. CASSINARI–Sea at Portofino, oil, in the Artist's possession.

178 E. MORLOTTI–Hill at Imbersago, oil, 32×32 in. (80×80 cm.), Guenzani Collection, Gallarate.

179 E. MORLOTTI–Evening in Brianza, oil, 36×36 in. (90×90 cm.), Riva Collection, Gallarate.

181 G. MELONI–The Church of S.M. della Salute, oil, 24×28 in. (60×70 cm.), P. Malcovati Collection.

182 G. MELONI–San Marco, oil, 28×22 in. (70×55 cm.), Private Collection.

183 G. MELONI–Cocks Fighting, oil, 32×24 in. (80×60 cm.), E. Hintermann Collection.

184 F. GENTILINI–Woman in the Café, 21½×29 in. (54×73 cm.), R. Maccolini Collection, Bologna.

185 F. GENTILINI–The Cathedral, 15×22 in. (38×55 cm.), Stefania Gentilini Collection.

186 F. GENTILINI–The Table, 26×32½ in. (65×81 cm.), Galérie Rive Gauche Collection, Paris.

187 A. CORPORA–Boats in the Argentario, oil, 38½×50 in. (96×125 cm.), G. C. Reda Collection, Rome.

188 A. CORPORA–Landscape, oil, 24×28 in. (60×70 cm.), Private Collection.

189 A. CORPORA–African Port, oil, 32½×40 in. (81×100 cm.), De Luca Collection.

191 AFRO–Scandal Sheet, oil, 40×28 in. (100×70 cm.), A. Cavellini Collection, Brescia.

192 AFRO–Ballet, oil, De Luca Collection.

193 AFRO–"Falso bordone", oil, 26×40 in. (65×100 cm.), A. Cavellini Collection.

195 G. SANTOMASO–Image in Green, oil, 26×42 in. (65×105 cm.), Private Collection.

196 G. SANTOMASO–Composition, oil, 18×24½ in. (45×61 cm.), in the Artist's possession.

197 G. SANTOMASO–At the Concerts of Arzignano, oil, 44×28 in. (110×70 cm.), A. Cavellini Collection.

198 E. VEDOVA–Cosmic Vision, tempera on board, 20×32 in. (50×80 cm.), Museum of Modern Art, New York.

199 E. VEDOVA–Unquiet Space No. 5, tempera on canvas, 44×44 in. (110×110 cm.), G. Giavi Collection, Venice.

201 T. SCIALOJA–June in Provence, oil, 25½×33 in. (64×82 cm.), in the Artist's possession.

202 A. MUSIC–Landscape, oil, 29×21 in. (72×52 cm.), G. Lizzola Collection, Milan.

203 G. AJMONE–Yellow Flowers, oil, 18½×22 in. (46×55 cm.), Private Collection.

204 A. CHIGHINE–Shapes in Contrast, oil, 26×33 in. (65×82 cm.), Private Collection.

The development of modern painting has been governed by one thing only: the effort to integrate new myths and idioms with the constant aim of all art—lyricism. In all ages there has been the pursuit of lyricism, but the outstanding feature of our own age has been the rapid rise, decline and fall of successive idioms and creeds, all prompted by the feeling that our restless search for an "absolute", combined with our newly won freedom, should produce an art of pristine purity. Formulas and programmes, however, by no means always produce great pictures, and often are significant only in so far as they are symptoms of, or contribute to, the cultural ethos of the time, or if they reveal intellectual vigour. Moreover, a pictorial idiom shared by a group of painters is not necessarily the outcome of a formula but of a whole complex civilization. A typical example of this is French Impressionism.

In Italy, ever since the battle over Futurism, the best painters have been aware of the various idioms in Europe, but as an indirect stimulus only. Groups have existed in Italy, of course, but they have been the exception. Moreover, there has been no widespread educated market to give Italian painting international status. The efforts of an occasional dealer and a few collectors, mainly in northern Italy, have helped, but it is only since the war that a really lively market has grown up to give Italian painters fresh stimulus and opportunity.

As a result of this, modern Italian painting shows a divorce between local or provincial forms of expression and the European idiom generally, a divorce of which Italian artists have been keenly aware, knowing as they do that a pictorial idiom is not born in isolation. Whether or not an artist thinks that he is free and independent, he is really subject to the cultural pressures that surround him. A culture may be tired and capable of offering only tired formulas, but an artist has to be aware of it; he has to be able to weigh it up for himself, preferably in the light of international competition.

But here a false myth may well arise—namely, that if you belong to an *avant-garde* culture you thereby avoid provincialism. In fact, a tired kind of provincialism can emerge even when formulas are a hundred per cent European—when inner compulsion, personal "involvement" and a deep, genuine response to life are lacking (and when this happens art falls into academicism). For the last fifty years Italian painting has swung on a pendulum between provincialism and internationalism, sometimes with a gulf between them and sometimes—in the case of outstanding painters—integrated, without any loss to local tradition. In fact, contact with Europe as a whole has served the purpose of goading artists on to new achievements precisely by encouraging the individual voice, even when its accent is dialect. This has happened with every genuine artist, even the most European ones. Picasso, for all the complexity of his idioms, has been inspired more than once by local Catalan tradition, without any direct imitation in style. He owes his success as a painter to Paris, where he has lived out his most vital experiences from Impressionism to Cubism and Expressionism, and yet his personality remains Spanish throughout. *Guernica* fulfils in a new way an ancient and forgotten Catalan tradition. Kandinsky remains a Russian even at his most abstract—we see icons and the popular traditions of his country in his allusive rhythms; while Chagall, the Parisian, recalls Russia no less, with his melancholy idylls and peculiar Jewish bitterness.

Many other examples come to the mind. But nowadays regional traditions tend to have an indirect influence only, for artists usually live in cities and lead complicated lives, and in Italy many of them have fallen for a new academicism. Others, however, stimulated by local tradition, still produce painting with a genuine and individual accent. So, to sum up, the development of modern

Italian art has had a double trend: innovation in the light of the European artistic climate, and the revaluation of ancient, local traditions as seen with a new eye.

At the beginning of the century innovation meant violence. In France and other European countries the figurative idiom was finding fresh stimuli, while in Italy official painting was dominated by the worst type of academicism.

In Italy, of course, we never experienced a genuine Romantic revival of the figurative arts in the nineteenth century. There were one or two outstanding artists, but on the whole there was no cultural development to compare with that in the other countries. Italy was far indeed from the world leadership she had enjoyed in earlier centuries. The first phase of Italian Romanticism was Romantic only in the most superficial sense. Its figurative side had no expressive value where colour was concerned, but was still inextricably tied up with neo-Classical academicism. Just a few painters in the second phase brought something fresh to their means of expression. Piccio was one of our best painters in the last century, and the fact that he had no immediate influence except on the so-called *Scapigliatura* movement is no criticism of him—the value of art cannot be measured by its cultural results. In a way he seemed out of date, with links with the eighteenth century, and yet since his revaluation by the critics he has influenced painters of this century, especially the Lombard ones, by his free use of colour. Ranzoni, too, has influenced a few twentieth-century painters—Tosi, for instance—while the Piedmontese, Fontanesi, certainly one of the most lyrical painters of the nineteenth century, has passed on his severe standards of composition. There was no real assimilation of French Impressionism in Italy, with the possible exception of Zandomeneghi, though his Impressionism was overlaid with the colours of Venice.

The most important school of painters in nineteenth-century Italy were the *Macchiaioli*, which included great figures such as Lega, Signorini, Sernesi and Fattori. Their outlook was different from that of the French Impressionists, a point that must be borne in mind if we are to understand the development of Italian art in the twentieth century; for what then happened was that some painters recast their style under the influence of international tendencies which presupposed the assimilation of French Impressionism. In other words, the Fauves' orgy of colour and the Cubists' reaction to this happened, and could only happen, because the whole experience of French Romanticism and Impressionism lay behind them. But in countries such as Italy, where this experience had made slight, if any, impact, the mere following of certain formulas, divorced from the circumstances that had brought them into being, gave rise to ambiguities of idiom.

The main difference between the *Macchiaioli* and the Impressionists lay in the fact that, for the former, colour was not the only valid means of conveying light and atmosphere—but by subtle use of chiaroscuro each *macchia* had a double value, as light or dark, and as colour. Hence, while setting themselves against the past, they in fact linked up with ancient Tuscan traditions, and in some smaller paintings achieved a purity almost like the inlaid work of fourteenth-century altar-pieces. The delicate harmony of composition and the colour—not made heavy by chiaroscuro—have influenced artists of our century, especially in Tuscany.

Following the *Macchiaioli* came the Divisionists with their complementary colours, their scientific presuppositions, their minute analysis of the sharpest effects of light. Apart from Segantini, who achieved a lyrical and crystalline luminosity in some of his mountain landscapes, the freest from scientific prejudice was Pellizza, whose *Mattina d'Estate* (Summer Morning) and *Panni al Sole* (Clothes in the Sun) are works in which the measure of the composition in no way impedes poetic freedom, though in some other paintings he failed to overcome the conflict between lyricism and sentimental anecdote. His sketches were a more successful vehicle for his social humanitarianism.

At the time of the Divisionists Italian painting was steeped in provincialism and rhetoric—both trying to cover up academicism. Official art was dominated by floral symbols, Wagnerian myths translated into insincere painting, and allegorical trees of life. Artists, whether they know it or not, are always sensitive to the machinery that exists to exploit their art—exhibitions, dealers, critics, patrons—for it creates the climate, of prejudice or toleration, in which their art has to make its way. It was this particular climate that the Futurists were determined to destroy.

It was the time when De Carolis was illustrating D'Annunzio's aestheticism; Sartorio, with a spurious and literary prettiness, was painting the frieze of the Parliament Hall in Rome; Ettore Tito was dominating the main Italian reviews; Bazzaro, Grosso, De Maria—to mention only a few—were upholding the academic compromise. Medardo Rosso, successful in Paris among artists and writers, was an isolated figure, while Gola, who never abandoned his Lombard traditions, seemed a mere dilettante in official eyes.

So we can understand the rage of the Futurists. Their task was to bring about the shock tactics that would put Italian art on the European map.

In the years before the first World War, the various *avant-garde* movements in Europe all seemed to answer to a common need. The centre of interest was no longer the object but the artist's subjective state. The object became a mere pretext or ceased to have any purpose at all. Such were the effects of crisis in an individualistic society. Space, though still captured within the two-dimensional canvas, became the symbol of a fourth dimension, outside time.

There was a flight from history. Gauguin's Tahiti myth, or Rimbaud's travels in Africa, typified the need to escape into the prehistoric past, to find absolute purity at the uncontaminated source. Professionalism became intolerable, and the Sunday painters, the new Primitives, emerged—Douanier Rousseau and Utrillo.

When the escape was not into prehistory, it was into a hypothetical future as with the Italian Futurists. The present was altogether too provisional. African idols and the masks of primitive peoples opened up new horizons. Purity of colour and form were pursued irrespective of any illustrative value. Exoticism, fostered by contact with the colonies and increased opportunities for travel, emphasized subtle intellectual aestheticisms. The influence of Bergson's intuitions was felt by artists as well as writers.

But the important point is this. The escape into prehistory, or, if you like, into the fourth dimension, resulted in a closer contact with history. The present became charged with the past, and charged with the future too, with manifestoes and proclamations aimed at opening up new avenues for expression. At the very moment when they thought they were fleeing it, painters and sculptors had their eyes on the historical past more than ever before. The whole of the past—Byzantine painting, Romanesque and Gothic painting and sculpture, the so-called Primitives, the fifteenth century, the Orientals, the Baroque, Hellenism, Ancient Greece and the Etruscans—all seemed actual and contemporary as seen through fresh eyes. Pure visibility, Croce's abolition of *kinds* of art, awareness of the relativity of the various idioms and the irrelevance of scales of value between periods and artists once a certain standard has been reached—all these things produced a new kind of criticism. In Italy Giotto, the Sienese painters, the Ravenna mosaics and fifteenth-century art underwent revaluation. Artists themselves became more and more critical as they rediscovered traditions that had long been forgotten.

The Fauves exhibited for the first time as a group in Paris in 1905, and the Brücke group was founded in Dresden in the same year. Though "savage", the Fauves were sensitive and intellectual, and their worship of colour seemed like a liberation of instinct. What they painted began to acquire plastic value just as colour, irrespective of what was represented. The gulf between objective representation and the "absolute image"—or the subjective vision of the artist—became wider, until more or less realistic imitation of the object gave way to pure creativity and the discovery of the relationships of colours as colour. In short, the Fauves opened the way that eventually led to non-figurative, abstract art. But the Fauves had behind them the colouring of the French Impressionists—made of light and air—and they had assimilated the refined taste of their predecessors. The Fauves, in fact—and particularly Matisse, who was their most lyrical exponent—felt and expressed pure colour. Yet they had no pedantic programme. For them Fauvism was an experience, the need to work in total freedom from preconceived ideas. In Italy the influence of the Fauves lay mainly in the free play of colour harmonies, but the Italians lacked the refined taste of the French which was the legacy of Impressionism.

It might be tempting to compare the Brücke group with the Fauves, except that it began in Dresden in 1905 and behind it lay all the exasperated feelings of German Romanticism. Though the Expressionism of the Brücke group, like that of the Fauves, had reached a point of revolt against all forms of Naturalism, it had arrived there along a different path. The idea of the Brücke painters was to look not at what was in front of them, but at what lay within them, so as to reach the source of impulse at the moment of emotion. They waged war against all forms of mere technical display in favour of a barbarous, elemental and expressive purity—and here again we come up against the prehistory myth. Goethe's words were fulfilled: "Painting represents what a man could and should see, not what he usually does see." Imagination was understood as inner productive force.

The revolt of these German painters began as aspiration in the moral order. They had no formulated theory. It is true that Kirchner, Nolde, Heckel, Hansen, Pechstein and Schmidt-Rottluff echoed the feeling to be found in the Fauves and shared their exaltation of colour, but they also reflected the Germanic tradition of symbolist derivations, aspiration towards an exotic Primitivism, and above all a high charge of emotion which in time became socially "committed"—especially with Grosz and, after the first World War, with the Neue Sachlichkeit movement. They were the heirs of the German tradition in its most aggravated form. True, Cézanne had already turned his attention to interior expressiveness, and Van Gogh had distorted his objective vision in the interests of subjectivity; but the inward eye of these German painters was the outcome of Romanticism.

With the Brücke group European painting took a sharp turn towards anti-Naturalism; colour was strident and discordant and there were no tonal relationships. Distortion of perspective, accentuation of particular details, the urge towards the grotesque, the wail of exasperation—all were a protest against the structure of bourgeois society and have had a considerable influence over modern painting.

In Italy Expressionism made itself felt as an influence as early as Boccioni. It was the mainspring of social revolt painting, and was to be particularly apparent in the work of the young *Corrente* group.

The exhibition commemorating Cézanne's death, which took place in Paris a year after the event, had a resounding success. No one now disputes Cézanne's supremacy as an influence on the development of modern painting. He surpassed the Impressionists by the intensity of his expression and the severity of his composition, which opened the way to Cubism and retains a following in our own time. Cézanne's power lay in his concept of reconstructing nature, but his use of colour had its influence on the Expressionists, and his ideas on the relationship between colour and form influenced isolated artists belonging to no particular school. In Italy Cézanne played a greater part than any other foreign painter in overhauling the pictorial idiom. The impact of his measured compositions coincided with a return to tradition in which form and colour achieved inner harmony.

In Paris in 1910 there were such masters as Seurat, Van Gogh and Gauguin, besides Cézanne. The methodical and luminous painting of the neo-Impressionists—Signac, Cross and Theo Van Rysselberghe—echoed the scientific theories of Henry. Simultaneous contrast of colours was pursued with mathematical care—here Seurat's example was more important than Van Gogh's. Somewhere between the Fauves and the neo-Impressionists came the last Symbolists who worked by a compromise of a more traditional kind. Yet all the new painters would have agreed with the famous words of Maurice Denis, the leader of the Symbolist group: "Bear in mind that a picture, before being a horse, a nude, or any other narrative affair, is essentially a flat surface covered with colours set out in a certain order."

This pursuit of the "absolute" pushed all the "descriptive" or "psychological" attributes of art into the background. The painting or the piece of sculpture became an object in itself, more and more free from any imitation of nature. As Matisse said: "For me expression does not consist in the passion that transforms a face or produces violent movement. No, it lies in the very arrangement of my picture—the place the shapes occupy, the empty spaces round them, the proportions; all that has its importance. Composition is the art of disposing decoratively of the various elements the painter has at his command in order to express his feelings. Every part of a picture ought to be visible and play its proper role, whether this be primary or secondary. Everything that is not useful in a picture is moribund for that very reason. A work carries with it the harmony of the whole; any superfluous detail takes the place, in the mind of the viewer, of an essential detail. . . ."

Detachment from the object was carried even further by the Cubists, who pulled it apart and put it together again with new rhythms so as to suggest the idea of it rather than its appearance. The intellectualism that all this involved was possible because of the Impressionists and the Fauves and also Cézanne, who, in his last years, had re-formed Nature in terms of cylinders, spheres and cones. Yet it would be mistaken to think that the early Cubists were entirely rationalistic in their approach; Picasso was much too open-minded to observe pedantic rules, and so were Derain and Braque.

Hence the Cubists were not so different from the Fauves as all that. The Fauves gloried in colour and contrasts of zones; the Cubists dealt more severely and constructively with colour, but never mathematically: there is always emotion of a subtle kind in their rhythms. The neo-Impressionists were much more methodical and rationalist by comparison. This is important because Cubist influence was strong in Italy at one time, but only so long as its idiom was not too rigid. The painters of the *Section d'Or*, which included Villon, Gris and Léger, pursued proportion values in a more mathematical way, but only as preparatory to the moment of creation. Geometry was never meant to produce frigidity.

And then at Munich there appeared the Blaue Reiter group, with Kandinsky, Klee and Franz Marc who gave European painting a new idiom. Klee was an extremely subtle, hermetic painter who used an allusive, private language. Kandinsky painted his first non-figurative watercolour as early as 1910, with an almost complete elimination of the object and autonomy of lines and planes. Yet the stimulus of allusion was still there—to be destroyed by the Dutch neo-Plastic group which was uncompromisingly abstract, making constructions of space with no reference to emotion. The last link with Romanticism was finally severed in the interests of a rationalistic and Calvinistic purity and a myth of structure—and this influenced a few abstract painters in Italy.

At the other end of the scale the Dada group, founded in Zürich in 1916, pushed another myth to its logical conclusion—that of emotional and intellectual anarchy, pure arbitrariness and the absurd; the precursor of Surrealism.

The coexistence in one and the same period of such opposite tendencies, yet all presupposing detachment from objective reality, was a clear proof of the state of crisis in society. Moreover, interest had shifted from the traditional conception of art as having a clear function of communication in society, to the formulation of idioms, statements, theories, creeds. And this, too, was a symptom of unrest.

In Italy, as we said above, lack of international outlets and consequent provincialism had a constricting effect. It was the task of outstanding individuals, rather than of groups, to bring about a change. Now, in the post-war epoch, Italian art from Futurism to the present day arouses interest everywhere. Standpoints have changed, a new taste has been formed among the public, and the commercial side is expanding and seems more able to meet the open and inevitable diversity of idioms.

FUTURISM

One of the most significant contributions to the revival of art was made by Futurism, though this movement was symptomatic of the times rather than productive of masterpieces—in other words its activity was "cultural". It was noisy and rhetorical and made pre-1914 Italy sit up. Unlike other *avant-garde* movements in Europe, it was not confined to aesthetics but entered the arena of politics and morals. It pressed for Italian intervention in the war and found the climate of Fascism congenial to its outlook.

When the Futurist manifesto was first launched in 1910 by the painters Boccioni, Carrà and Russolo—with whom Balla and Severini had joined forces—its primary aim was to bring Italian painting on to the European scene and oppose all forms of provincialism. The idea of Futurism had emerged a year earlier with the publication of Marinetti's declaration in the *Figaro*. In the field of painting Umberto Boccioni was Futurism's main inspirer. For Carrà the movement had no more than experimental value; while Severini, who had graduated through neo-Impressionism and was living in Paris, was painting those static compositions of classical inspiration that linked him with the Cubists. Balla, originally Boccioni's and Severini's master, was the most abstract of them all and remained rather outside the movement, while the impact of Futurism on Soffici, Sironi and Rosai, who joined the movement later, was not sufficiently strong to make them alter their idiom. As for Russolo, there are only one or two of his pictures worth remembering; he was no real painter. In the second phase of the movement, Prampolini was the liveliest figure; but his inclinations led him finally to Abstraction.

Was there a Futurist "creed" for painting and sculpture? Were the first Futurists trying to solve the problem of form or the problem of politics?

Besides the manifestoes, we can find a clear "statement" in Boccioni's writings, yet even this applies to his own works rather than to any others. His Futurist "statement" proclaims first and foremost a determination to belong to the modern world with its machinery and dynamism. He makes common cause with the Impressionists and the Divisionists in maintaining that a painting is not something to be looked at but to be lived with a total physical participation—"We will put the spectator into the middle of the picture." The Impressionists had broken up form into atmosphere and light to suggest movement; the Futurists took from them the desire to create movement, but they achieved it more intellectually and dynamically by breaking up the object into planes and volumes which, by their interplay, would suggest movement.

But Boccioni's deepest aim was always that of reconciling colour and form along the lines of Cézanne's later work. Both the Impressionists and the Fauves had gloried in vibration and colour at the expense of form, whereas the Cubists (according to Boccioni) had rejected colour as an element in the construction of an image. But "plastic dynamism", Boccioni contended, with its instantaneous breaking-up of the object, would lead the way to the fourth dimension, to the rhythm of space, to space-time, with dynamic colour playing an equal part. Plastic and chromatic dynamism would reconcile colour and form in a new way. But it was this very demand for a synthesis that showed up the inner conflict and the limitations of Boccioni's Futurist creed. Colour, whose dynamism lies in its physical and atmospheric sensuality, has a vibration independent of intellectual formulas. Form, achieved by breaking up the object into significant lines and planes, conveys the idea of movement, but if it is to remain as an abstract entity it must reject sensuous, atmospheric

Gino Severini *14 July 1913*

Carlo Carrà *Study in black and white for "La Galleria" 1912*

colour, for this finally destroys all sense of form. Hence, what was intended to be a synthesis became an antithesis, a dualism.

Apollinaire ended his somewhat critical notes on the Paris exhibition as follows: "The Futurist exhibition will encourage our young painters to be still bolder. Without their sheer boldness, the Futurists would never have dared to exhibit their pictures." Yet the fact is that in spite of this "boldness" there was something of a reversion to formal schemas in the "theory" of Futurism. In spite of the breaking-up of the object, and chromatic dynamism, imitation of nature had not yet been superseded, total reconstruction not yet achieved. There was, in fact, an unconscious compromise. The attraction to the subjective state of mind—an important factor in the Futurist theory —did not find satisfaction in purely abstract symbols; Naturalistic stylization had pride of place, and

Giacomo Balla *Rifle Shot 1915*

the symbolism became charged with psychological values which at times came near to "art nouveau" taste. In fact, few of the early Futurist paintings rose above the polemical level.

As Severini put it, Futurism was not a painter's movement in the strict sense but an intellectual attitude that aimed at bringing new life to a cultural climate that had become narrowed by clichés and provincial compromises.

Giacomo Balla's brand of Futurism puzzled people for some time owing to his picture *Cane al Guinzaglio* (Dog on a Leash) (1912). Here movement is expressed in an "illustrative" succession of moments without any real breaking-up of the object or any intention of overcoming Naturalism.

Giacomo Balla *Flower Show in the Piazza di Siena 1912*

This picture apart, Balla's work was the most abstract of all the Futurists', with no trace of Naturalism. He was the first to reject the expression of space in terms of tone, his design relied entirely on breaking up, and his colours had no sensuous content—hence there was no conflict between colour and form. And yet his work lacks Boccioni's overwhelming vitality; he achieved coherence in a subtle, cerebral way, as if he was a draughtsman endowed with a rich inventive fancy rather than a painter.

All this was the result of his taste for analysis, his meticulous care, his scrupulosity about method, his clarity of mind. His abstract forms, suggesting non-Naturalistic motion, are defined by rhythmic outlines and clear, almost transparent, colours. His abstract pictures were the outcome of a blend of the Impressionism he had absorbed in Paris, and Divisionism. As Carrieri has pointed out, he is Kandinsky's precursor. In *Dinamismo d'Automobile* (Automobile Dynamism) (1912) at the New York Museum of Modern Art, there is no object in a Naturalistic sense—it has been broken down into ellipses and other delicate, luminous shapes. *Corso dei Fiori a Piazza di Siena* (Flower Show in the Piazza di Siena) (1912) is also worked out in gay colours and dynamic rhythms. His compositions of 1913—for instance, his *Volo di Rondini—Compenetrazione di Grondaia* (Flight of Swallows —Interpenetration of Raindrops), or his *Velocità Astratta* (Abstract Speed)—are diagrams in which there is no recognizable object, merely the idea of pure movement, a fourth-dimensional world that makes us think nowadays of nuclear physics.

His compositions of 1914, however, sometimes strayed from pure Abstraction, as with his ballet scenes. In other works—such as *Insidie di Guerra—Forme di Stato d'Animo* (War Stratagems—States of Mind), *Colpo di Fucile* (The Rifle Shot) or *Dimostrazione Interventista a Piazza Venezia* (Demonstration for Intervention in the Piazza Venezia) there is an effect of mosaics and architecture—there are surfaces and volumes in symbolic movement and colours of marked plastic significance. In yet other pictures of the same year there is a frank reversion to Naturalism—for example, his *Ritratto della Contessa Castelnuovo De Luca-Cinque* (Portrait of Contessa Castelnuovo De Luca-Cinque). In

Alberi Tagliati (Felled Trees), however, we have a combination of abstract elements with boughs of Naturalistic trees, but unity is provided by the alternating cold colours that give a Surrealist impression of light. Finally in *Pessimismo e Ottimismo* (Pessimism and Optimism) (1922) and *Turbine della Vita* (Whirlwind of Life) (1929) he reverts once more to pure Abstraction. But on the whole Balla terminated his Futurist experiments later than the other signatories to the manifesto.

Umberto Boccioni *Muscular Dynamism 1913*

Luigi Russolo has already been mentioned as one of the painters who believed that Marinetti's ideas could be applied to painting. He had a fanciful, inventive but scattered genius, and his pictures are on the whole symptomatic of the time rather than works of art in their own right. Worth mentioning, however, are *La Rivolta* (The Revolt) (1911—the year Boccioni painted *Forze di una Strada*), *Autoritratto* (Self-Portrait) and *Volumi Dinamici di una Testa* (Dynamic Volumes of a Head) (1912). But Russolo was not really satisfied with the medium of painting. He made intensive studies of musical instruments and invented the *intonarumori*—which interested Stravinsky and Ravel. He wrote *L'Arte dei Rumori* (The Art of Noises) in 1916, and gave concerts with his *rumorarmonio*. After his one-man show of paintings in Paris in 1925 he abandoned Futurism.

Carlo Carrà's experiment with Futurism was a more genuine one, not only in the polemical but also in the pictorial sense, even though the spirit of Futurism was only accidental in his style. His works have little movement and he makes no use of plastically significant colour; his colour is tonal in the Lombard tradition. In fact, some of the Futurist paintings show Cubist influence and later his feeling for the static led him to the Metaphysical idiom. But Carrà was too much of a painter to be dominated by formulas; he was almost aggressively open-minded and moreover never turned his back on the Lombard tradition.

After his *Ritratto del Poeta Marinetti* (Portrait of the Poet Marinetti) of 1910, which is distorted in the interests of expression, came *Ritmi di Oggetti* (Rhythms of Objects), a picture foundational in the evolution of Futurism—yet its static composition is more suggestive of Cubism despite the fact that the rhythms are strong. In *Funerali del Anarchico Gallo* (The Funeral of Gallo the Anarchist) (1904–11), we have another example of the Naturalist influence, while in *Sobbalzi di Carrozella* (The Bumping Carriage) and, to a lesser degree, in *Tram*, we see Carrà's efforts to convey an "impression" of movement—the figurative object is glimpsed through an interplay of light and shade (here we see Tallone's influence). *Galleria di Milano* (The Milan Gallery) (1912) has a Cubist, vertical design once more, but the warm subdued tones, alternating with cold greys, give the movement "impression" again, and this is borne out in the rhythms. Between *Uscita dal Teatro* (Theatre Exit) (1910–11), which was still Divisionist and Symbolist, and *Donna e l'Assenzio* (Woman and Absinthe) (1911–12), which has force and form, we can see to what an extent Carrà had revivified his idiom. And though *Cavallo e Cavaliere* (Horse and Horseman) in *Guerra-Pittura* (Painting the War) (1915, Mattioli Collection) still shows the influence of Futurism in the conveying of movement and the use of collage, the path had been opened on to the field of Metaphysical painting.

BOCCIONI

Umberto Boccioni's idiom was highly original; uneasy almost to exasperation, and with the vitality of a primitive.

His painting shows a gulf between his detached way of seeing things and the urgency with which he painted them, but he was able to overcome this by means of movement—symbolic rather than physical, though he often found himself a prisoner of physical movement and Naturalism. He lacked the power to transmit what he felt direct to the canvas: it had to pass through his intellect, which checked his violence and impetuosity and prompted him to evolve theories and seek a method that would be permanently valid. This double-edged conflict was reflected in his character. He despised provinciality; he wanted to belong to the international vanguard; yet he felt a certain pride in being a provincial and in the position of having to break through the barriers set up by certain milieux. He used colour harshly; his aim was to achieve a new synthesis of colour and form.

But painting was not enough for him; the time came when he felt the need to express himself in sculpture. Others have done the same, but with him the explanation lay in his dissatisfaction with colour. He also felt drawn to write, to involve himself in the active political life of the times. These alternating moods of creative urgency, critical reflection and the impulse to action gave a certain element of unrest to his personality.

They also explain why French Impressionism never satisfied him and why he felt the appeal of the Expressionists of the German Brücke group. In his pre-Futurist days he thought he had found a solution to his conflict by adhering to the Lombard tradition which enabled him to achieve results impulsively and hurriedly without stifling the *élan* of his inspiration. Yet although he had previously been two years in Paris, had seen the Impressionists and Seurat, he did not realize that the clumsy colouring that weighted his pictures was in fact a legacy from the Lombard provincial tradition. The trouble was that Seurat's *Pointillisme* was a carefully calculated idiom with no urgency of expression whereas Boccioni had to express himself by means of shock and drama; he had too much dash to be satisfied by sensibility and contemplation alone. He was a primitive man from Calabria,

Umberto Boccioni *Dynamism of the Human Body 1913*

consistent and straight-forward; if there was a danger of rhetoric, it was the youthful rhetoric of a late Romantic.

Before joining the Futurists, Boccioni had already had various experiences in connexion with his art. At the beginning of the century, after the quarrel with his father who did not want him to be a painter, he went to Rome. There, like Severini, he frequented the studio of Giacomo Balla, who had recently returned from Paris full of Impressionist ideas. "Giacomo Balla became our master," wrote Severini, "and it was he who first introduced us to the technique of Divisionism though without teaching us its basic scientific laws." Balla fired them with French ideas. But in Italy Seurat's Divisionism was transformed into a fussy and detailed kind of scientific calculus used in the service of ponderous Naturalism; though Pellizza had achieved lyrical effects in some of his landscapes by means of the Divisionist technique. But beyond and behind his influence over Boccioni lay the shadow of Cesare Tallone, the Lombard. As with Pellizza, social preoccupation was apparent in Boccioni's Futurist works, though with him it took the form of wanting to shake society up from its lethargy; the task of art was to give society a shock.

Boccioni went to Paris in 1902 after winning an art prize in Rome, and so at last he was able to get really to grips with the work of Monet, Seurat, Pissarro, Cézanne and, to a lesser degree, Toulouse-Lautrec. But though he recognized the importance of these painters, he was not satisfied with Impressionism. As Argan puts it, the choice had to be made between "art as vision and art as expression, art as contemplation and art as action, Impressionism and Expressionism". He favoured Expressionism and later the influence of the Brücke group was to corroborate his choice. Nevertheless, direct contact with French painting at an early age could not but leave its mark: hence his uneasy tensions and his need to forge a new method. "I want to paint what is new: the fruit of our industrial age," he wrote in his diary in 1907.

After his visit to Russia he worked for two years in Padua and Venice and in 1908 was back in Milan. *Ritratto dello Scultore Brocchi* (Portrait of the Sculptor Brocchi) (1906) shows the conflict between the detailed *Pointilliste* technique of the landscape and the rather summary drawing of the figure in the foreground. Another example of the Lombard idiom lurking behind Pellizza. In *Autoritratto* (Self-Portrait) and *Officine a Porta Romana* (Workshops at Porta Romana)—both of 1908—interest is concentrated in the perspective which is foreshortened from above. Naturalism and Lombard provincial influence are to be found in all the paintings of this period down to *Tre Donne* (Three Women) (1909-10). But in *Figura al Sole* (Figure in the Sun), a portrait of his mother, the expressiveness is accentuated and the colour is non-Naturalistic. The influence of Toulouse-Lautrec is already there. With *Lutto* (Mourning) (1910) the German influence asserts itself—Munch and the Expressionism of the Brücke are at work, turning his colour into a symbol of a state of mind. Distortion has replaced perspective. By 1909-10 Boccioni's pre-Futurist idiom had reached a happy moment of equilibrium.

1910 was one of Boccioni's decisive years. Both Impressionism and Expressionism were groping towards new attitudes to movement. Hence he joined the Futurists at a time of acute crisis—the Futurist creed provided the answer to his deepest needs, and he became the theoretician of the movement. *La Città Sale* (The City Rises)—as well as *Lutto*—belongs to this year. Here the Expressionist whirlwind, weighted with symbols, is served by the luminous effects of Divisionism. The point of perspective is from above, and all the rest whirls with an undulating centrifugal movement.

Henceforward all Boccioni's compositions were turbid with the sense of movement. Unlike the Cubist painters, with their breaking-up of the physical object, some of the details of Boccioni's physical objects are retained—such as the head, the bottle, the table, the glasses in *La Risata* (Laughter)—but the setting, or surrounding, is fragmented into a geometry that creates a new dimension. The effect is more Surrealist than Cubist, for the Cubists cared less for Expressionism and Symbolism. *La Strada entra nella Casa* (The Street goes into the House), *Visioni Simultanee*

Umberto Boccioni *Dynamic Decomposition 1913*

Umberto Boccioni *Beneath the Pergola in Naples 1914*

(Simultaneous Visions), the series called *Addii* (Good-byes) and *Forze di una Strada* (Forces of a Street) are all states of mind in which the physical objects are not destroyed but acquire a new significance by their relationship with the surround. Space, thrown into a new dimension, opens out, is turned upside down, brings out the characteristics of some objects, pushes others into the shade. *Elasticità* (Elasticity) is more abstract: the rhythm has an undulating and centrifugal move-ment that breaks down the objects, and there is a new spatial dimension.

Boccioni's experiments with sculpture were born of his urgent need to clarify his idiom, and to what extent they succeeded is shown by the structure of the design, and the order of the colour, in the series of paintings and drawings called *Dinamismo del Corpo Umano* (Dynamism of the Human Body). Potential movement is suggested by the clear rhythm of the contours within which the colour, with its gradations of light and shade (following Cézanne), has a texture we can almost touch; this is particularly true of the huge *Dinamismo del Corpo Umano* in the Gallery of Modern Art in Milan. There is also a great deal of life in some small temperas in the same gallery; they have the same dynamic motif, but the monochrome effect makes them more sober and severe. From 1912 onwards, after the exhibition organized by Marinetti in Paris, Boccioni exhibited with other members of the Futurist group in various countries. But little by little Cézanne's influence gained ascendency over him. *Costruzione Spiralica* (Spiral Construction), *Bevitore* (The Drinker), *Sotto la Pergola a Napoli* (Beneath the Pergola in Naples) (1914) show how he had passed beyond Futurism; all that remains is the whirling, rotating composition, and the interpenetration of the objects and their surroundings. His last work, *Ritratto di F. Busoni* (Portrait of F. Busoni), which he finished before his fatal fall from a horse when doing military training in 1916 at Verona, for all its awareness of the new trends, marks the return to his pre-Futurist days.

LA VOCE and *LACERBA*

During this period the Italian *avant-garde* reviews played an all-important part in the cultural life of the country. Since the beginning of the century, writers, critics and artists—as distinct from official circles—had grouped themselves together to make the new movements and ventures known. Reviews of literature and the arts gave the reading public a new awareness, moral and political, as well as aesthetic; and it became plain that painters could not only paint but also write trenchant critical articles. Stimulus was given to the quest for new formulas. The artist, with his new sense of freedom, sought to change his angle of vision and his way of seeing things, to forge a new syntax. The move towards lyrical purity went hand in hand with a sharper critical sense. Old and forgotten traditions were examined and seen in a new light. Artists wrote essays on early painting, drew up manifestoes, overthrew time-honoured idols. Sometimes critical activities had pride of place over creative activities, as, for example, with Ardengo Soffici.

Carlo Carrà *Horse and Horseman* (collage) *1915*

25

Ardengo Soffici *Still Life* (collage) *1913*

In the early years of the century, when Florence was outstanding for artistic vitality, there was a Florentine review of the arts called *La Voce* edited by Prezzolini, and then, for a short time, by Giovanni Papini. It lasted from 1908 to 1916. In the first number Papini wrote: "Our task is twofold: to bring Italy into contact with Europe, and to reawaken her sense of her own heritage as a vital contribution to European culture." So the urge towards internationalism was not to be at the expense of national pride. Soffici was the principal artist writing for *La Voce*. He wrote on Medardo Rosso, on the Venice exhibition, on Impressionism, and he tore to pieces the painters and sculptors officially in fashion. *La Voce* took its stand against all that was spurious: it challenged D'Annunzio's aesthetics and Wagner's mysticism. In painting, the enemies were the heirs of the pre-Raphaelites, Symbolism derived from Wagnerian myths, trees of life and floral allusions; in fact, every kind of false Romanticism.

Against all this Croce was the surest arm. His *Aesthetics*, published in 1902, made its influence felt on critics and artists alike. His "art as intuition" helped artists to form a new critical awareness, and let loose a new freedom of idiom. Under Croce's influence Prezzolini upheld "man's conquest of himself . . . the duty of effort, the necessity of discipline, the sense of heroism in prosaic and pedestrian life". He saw a humble day's work as a mission. "To be a man", to rediscover simple and long-suffering humanity, was the core of *La Voce*'s moral message.

Gino Severini *Composition 1917*

It was under the auspices of *La Voce* that Soffici organized the first exhibition in Italy of French Impressionist painting, with works by Degas, Monet, Pissarro, Cézanne, Renoir, Van Gogh and Gauguin. He also organized an exhibition of sculpture by Medardo Rosso; and it was at the premises of *La Voce* in Florence that the first exhibition of Futurist painting was held in 1913, with work by Balla, Boccioni, Carrà, Russolo, Severini and Soffici.

Even more important for its direct effect on the figurative arts was another review, *Lacerba*, founded in Florence in 1913 by Papini and Soffici. This review welcomed the Futurists with open arms. Contributors included Carrà, Russolo and Boccioni, besides Soffici. "Freedom: that is all we seek" was *Lacerba*'s cry. In 1915 it made propaganda for Italy's intervention in the war.

Like Futurism, it was noisy and rhetorical, but it helped to clear the air. Futurist and Cubist drawings alternated with free verse, revolutionary typography and attacks on traditions that were over and done with. Soffici boosted the Paris *avant-garde* movements and also examined technical problems of art. Boccioni published his *Plastic Foundation of Futurist Sculpture and Painting*, and also his *ABC of Painting*. Carrà weighed in with his manifesto in favour of Total Painting (colours, sounds, smells), while Russolo tried to popularize his *intonarumori*.

This was the peak of Soffici's career; his imagination had been set free by contact with the European idioms. In 1913 his *Sintesi di Paesaggi* (Synthesis of Landscapes), though heavy, showed that he had learnt a lot from Cézanne, while his still lifes, done in the Cubist and Futurist atmosphere of *Lacerba*, show a fanciful imagination, a clear sense of rhythm, and lively clean colouring. But by 1919 he was no longer following in Cézanne's path. His "return to order" meant the end of all power of renewal. The flaws already latent in some of his pictures during his Futurist period, particularly a certain heaviness in the painting, became more apparent as the years passed, until the present time when what predominates is mere technical skill.

His brilliant and really successful polemical period is associated with *La Voce* and *Lacerba* and the struggle against the constraints of provincialism; his influence was mainly of a cultural character —letting in the fresh winds from Europe.

SEVERINI

Gino Severini stands out among his contemporaries for the coherence of his idiom. He has tried to adapt the ancient traditions of his country to his own needs; but sometimes his imagination and sensibility as a painter have been at odds with his intellectualism, professionalism and skill as a craftsman. Controlled measure has been his watchword and has curbed any impulse towards sentimentality: his Futurism reveals the greater attraction of Cubism. Further figurative experiments, which some critics have incorrectly called neo-Classical, followed on his years of Futurism, but recently his tendency has again been towards a non-figurative idiom, with the use of abstract symbols. As Umbro Apollonio has put it: "Severini's periods always occur at the right time and season. . . . His experiments live and work inside a European movement that he foreshadows and upholds. . . ."

He left his native Cortona for Rome before he was twenty. There he struck up a friendship with Boccioni, and met Balla, who was back from France and full of enthusiasm for Impressionism. In 1906 Severini went to Paris (Modigliani arrived there in the same year), and found in Seurat's splitting up of colour the answer to his deepest needs—he found the theory of division of form all-absorbing. *Boulevard* (1910) in the Tate Gallery, London, is symptomatic of his work at that time, from which Naturalism had not yet been entirely eliminated. In that year Severini joined the Futurists. From Paris he wrote to friends who, like himself, had signed the manifesto, exhorting

Gino Severini *Rythme d'une Danseuse au Tutu Violet 1953*

them to be less rhetorical in their forms of expression. Though under Futurist influence to the extent that his geometrical rhythm became more *mouvementé*—as with his famous *Danza del Pan-Pan* (Dance of the Pan-Pan) of 1911 or *Festa a Montmartre* (Holiday at Montmartre) and the *Danzatrici* (Dancers) of 1912—Severini reflected Futurism only in part; his intellectualism made him fight shy of rhetoric and clamour especially as, being now in Paris, the need to kick against provincial fashions had been removed. As I said before, he was really more attracted by Cubism, not only on account of its static sense but also because the Cubist type of rearrangement offered him an idiom more in accord with his meditative intelligence. In the *Danza del Pan-Pan*, which Bazin considered "the masterpiece of Futurism", the rhythm owes its origin to neo-Impressionism and has a movement of forms as well as of colour, but in the *Gatto Nero* (Black Cat) there seems to be no search after movement in the geometry. *Autobus* (1912), *Crollo* (Collapse) and *Treno Blindato* (Armoured Train) (both of 1915) show more obvious Futurist emphasis, though expressed with the dynamic force of abstract form, for Severini had already realized that a Naturalistic motif, even if inspired by machinery and move-ment, could not have value in a painting; what mattered were the symbols, the colour and the rhythm. In the *14 Lulio* (14 July) of 1913, and the *14 Lulio* and *Guerra* (War) of 1915, the com-position could not remotely be called Futurist: the surfaces have a dimension which is symbolic and abstract.

In an article in the *Mercure de France* in 1916, Severini wrote some notes on plastic Symbolism which are useful as giving us an idea of the way he was going. "One of my first Futurist paintings, the *Danza del Pan Pan a Monico*—in which I made the shapes of things join in the movement of the human forces—was called by Dufy 'Unanimist painting'. At that time I was unaware of the exact meaning of Unanimism—my efforts to portray movement were almost unconscious. Later I derived strength and confidence from this new point of contact between literature and painting.

"Human movement, our movement, when projected onto objects, is capable of traversing the whole universe on the hertzian waves of our sensibility and intelligence. With the help of will, memory and imagination, we are capable of projecting our idea-sensation not only onto the beings and things in the same surroundings (first Futurist period: object *plus* surroundings) but onto everything in the universe (second Futurist period: object *plus* universe). I grasped that an idea-sensation could be transmitted, by its affinities and by analogy, into a different species as I looked at the waves of the sea, for in them I saw the image of a dancer.

"The contrasts of form and colour which derive from the perception of one reality—'the dancer'—can also be found, by affinity and analogy, in the spiral flight of an aeroplane or the shimmering of the sea. So here we have the two terms of comparison—dancer-sea—confirming the maximum of life in the universe."

Once the unity of time and space has been destroyed in a picture, Severini concluded, "modern plastic painting can express not only the idea of the object and its continuity, but also a kind of plastic ideogram or synthesis of general ideas . . . for instance I have tried to express the idea of war by means of a plastic whole composed of cannon, workshop, flag, order of mobilization, aeroplane, anchor.

"According to our conception of idea-realism no naturalistic description of a battlefield or slaughter can give the synthesis of the idea—War—better than these objects which are the symbol of it." We can detect in this premise—which typifies the second Futurist period—the danger of the poster, yet it was precisely in those years that Severini's compositions were at their best. The subtle vibration of colour, especially the silvery greys, and the luminosity that came from neo-Impres-sionism, make his pictures of that period outstanding.

But after a few years Severini drew nearer and nearer to the Cubists. His surfaces became severer and cleaner, the greys and browns alternated with a balance that was far indeed from any form of rhetoric. Geometry and a stern mathematical relationship of forms distinguish his compositions from

Gino Severini *Still Life 1923*

those of other Cubists. His *Composizione* (Composition) (1918) in the Jucker Collection is one of the best paintings in the history of French Cubism.

His experiments with figurative art after 1920 also reflected a tendency current in Europe as a whole. Important in this connexion was Picasso's return to Pompeii, Ingres, and traditions that had been long forgotten. But though in that period Severini's metre of composition was severe and his rhythms of Cubist inspiration, many of his works showed signs of compromising with a descriptive type of decoration.

In recent years Severini has reverted to the non-figurative idiom. *Rythme d'une Danseuse au Tutu Violet* (1953), in the Schettini Collection, makes a link with Severini's first *avant-garde* work. But the latter is more living.

MODIGLIANI

Amedeo Modigliani's intense and legendary life has been the subject of many books since his death in 1920 at the age of thirty-eight. Outstanding among his biographers and critics are Lionello Venturi, one of the earliest Modigliani enthusiasts, Raffaele Carrieri and Lamberto Vitali.

Though Italian characteristics were always present in his work, Modigliani was essentially a European. It is difficult to nail down the influences that went to the formation of his idiom because he was, in fact, beyond and above the group tendencies of his time. It is never easy to trace the cultural background of an original artist: preferences and affinities are, perhaps, tracked down, but nothing can take away from the fact that the final idiom is entirely original. In Modigliani's case various influences have been hinted at—notably those prevailing in the Paris of 1906: Cézanne, Negro art, fourteenth-century Sienese painting, Botticelli, Carpaccio, the Fauves. Mention has also been made of his contact with a late and minor *Macchiaiolo*, Micheli; of linear arabesques, decorative art, compositions constructed with ovals and cylinders; and of the Cubists.

Cézanne's influence is observable in *Mendicante di Livorno* (The Beggar of Livorno)—the only picture Modigliani painted during his short stay in Italy in 1909. But Modigliani's temperament was poles apart from Cézanne's: his figuration is pure and delicate and his sensuality is so filtered and sharpened by his mind as to brush near to stylism. Indeed Cézanne's work was less an influence on the evolution of his idiom than an example of a type of structure—he built his compositions as a solid man of the soil, not as a cultivated Mannerist. Lionello Venturi draws attention to Modigliani's independence when he notes that with him "the feeling for the ideal line precedes the execution of the actual line", and concludes, "his lines never develop on one and the same plane; with a two-dimensional surface appearance they achieve a three-dimensional vision".

In the Negro art which Picasso and Matisse were introducing in those years, Modigliani could certainly see examples of freedom of composition and expression. His sculptures, which must be viewed as experiments for perfecting his style, and his *Cariatidi*, reflected this influence but, as always, they carried his own individual imprint. Negro art pushed primeval expressiveness to its extreme; but in Modigliani a conscious refinement took place through the mediation of decadantism —in the best sense of the word—and this inclined him to allusion, love for sharp sensuality, withdrawal into himself, and a subtle intellectualism.

It is true that when Modigliani went to Paris from Italy he took with him reproductions of the work of fourteenth-century Sienese painters and one or two fifteenth-century Tuscan painters, and Carpaccio. But these remote Italian traditions could not become urgent or actual without Modigliani's personal imprint: he was anything but a "museum" painter. He studied Simone Martini, Carpaccio and Botticelli, yes, but his vision was contemporary. This is apparent in the style of his composition, the presupposition of the new freedom inherent in the concept of the object being viewed as a pretext only, the clash of colour, the distortion arising from the artist's subjective vision rather than the model.

He was far removed from theories and formulas. The furious colouring of the Fauves, or paint spread on the canvas directly from the tube, were not for him. Neither was the geometry of the Cubists. Yet these innovations and excitements had an indirect influence on his evolution in that they gave him examples of pure creative freedom and the escape from tradition. Picasso of the Blue period, Klimt and the Japanese, Utamaro, could have suggested freedom from models and concentration on the essential in line. But we know from the few letters of Modigliani that have survived that his greatest admiration was reserved for Picasso and Douanier Rousseau. Another source of influence was doubtless the contemporary poets who were his friends, and perhaps earlier poets whom he loved to read; he knew Apollinaire and Max Jacob and read Petrarch, Mallarmé, Rimbaud, the Parnassians, the Symbolists and Lautréamont. Among his artist friends in Montparnasse and Montmartre were Picasso, Brancusi, Utrillo, Kisling and Vlaminck.

Modigliani, then, sought for his own personal idiom—an idiom of perfect lyrical purity that expressed his own particular vision of the world. He liked naked women, he abandoned himself to his moods, he had moments of acute melancholy, he felt the joy of life but also a secret suffering that enabled him to see the pathos of the human condition. His figures were melancholy terrestrial angels caught in their short spell between birth and death. The idea that his art was born of alcohol and drugs is a myth which has been definitely exploded—there is too much measure in his style, too much subtle and lucid control, for that to be possible: abuses, if they existed, had no connexion with the moments of poetic creation that demanded, in Modigliani especially, an absolute mastery over the means of expression.

We can observe the discipline of his style in the relationships of ovals and cylinders in his compositions. Lamberto Vitali has pointed out the extreme transfiguration of his models in the works of his last period. "Transfiguration by means of ovals and cylinders: the eyes in the elongated faces bend over the cylinders of the swans' necks and join in harmonious rhythm with the ovals of the bodies." But this comment is ambiguous, for there is never a pure geometric relationship for its own sake, complete with symmetry and calculation in Modigliani's work; his emphasis is on expression

Amedeo Modigliani *Head of Madame Hasting 1915*

Amedeo Modigliani *Portrait of Madame Hasting with red background 1915*

with a metre of its own, often asymmetric in movement and with a distorting accentuation of certain details. Colour is the essential element in his delicate and lyrical vision, and there is even colour in the pure lines of the drawing. That is why it is misleading to talk of the arabesque in connexion with Modigliani: his work lacks the detachment of the arabesque because he moulds his composition at various levels, and even when it appears to be arabesque the intensity of the expression brings out elements of colour that are emotional. The blacks, pinks, greens, reds and greys are never set down in firm abstraction; they move and vibrate and have variations of luminous intensity even when spread over wide surfaces.

The balance of colour and line—the two fundamentals in Modigliani's idiom—in no way excludes human feeling which is at times poignant in the extreme. Sensuality, as filtered by emotional purity and mental control, alternates with human understanding and compassion. Besides the famous nudes—the *Nude* in the Mattioli Collection is undoubtedly one of the finest in all modern art—the series of portraits from *Kisling* to *Paul Guillaume*, from *Madame Hasting* to *L'Enfant Gras* show the coherence of Modigliani's style. While typically European, he preserved the individual metre of the Italian line.

GINO ROSSI

The final break with officially sponsored art in the early days before the first World War was brought about not only by the battles fought by the Futurists and the Metaphysical painters who followed them, but also by individual artists belonging to no specific group. Outstanding among these was Gino Rossi. His temperament, though gentle, was proud, resolute and intransigent. His romantic nature endowed him with a free and subtle lyricism and sensitivity for colour, while his self-critical and intellectual control led him to see form as something to be achieved at all costs. His difficult life—for more than twenty years he was mad—made him diffident and retiring.

His work falls into two periods. Even before his comprehensive one-man show at the Venice Biennale in 1948, a year after his death, some critics preferred his "constructive" period to his more formal one. Certainly in the first period his work had power, but it did not reveal the inner lyrical spirit of Gino Rossi. His form sometimes seems contrived and almost theoretical, stemming from his fear that his temperament might lead him into an over-emphasis on sensitive colour. He certainly indulged in orgies of self-criticism. In the summer of 1921 he wrote to his friend, Barbantini: "As for believing that salvation lies in Impressionism, I now deny it categorically. I am not saying that Monet, Pissarro and Guillaumin have not left some fine things from the colour point of view. But construction is not achieved with colour but with form. To go on painting as if Cézanne had never lived is impossible. A painter who fails to realize this is dead. That's all I have to say."

And yet, if we are to judge by results, Rossi's unquiet personality is better reflected when he listens to the suggestions made by colour. He was a Venetian with a sense of form and early in life acquired ability to construct, yet his most lively and personal paintings are those in which colour is freed from any formal system. Some of the landscapes which he called "descriptions" are not only more lyrical but also less descriptive than much of the rest of his work.

Gino Rossi arrived in Paris in 1907, the year after Modigliani. It was a time of lively controversy. The Fauves were in the saddle; Vuillard was putting Cézanne on to the world market, and Picasso had started the experiments which led to Cubism. Rossi must have felt out of place—except that his Venetian instinct for colour drew him to Gauguin, Van Gogh and the East. He renewed an erstwhile contact with Byzantine mosaics. Gauguin had no deep influence over his idiom, but

Gino Rossi *Cottage 1910*

encouraged him to throw off a local sense of colour. Van Gogh taught him the vibrations of living expression, and from Japanese, Indian and Persian prints he learnt that space need not be naturalistic, but two-dimensional.

"Rossi's novelty lies in the rejection of local colour," Marchiori points out; "that is to say, of the literary Realism favoured by the Venetian school still bound up with the end of the nineteenth century; and in the discovery of colour as invention and fantasy on a two-dimensional plane. It was only later, after 1919, that Rossi took up the idea of space constructed by means of a rational analysis of forms that he placed and rearranged to make a new dimension."

The highly colourful *La Petite Paroisse* (1908) and *La Fanciulla del Fiore* (The Child with the Flower) show Gauguin's influence. In *Colline Asolane* (Hills at Asolo) (1911) the drawing is itself ornamental; and in the figures of fishermen in various other paintings the outline circumscribes, but does not harmonize with, the colour. But in landscapes in which the drawing is less insistent the colour takes on a plastic quality of its own and becomes evocative and keenly lyrical.

After a period in Paris and in Brittany, Rossi returned to the solitude of Burano and, later, to the greater solitude of Asolo. The stimulus of nature drove him less to description than to evocation, especially when his works were born of intense emotion and suggested by a state of mind. He forgot all his intellectualism and gave a fuller rein to colour which was neither naturalistic nor descriptive. Once his taste had become conscious he never again made use of local colour. After his experiences of war and prison—that is after 1919—Gino Rossi's constructions became more formal. If the ideas of the Cubists meant more to him than Metaphysical painting, it was Cézanne's last period that remained the basic influence on his work. The drawing became constructive, the plastic value of the colour marked, the light clean and bright.

Some of his *Costruzioni di Nature Morte* (Constructions of Still Lifes) which he did in 1922 have a severe and solid beauty: outstanding among them is *Violino e Bottiglie* (Violin and Bottles). They could be ranked among the most significant paintings done at a time when the return to order was only too often more superficial than real. Other paintings of this series are mainly interesting as formal exercises, and sometimes the drawing is so overstressed that he would seem to be in the grip of some theory or formula. His deepest poetry was achieved perhaps in some of his minor works, in little landscapes with clear colours and without decorative outline.

Gino Rossi *Violin and Bottles 1922*

METAPHYSICAL PAINTING

Metaphysical painting, unlike Futurism, announced its birth by no noisy manifestoes. It began when a group of pictures, presupposing a totally new way of looking at things, had already created a new taste in painting—for it was not until 1919 that Giorgio De Chirico published his basic concepts for a "Metaphysical aesthetic" in the review *Valori Plastici*. "My mind was obsessed, and still is, by carpenters' squares: I saw them rising like strange planets behind all pictorial designs. . . .

"The structure of cities, the architecture of houses, squares, gardens, public walks, gateways, railway stations, etc.—all these provide us with the basic principles of a great Metaphysical aesthetic. . . . We, who live under the sign of the Metaphysical alphabet, we know the joys and sorrows to be found in a gateway, a street corner, a room, on the surface of a table, between the sides of a box. . . .

"Perfect knowledge of the space an object should occupy in a picture, and of the space that separates one object from another, establishes a new astronomy of things attached to our planet by the magic law of gravity. Canons of the Metaphysical aesthetic lie in the minutely-accurate and precisely-estimated use of surfaces and volumes. . . . We are building in paint a new Metaphysical psychology of things. . . ."

This new idiom was born with the works of De Chirico. Later Carrà and Morandi joined him and brought fresh life to the movement with their own discoveries. Metaphysical painting had an impact not only on Italy—where it created more stir than Futurism—but on Europe as a whole. It lasted as a movement roughly from 1910 to 1921, but its influence since then has been great and still exists. It is important not only for its static sense and architectonic precision, but also because it resurrected forgotten traditions of the Renaissance from which the Futurists had tried to break loose. Futurism, with its mystique of speed and machinery, reflected one aspect of the Italian character, but the Metaphysical idiom reflected one that is perhaps deeper, the one manifest in the Primitives —meditative, quiet, absorbed by problems of composition.

Oddly enough De Chirico reflects this aspect less than the others, though he was the inventor of the idiom. His Metaphysical paintings take us back through Böcklin to neo-Classicism, while his later works recall the seventeenth century and the Dutch and Flemish painters, but in all of them there is a feeling of artifice and Baroque theatricality.

Too much has been written both in Italy and abroad about De Chirico's Metaphysical painting. The usual practice is to draw a sharp dividing line between his work of the 1910 to 1920 period, and everything he has done since. Eluard places De Chirico and Gérard de Nerval side by side as the two pioneers of Surrealism. Soby underlines De Chirico's influence on Max Ernst, Tanguy, Salvador Dali, Delvaux, Magritte and other Surrealists. Marco Valsecchi rejects the theory that the early De Chirico paved the way for Surrealism, for, he says, Surrealism is "monotonous" compared with the "unexpected associations of images" of Metaphysical painting which reveal deep premeditation, and hence open the door on to an intimate and private world. This last comment applies especially to Carrà and Morandi in their Metaphysical period; it hardly fits De Chirico in whom Valsecchi notes a "cold bright tone conducive to, yet freezing out, magic", a climate of "universal symbolism", and the effort "to get right away from human limitations"—as De Chirico himself put it. "The objects detach themselves from any relationship, and isolate themselves in detached sensations" (Valsecchi). So we find ourselves in a world of externally decorative Baroque, which is not at all the case with the Metaphysical idiom of Carrà and Morandi, whose results are painterly and unified and spring from deep inner necessity.

Giorgio De Chirico *Piazza d'Italia*

De Chirico's Metaphysical idiom owes much to literature. He was a friend of poets and critics such as Apollinaire, and it was with the help of his brother, Savinio, that he invented some of his recurring images. For instance, it is well known that the origin of the tailor's dummy is in the play *La Chanson de la Mi-Mort*, written by Savinio in French and published in 1913 by Apollinaire in *Soirées de Paris*.

But De Chirico's literariness derived, too, from various other currents in vogue at that time. I am thinking of the emphasis on the importance of dreams and memory, the cult of "the absurd" and the effort to break away from human limitations. Though the object in De Chirico's paintings gives the impression of being detached and recognizable, it is in fact part of the subjective conscious-ness, it is an emotive pretext. Whether an artichoke, a biscuit, a glove, or a tailor's dummy, it is a symbol of the uneasy silence of the universe—a universe which is always a state of mind. The concreteness of the detail, thrown into relief by the abstract lines and surfaces, accentuates our feeling of witchery. But the real motif is not the object; it is what we are reminded of, and silence, solitude and brooding melancholy. That is why the highly defined lines, the geometric spaces and the sharpness of the shadows have a Romantic significance. The "absurd", which was to find its extreme expression with the Dadaists and Surrealists, was less important in the Metaphysical idiom than the need to escape into a world transcending history and human limitations. Such, roughly, was the "literary" background to De Chirico's work.

A certain "capriciousness" in his flights of invention can also be found in De Chirico's Meta-physical paintings, and while some of the spatial relationships seem to suggest classicism, they are really neo-Baroque in spirit. On top of all this his compositions often give the impression of a stage set. And it is precisely the light—unreal, brooding, cold, fraught with disturbing illusions—that enables such heterogeneous elements—some hallucinating under the mask of Realism, some set out geometrically, some drawn with an illustrative outline—to coexist in one and the same painting. And behind De Chirico there always lies the theatre—love of contrasts, of contradictions, and of surprising and spectacular effects. But though De Chirico was an innovator in theory and taste and as such influenced the history of modern European painting, it cannot be claimed that even the works of his Metaphysical period achieved a true painterly unity.

A painter must be judged by the totality of his work, so we must move on to De Chirico's more recent paintings and see his whole output (to date) in perspective. A painter who has created a new idiom has a perfect right to denounce it later if he wants to. But the fact that De Chirico now denounces all modern art and signs himself "Pictor Optimus" on paintings that show nothing more than technical ability suggests that his Metaphysical work reflected only part of his personality. De Chirico loves paradox and the spectacular, and he loves to provoke; herein lies the strength which enabled him to influence taste by his imaginative invention, and herein, too, lies his limitation, for mere cleverness has finally won over poetry and fancy, and the influence of "museums" has become more and more marked.

For years now he has claimed to have rediscovered the true paint of the past—a special emulsion guaranteed to produce great and lasting pictures. But obviously the value of a technical means is only relative. His recent paintings are not only fat and oily and lacking in delicacy, but they are devoid of any poetic imagination for they are too closely based on the past. The interplay of plumed hats, breastplates, helmets, Baroque, Oriental or Spanish costume—even his still lifes—show his masterly technique, but they lack inner compulsion.

When we look back at his Metaphysical work in the light of his latest pictures and his whole personality, we realize that even their outstanding inventiveness was lacking in real formal unity. Both Ragghianti and Umbro Apollonio have perceived this and agree that a picture of his is rather an "aggregate" of its component parts than a true "composition". This does not alter the fact that De Chirico's Metaphysical paintings were incomparably more suggestive and rich in fancy and invention than the "museum" *tours de force* of recent years.

De Chirico was born in Greece of Italian parents, but his impressionable years were spent in Munich. Here he was deeply impressed by Böcklin, whose most significant works are in the Neue Staatsgalerie and the Schackgalerie. His *Triton and Nereids* inspired De Chirico's painting of the same name, and his *Battle of the Centaurs*, in the Basle Museum, inspired a similar interpretation of the same subject. "He liked everything in Böcklin," says Carrieri, "his inspiration, his execution, his fine materials, his drawing and his composition. He admired the patience and conscientiousness of Böcklin's finish, his laboratory secrets, his technique. . . ."

For two years he was a pupil at the Academy of Fine Arts in Munich. Besides his enthusiasm for Böcklin, he came to admire Max Klinger for his stylized symbols. It was here that he learnt about optic illusion and developed his preference for inventive painting with "poetic" intentions. His love for images charged with a brooding uneasiness, and a "symbolic universe", was stimulated by reading the philosophical works of Nietzsche, Weininger and Schopenhauer—whose essay on apparitions and the objective character of dreams had an especial appeal.

In the *Enigma di una Sera d'Autunno* (Enigma of an Autumn Evening) and still more in the *Enigma dell' Oracolo* (Enigma of the Oracle) (1910) one could deny the literary overtones, but they have a disturbing spectral unity, again almost like a stage set. With *Meditazione Mattinale* (Morning

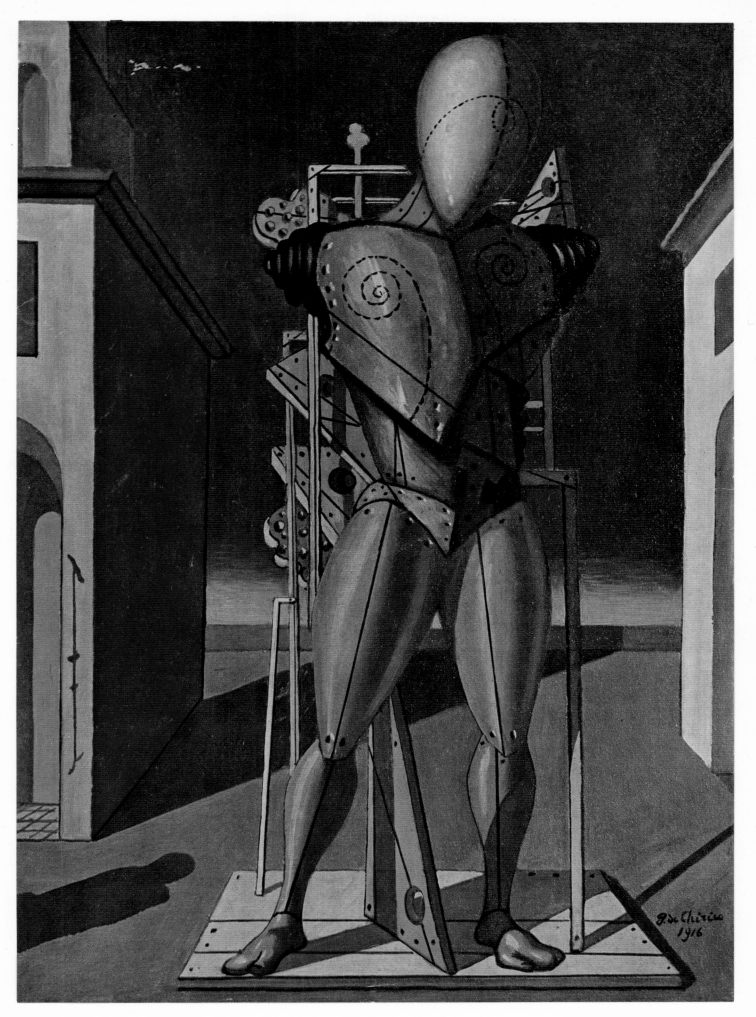

Giorgio De Chirico *Hector 1916*

Meditation) which he painted in Paris in 1912—he had moved there the year before after a period in Florence—the composition suggests the wings of a theatre with statues to stress the impression of neo-Classicism. The lines of the surrounding architecture create the illusion of space in a brooding light of expectant void. The sense of stage is beginning to get the upper hand.

Autoritratto (Self-Portrait) of 1913 is one of his most homogeneous paintings. In *Canto d'Amore* (Love Song), of the same year, the elements in the composition are placed coldly side by side. The picture is first and foremost illustrative. The foreground, the background with the train, the portico on one side—all make up an aggregate lacking any deep compulsion of style. *Malinconia e Mistero di una Strada* (Melancholy and Mystery of a Street) achieves a more intense lyricism in which the portico, the cart, the girl with the hoop, in contrasts of light and shade, are presented with more painterly unity, though here too the background sky has something of the suggestiveness of a stage set.

The same sort of comment can be made over and over again in discussing De Chirico's work. Even the famous *Muse Inquietanti* (The Disquieting Muses) of 1916, which ranks among De Chirico's best work, stresses the spatial illusion, but between the various elements in the composition—bright and plastic in the foreground, descriptive in the scenic background, with castle and sky gleaming like an oleograph—there is a casual relationship which is not entirely worked out in terms of plastic unity.

So in De Chirico's Metaphysical work there is invention, originality, imaginative flight, and a strong inclination towards poetry. What is lacking is a central core to the composition which too often is just a brilliantly contrived aggregate of its parts.

Carlo Carrà's place in Metaphysical painting is of quite another kind. Though influenced by De Chirico's new idiom with its ambiguous and literary overtones, Carrà was at all times first and foremost a painter, and some of his Metaphysical compositions are remarkable for their simple and severe purity of style. *L'Idolo Ermafrodito* (The Hermaphrodite Idol) and *Penelope* could be ranked among the best paintings of our time. Nevertheless Carrà learnt his new mythology from De Chirico, and followed him. *Solitudine* (Solitude) stems from *Indovino* (Conundrum), *Penelope* from *Ettore* (Hector), *Andromaca* and *Trovatore* (Minstrel), and *L'Ovale delle Apparizioni* (The Oval of the Apparitions) from *Le Muse Inquietanti* (The Disquieting Muses). But though De Chirico invented the new taste, Carrà's results were more lyrical and painterly in the strict sense.

When De Chirico returned to Italy in 1915 he was stationed with the army at Ferrara until 1919. Carrà arrived in Ferrara in January 1917 and met De Chirico and De Pisis. So it happened that this Renaissance city became the centre of the Metaphysical movement. Carrà painted his first group of Metaphysical paintings in the Hospital for Nervous Diseases where he was a patient: they were *Solitudine* (Solitude), *La Camera Incantata* (The Enchanted Room), *Madre e Figli* (Mother and Sons) and *La Musa Metafisica* (The Metaphysical Muse).

Carrà's formation up to that time had followed a totally different course from De Chirico's: there had been no Böcklin and no Munich, but Divisionism, Lombard painting, Cesare Tallone and Futurism. Moreover, he was a critic and in 1916 published his "Talks with Giotto and Paolo Uccello" in *La Voce*. *Le Figlie di Lot* (The Daughters of Lot) (1915) was a prelude to Metaphysical painting, but reached by a careful study of the school of Giotto, while the *Gentiluomo Ubriaco* (The Drunk Gentleman) (1916) and *Composizione con TA* (Composition with TA) are examples of construction which is in a sense a Metaphysical statement, yet made independently of De Chirico. It was in 1917, the year he met De Chirico, that Carrà produced his most typically Metaphysical works—*Penelope*, *L'Idolo Ermafrodito*, *Cavaliere Occidentale* (Horseman of the West) and *Natura Morta con Squadra* (Still Life with Carpenter's Square).

Carlo Carrà *Composition with TA 1916*

When discussing Carrà it would be unthinkable to refer to "contrived illusions" or "the aggregate of the parts". His compositions of this period have a coherent centre, and the bright Lombard colours are anything but oleographic. For Carrà the Metaphysical idiom was a search for pure, essential forms in a strict metre of style, an attempt to resolve the form-colour relationship in a concrete way.

Giorgio Morandi's experiments in Metaphysical painting were far removed from De Chirico's influence and a perfect reflection of the personality of this pure painter from Bologna. Though we can see his Metaphysical period as a distinct painting experience, it cannot be detached from the rest of his activity as a painter. Unlike De Chirico, Morandi always manifested absolute coherence, and the results have been great painting in the purest style. So we shall discuss his Metaphysical period presently, in the special section devoted to him.

Giorgio Morandi *Still Life 1919*

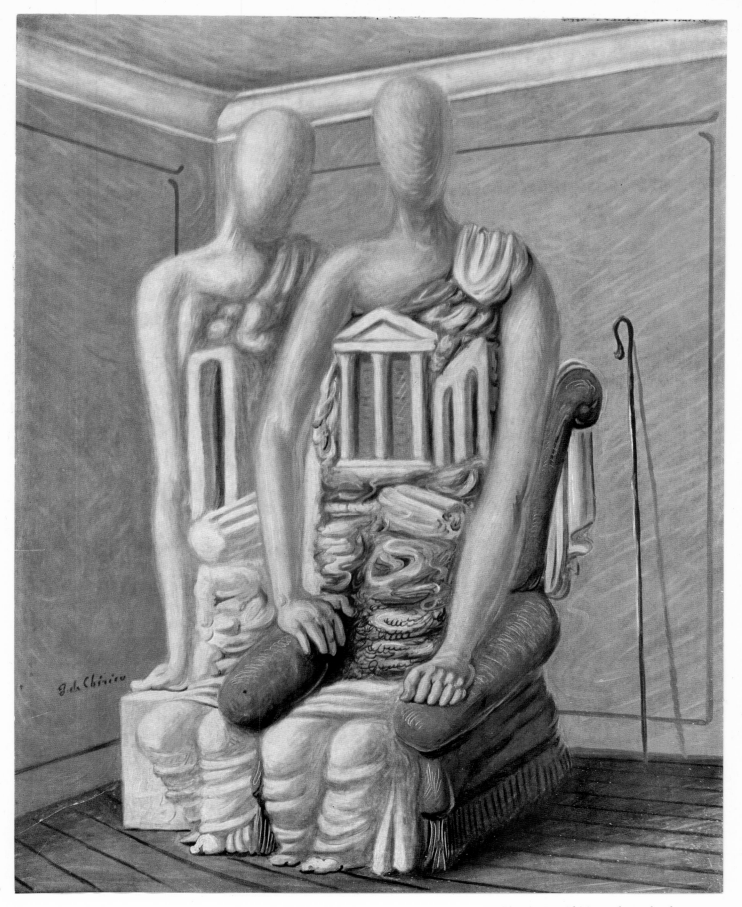

Giorgio De Chirico *The Archaeologists 1927*

VALORI PLASTICI

After the first World War, there were changes in the Italian scene. Boccioni had died in 1916; Severini was definitively classed with the French Cubists; Metaphysical painting had reached its peak, and the *avant-garde* had outgrown its war against tradition.

The critical reviews shifted from Florence to Rome. In 1919 a literary review which also discussed the figurative arts was founded, called *La Ronda. La Ronda* exalted form, spoke of a new classicism and of the search for a "noble" style. Architectural values were preferred to pictorial ones, as prose was to poetry. *La Ronda* published articles by Carrà on Cézanne and Derain. De Chirico, in 1920, referred to a "demon of classicism" and the "magic of line": "Our aim today is to be sufficiently mystical to bring about a revival of classicism." Obviously he had in mind his own Metaphysical classicism (which was in fact seething with Romantic subjectivism). But a still more important review was founded in Rome in November 1918 and edited by Mario Broglio—*Valori Plastici*.

Valori Plastici is more important than *La Ronda* in the history of modern Italian painting not only because it helped to establish Metaphysical painting—it carried articles by, and reproductions of De Chirico, Carrà and Morandi—but also because it brought information about the main European idioms to the Italian public. Carrà was one of the most active contributors, but both De Chirico and Savinio wrote for it, as well as Cecchi, Broglio, Morandi, Melli, Soffici, Picasso, Braque and Archipenko.

One of the 1919 numbers was entirely devoted to French Cubism with illustrations by Braque, Picasso, Severini, Léger, Juan Gris and Metzinger, and with poetry by Salmon, Cocteau, Jacob, Breton and Aragon. There were also articles on Chagall, Kandinsky and the Dutch neo-Plastic painters.

But the primary function of *Valori Plastici* lay in its desire for a return to tradition. Its critical estimate of the international scene was intended to establish comparisons, and to indicate signs of a return to tradition—especially that of the fifteenth century—among Italians. This return was in fact implicit in Metaphysical painting, but the articles in *Valori Plastici* made it explicit. French Impressionism was judged on the whole unfavourably; De Chirico outlined the premises for a "Metaphysical aesthetic" and exhorted a "return to the métier". Carrà wrote of an "Italian principle" and of "an Italian spirit in the arts" and inveighed against the innovations of *avant-garde* movements that rejected contact with Italian tradition. In 1920 to 1921 Soffici reproduced some of his paintings which openly proclaimed a return to traditional order. Cecchi wrote an essay on Fattori, who was later reviewed by Soffici, and De Chirico got involved in a huge war of words about the "mania for the seventeenth century". In it he tried to establish dogmatically that the true Italian tradition was that of the fifteenth century (but subsequently he was to contradict himself when he took his stand by seventeenth-century "museum" art).

Both *La Ronda* and *Valori Plastici*, then, looked to the past. Museums must not be destroyed—as the early Futurists had contended (though the pitfalls of "museum-ism" did beset some second- and third-rate painters who lacked the personal inspiration that could renew and deepen tradition). In brief, *Valori Plastici* provided artists with a new critical awareness.

Carlo Carrà *San Gaudenzio di Varallo 1924*

CARRÀ

Carlo Carrà is a highly representative figure in modern Italian art and has played a crucial part in all the main idioms between Futurism and the second World War. At each of his various stages he, like others, has had to pay his toll to the critical self-consciousness of the time, but from each stage he has left paintings full of vitality and style. We find in him not only control and the slow bringing of the image to maturity before settling down to the *tabula rasa* of the canvas, but also evidence that his conscious will dominated over the creative art. But whenever he reached a balance between criticism, willed intention, and free creative imagination, his painting is outstanding for its individuality and lyrical compulsion.

I have already discussed his Futurist paintings—after his contact with Cesare Tallone at the Brera Academy—and his Metaphysical period, but it is worth noting that in both these periods —though an exponent of the creed—his *élan* was genuinely European: indeed we have seen how in both these periods his own personal stamp distinguished him from other painters of the group in question. Even when his colours tended to be thick, they had a limpidity of their own, authentic and painterly. When he left Lombard provincialism behind him, his instinct prevented him from altogether abandoning its gentle, liquid resonances of colour.

Carrà was deeply influenced by Giotto, Paolo Uccello, Masaccio, Seurat—from the point of view of composition rather than colour—Derain, and above all by Cézanne. But he saw these painters in an Italian way, as exponents of a constructive relationship between form and colour. "We want Italian art to return to order, method and discipline; we want to acquire an assured form, with body and shape, form that resembles and yet—following the demands of our time—differs from that of the old masters. . . . It can be seen over and over again in the history of Western art that whenever a European painter wants to make a radical statement about the constructive impulse of his work, the 'Italian principle' comes into its own. . . ."

Under Giotto's influence Carrà tended to whittle the elements in his picture down to the bare essentials, to over-economize the means at his disposal—as in *Pino sul Mare* (Pine Tree by the Sea) (1921). Self-imposed rules of this kind obviously act as a check to broad creative freedom, so that while some of his works of this period are poetic, others are contrived and formulistic. In *Attesa* (Waiting) (1926) it is rather a survival of his Metaphysical period that causes him to deliberately denude his composition. Roberto Longhi says that "the solid houses on the hills gleam in the naked light". But the fact remains that this bareness is not suited to the type of landscape painted. In short, a particular idiom should ideally be charged with universal value, whereas sometimes Carrà did the opposite—he tried to compress the universal into the particular, thus depriving his composition of compulsion and poetic urgency. *Le Vele* (The Sails), also of 1926, shows a similar extraneous effort to resolve the problem of colour and form. In these cases tradition was impairing rather than stimulating the imagination.

Carlo Carrà *The Boat 1928*

But in the same year Carrà obviously felt the need to break with systems of composition and give himself up more freely to colour. The famous *Cinquale* of that year shows a revolt against pre-established systems and marks a turning-point in Carrà's idiom. Yet it opens the door to nothing fresh as regards colour itself. He has reverted to the Lombard palette and there are echoes of Tallone and Gola. *Cinquale* cannot be ranked among Carrà's really new and original works.

But with *La Foce del Cinquale* (The Mouth of the Cinquale) (1928) Carrà steps into his great period. The spaces are delicately calculated and the composition is worked out in tone areas with no lines at all. The result is visionary and the horizon, where sea and river meet, opens out into infinity. This painting has a poetry that is far indeed from his early Futurist compositions. There are no external signs of Naturalism and the colours—the glowing browns and reds, the discreet greens, the obtrusive blues, and the whites—are fresh and lyrical. *Mattino al Mare* (Morning by the Sea) (Mattioli Collection) also done in 1928 can be ranked among the most outstanding landscapes of the age. Other examples of Carrà at his happiest include some of the still lifes up to 1935, the *Marina di Carrara* (Seaside near Carrara) (1930) and various Venetian seascapes. Here tradition blends with the direct experience of modern idioms; there is nothing superficial about the return to order. In other pictures, for instance the well-known *Nuotatori* (Swimmers) (1932) and *Composizione* (Composition) (1938) the layout of the composition is more deliberate and forced. In others again, such as *L'Attore* (The Actor) (1935) we see traces of *Novecento* influence in the monumental and rather rhetorical construction: works of this kind are chiefly valuable in that they indicate the spirit of the age. Carrà was always representative of some Italian "period" up to the last years before the second World War. Since then his painting has tended to go into a minor key with a certain repetition of subject and without the tension of his great years.

MORANDI

For a long time critical writing about Morandi was confused by misunderstandings about his reserved and contemplative temperament, his lack of interest in creeds—he interpreted the Meta-physical theory in his own way. So there came into being a mythical Morandi, isolated in his ivory tower and revelling in the dust on bottles and lamps, and the bric-à-brac of his studio. But the better-informed critics could not delay indefinitely before recognizing the poetry that makes him one of the greatest artists of our age. The first to appreciate him were men of letters and poets like Bacchelli and Cardarelli; but, without intending to, they helped to build up a literary myth round him. In 1935 the critic Roberto Longhi praised the outstanding quality of Morandi's painting in his introductory lecture to his course on the history of art at Bologna University. The next step came with some trenchant observations by Arnaldo Beccaria. But it is to Cesare Grandi in his essay published in *Arti* (1939) that we owe the first comprehensive critical appreciation of Morandi's work. Since then further critics have made their contribution, including Giuseppe Raimondi, Gnudi, Lamberto Vitali, Marchiori, Argan, Arcangeli, Ragghianti, Umbro Apollonio and Carrieri. Perhaps more illuminating than all the criticism was the exhibition of fourteenth-century Bolognese painting held in 1950, for the colour-scheme of the fruit basket with flowers, painted by Vitale da Bologna, instantly called to mind Morandi's delicate colour-schemes.

This, of course, must not be taken as axiomatic, and we must not assume that it was a direct influence. But what would be totally mistaken would be to see Cézanne's influence even in Morandi's earliest landscapes. Morandi had seen few reproductions of Cézanne before the second Secessionist exhibition, Rome 1914. Then there was another factor: Morandi was a meditative artist, slow to assimilate an influence. Morandi's palette can best be understood when we call to mind the midday light on the hills and plains round Bologna.

Giorgio Morandi *Still Life 1936*

This may cause confusion, for we are not concerned here with the imitation of Nature. There is no local colour in Morandi's painting: it is the fruit of a slow meditated assimilation, as with the most lyrical Primitives. Giotto, Simone Martini, the Lorenzetti and Vitale never imitated Nature in their backgrounds. With them again memory stimulated imagination. Morandi has never ceased to see the poetry of the values of light in the place where he has always lived. In his early youth he studied Vitale and other Primitives, but his idiom has no link whatever with painting in Emilia in the nineteenth century. Once he had rejected Naturalism in favour of memory, so as to render the inner resonances, he had complete freedom to pass from landscape to still lifes. It is mistaken to suppose, as some critics do, that his landscapes and still lifes were motivated by a conscious desire for research: they were a lyrical means of conveying new images whose poetry expressed a particular emotion.

In all this he was helped by Cézanne—not as regards colour, but as regards composition. Indeed if we find Cézanne's influence in his first landscape of 1911, it does not lie in the evocative and harmonious colour but in the slanting angle of the composition. He had seen Cézanne only in black-and-white reproductions.

But it is important to bear in mind Morandi's favourite painters as listed by Roberto Longhi: Giotto, Masaccio, Piero della Francesca, Bellini, Titian, Chardin, Corot, Renoir and Cézanne —in that order. Various critics have seen other influences, notably Kandinsky and Derain.

But in a meditative and lyrical artist like Morandi influences are never cut and dried. His starting-point lies in the poetic compulsion within himself. His preferences for certain artists arise from affinities of sympathy and depend on sensibility and intuition. Of course no artist can be formed altogether outside the cultural stream of his time—but this is more marked with less lyrical painters.

Morandi also admired the Italian painters of the fourteenth and fifteenth centuries. Besides Vitale da Bologna and the others on Longhi's list, he was impressed by Carpaccio. But he studied their method only, he did not imitate their results; and his freedom has always been typically "modern".

Morandi is a coherent painter. He has no time for the surprises of rhetoric. He is anti-theatrical. He expresses his vision of the world in flowers, landscapes and still lifes, and then expresses it again, by subtle rearrangement of these recurring motifs in terms of space, colour and light.

He has been criticized for "poverty". But this is because he reduces his keyboard of expression and awareness to the minimum to convey the bare essentials of his vision. The lyricism is confident and far removed from the noise and rhetoric of the age.

Morandi is unique, and occupies a quiet and impregnable place in European culture. Any fragment of his painting has its own architecture and purity. He has been called "limited". But he loves limits within which to attain freedom. He is not discursive or polemical in his painting, which is vertical rather than horizontal. His lyricism is born of a new kind of religious feeling; his still lifes enclose the whole universe. The detail, the hidden and humble corner, takes on universal value without a trace of literary overtone. That is why he avoids portraits. He has done a few, but they are not the paintings he himself prefers. Morandi represents detachment from the object in itself, from the personality of the object; with him dialogue inevitably turns into monologue. It is equally easy to see why he has never indulged in abstract art, for abstract art sets out from universal laws,

Giorgio Morandi *Still Life with Lamp*

whereas Morandi sets out from detail, and through detail embraces the universe. Morandi is a lyricist who, with apparent "poverty" of means (cups, bottles, lamps), expresses his interior world.

In his early landscapes and still lifes before 1916, with their subtle grades of colour ranging from burnt browns to opaque and tender greens and subdued greys, the spaces did not really isolate the masses, though forming architectural cadences of their own. But by 1916 "the spaces have become isolating", as Brandi puts it. Let us look at *Bottiglia e Fruttiera* (Bottle and Fruit Bowl) (1916). The chalky tones range from ash-grey to faded rose; the spaces, between the images on which falls the light, have an architectonic clarity. The image is not coloured, it is colour; it is defined by its colour and the outlines themselves are drawn in delicate colour. All Impressionistic effects have been transcended. Cézanne's example—not as to colour but as to composition—and the indirect influence of the Cubists—from whom Morandi differed both in his use of colour and because he avoided the analytical breaking-down and rearrangement of the object—here blend with the enchanted rediscovery of Giotto, Paolo Uccello and Masaccio. Thus we see that Morandi's Metaphysical period was not born of De Chirico or Carrà, but coincided with his inner need for clarity of composition and architectonic discipline. In his paintings between 1918 and 1920 we never find, as with De Chirico, a discordant juxtaposition of the various figurative elements. Even Morandi's dummies are forms of the purest kind. Yet when, in 1920 and 1921, he began painting flowers and other still lifes with a light that penetrated the colour while avoiding all brightness, Morandi was a freer and more personal painter. The Metaphysical period was, by and large, a means of deepening his expression.

Since 1920 there have been no sudden changes in his work. As Raimondi points out, the modifications and refinements of his different years cannot be divided up into different periods. The outward form of his work may vary from sensitive impalpable images to bold geometric structures or canvases covered with silky greens; but what matters is the unfailing harmony between his painting and his inner world.

In this estimate I have not touched on those inevitable moments when Morandi's work has fallen below his own high standard. Some of his recent pictures are rather repetitive, but they in no way detract from the high poetry of his output as a whole.

Giorgio Morandi *The Haystack 1938*

◄ Giorgio Morandi *Still Life 1946*

Arturo Tosi *Lake Iseo 1952*

TOSI

We can judge a painter's general coherence by looking at his most recent work. Apart from inevitable changes in idiom, this should have a basic direction corresponding with that of his early work. Few artists live up to this standard, which presupposes that age should bring, not compla-cency, but renewed inspiration. Tosi is among the most coherent painters in this respect.

He spent over sixty years trying to deepen his vision of a few fundamental themes. These were landscapes of the valley of Bergamo with mountains and freshly ploughed earth, seascapes of the Ligurian coast or Lake Iseo, a few still lifes, and flowers.

Tosi was a natural painter, drawn to warm colours and without any intellectual preconceptions. His typically Lombard simplicity came from a harmony of mind and emotion, of critical control and instinct, which brought about a balanced serenity.

We can trace the coherent path from his early formation under Lombard influences to his last works with their more lyrical colour and light. Arturo Tosi was born at Busto Arsizio near Milan in 1871. He admired Piccio's luminous colour, Gola's colour vibrations, and Fontanesi's severe compositions. To a lesser degree he admired Cremona and Bazzaro, and he was a close friend of Grubicy, who taught him about the value of light. Some of his early landscapes reflect aspects of these painters' work. Between 1909 and 1912 Tosi did his series of lively pastels and drawings at

Rovetta, which show that he had found his idiom. The lines are full of colour and atmosphere and reveal pure feeling inspired by nature. Of course he could not escape the influence of Cézanne but, as Argan points out, this was "affective" rather than "intellectual". "He pondered over the lessons of Cézanne and the Impressionists more than anyone . . . and was able to establish a point of moral cohesion in the confusion of Naturalistic sensism." He differed from Cézanne in his colours which were warm and harmonious, never harsh.

His first positive statement came after the exhibitions held in 1926 by *Novecento Italiano*, of which he was a member of the organizing committee. It was apparent that his absorbed, though relative, solitude had served to mature him inwardly—his landscapes had more structure and the masses more weight. His loud colours caused critics to hint at Fauve influence, and there is no doubt that Tosi had seen the Fauves, but only incidentally.

His landscapes, still lifes and compositions with flowers became increasingly limpid as he grew older; and if there were moments of diminished lyrical tension in the course of his long painting life, these certainly did not occur in the years before his death in 1956 when his work was pure and lyrical. *Lago d'Iseo* (Lake Iseo) and *Fiori* (Flowers) with their free brushwork and diaphanous light, together with *Terre Arate* (Ploughed Land) with olive trees, mountains and the Ligurian sea in the sun, are among his greatest achievements.

Arturo Tosi *Still Life 1940*

Arturo Tosi *Ripe Corn 1951*

There is no visible effort in his painting. It derives from meditation and analysis, yet has an apparent spontaneity. The starting-point is a dialogue with nature, but his work transcends descriptive nature painting in that the places he painted had entered deep into his conscious and subconscious mind and become part of his personality. Only when this had happened could he trust the emotion evoked by light, mountains, ploughed land, ripe corn, olive trees, boats on the water, petals of a flower, or still lifes. Hence the serenity and urbanity of his communication. He does not reflect the crisis of our time.

NOVECENTO

The *Novecento* movement had no real programme for painting. It began as a moral attitude and welcomed to its ranks artists widely differing in temperament and idiom. Within the Fascist ethos it became the more or less official tendency, and was opposed, from 1930 onwards, by anti-formal groups such as the Roman School, the "Six" of Turin, the Lombard *Chiaristi* and *Corrente* (all of which I shall discuss in future chapters). The Fascist outlook advocated a return to "Mediterranean" traditions, the myth of heroism, and monumental art, and this was a fertile breeding-ground for the *Novecento* movement.

As we have seen, the spirit of restoring past glories had been at work for some years. De Chirico's neo-Classical yearnings, the rediscovery of Primitive and Renaissance art by the new painters, *La Ronda*'s search for a "noble" literary style, the revaluations of the old masters made by *Valori Plastici*—all these heralded a reaction against the polemics of the *avant-garde* and their rupture with the past. This attitude also existed in European countries other than Italy after the first World War. Picasso went back to Ingres and discovered the frescoes at Pompeii; Léger admired the frescoes of

Luca Signorelli and the Ravenna mosaics; and various Expressionists, from Rouault to Permeke and Hofer, emphasized form which they charged with expressive energy.

At the same time from all sides eyes were turned on Cézanne who was interpreted in two opposite ways—as the discoverer of forms detached from nature and constituting pure architectonic masses, and as the traditionalist painter who continued the dialogue with reality and who held that "we must return to the old masters through nature".

Where the limitations of the *Novecento* movement lay was in its conscious effort to re-create an Italian and "Mediterranean" art, to smooth out differences between old and new, and to overlook the importance of inner poetic urgency. Only the greatest painters, for example, Sironi—who was typically representative of *Novecento* painting—could burn up theories coming from outside in the fire of their native imagination and forge a valid idiom. Others were Campigli, Carrà, Funi in his first period, and Rosai: they, who had experienced Futurism and Cubism, would not be likely to allow the myth of epic grandeur to stifle their own inventiveness.

Achille Funi *Composition 1920*

Mario Sironi *The Sculptor and the Model 1928*

I said above that the *Novecento* movement had no formulated programme. Nevertheless its character became clearer with the passage of time. Its characteristic marks were a revaluation of form with a bias towards volume distorted in the interests of expression, and a liking for architectonic composition and monumentalism. The monumental side of the movement was encouraged by Fascism and easily fell into rhetoric.

The *Novecento* movement had another function. Its best exponents made a decisive break with late nineteenth-century taste in Italy, from flowery influences and those coming from Klimt. It helped to make Italian art better known abroad and, still more important, it accustomed people to look at painting and sculpture not in terms of representation, but as shapes existing in their own right. The first *Novecento* group was formed in Milan in 1922 at the Pesaro Gallery. It was composed of Anselmo Bucci (who thought of the name *Novecento*), Leonardo Dudreville, Achille Funi, Emilio Malerba, Piero Marussig, Ubaldo Oppi and Mario Sironi. The first exhibition was held in the same gallery the following year, and there was another two years later at the Venice Biennale. Meanwhile numbers of artists of different tendencies joined the movement, including Carrà,

Campigli, Semeghini and Tosi. There were further exhibitions both in Italy and abroad, including two in Milan in 1926 and 1929.

Critics have insisted too much on Achille Funi's neo-Classicism and echoes of Ferrarese masters in his work. But it is not as simple as that. A native of Ferrara, he studied the frescoes in the *Officina Ferrarese*, and the Mantegnas at Mantua, and developed a fascination for time-resisting materials and large murals. But his contributions to the *Novecento* movement came less from these than from other works less evocative of the old masters. In his early days he founded a group known as *Nuove Tendenze*. At that time he specialized in rhythmic colour sensations, abstract forms and breaking-up of the object, and was labelled a "temporary Futurist". Boccioni called him "one of the champions of Italian painting".

Soon after the first World War he followed Picasso's example and sought inspiration in Ingres and Pompeii. *Eva* (1927) shows his nearness to Picasso—the figure is abstract, with distortion of an almost Metaphysical kind. But *Il Ritratto del Padre* (Portrait of my Father) shows what he had learnt from Cézanne in the solidification of form and the disharmony of his greens, greys, purples and browns. It was his *Autoritratto* (Self-Portrait) of 1924 that first revealed his affinity with the frescoes of the Ferrarese school, especially in certain colour harmonies. But he was saved from "museum-ism" by the summariness of the construction and the distortion in the interests of expression.

Massimo Campigli *The Amazons 1924*

I listed Piero Marussig above among the foundation-members of the *Novecento* group, but *Novecento* was not a permanent influence on him—fortunately. *Donne al Caffè* (Women in the Café) (1924) in the Gallery of Modern Art in Milan, and the large number of monumental figures and still lifes, cannot be ranked among his most interesting works. Although Marussig's *Novecento* period coincided with his admiration for Cézanne's ability to solve the dualism of colour and form, he himself was far from solving it in these works: their formalism makes colour seem an adjunct to the image, instead of constituting it. In fact, the less monumental he was, the better.

Mario Sironi *City Outskirts 1949*

SIRONI

The most representative figure of the *Novecento* movement was Sironi. But he was more than this, for his oils and temperas give him a place among the most vital painters in Europe today. Instinctive and impetuous by temperament, he reaches his synthesis by means of contrasts in his summary colours and plastic masses.

Willed energy of expression and concreteness of space values are the secret of his language. His need to master his spaces and charge them with "palpable" expression makes him put the problems of composition first. His strength as a designer is obvious, and he has turned his attention to illustration, décor, sculpture, posters and the arrangement of exhibitions—which shows how closely involved he has been in modern life; there is nothing of the ivory tower about him. His best paintings are those in which he has left aulic eloquence behind and charged his idiom with disquieting overtones—such as the colour of ruins and remains corroded by time, evocative and acutely lyrical. Works such as the fresco in the Aula Magna of the Studium Urbis, depicting *Italy between the Arts and Sciences* (1935), or the one in the Palace of Justice in Milan—*Law between Justice and Strength*

Mario Sironi *Composition 1947*

(1936)—are noteworthy for their grandiose oratory, even if they do not reveal the essential Sironi. The essential Sironi is to be found in small paintings, in oil or tempera, depicting various aspects of city life, usually in the seamy outskirts. In these he escapes from declamation and epic splendour and works in a small confined space. Not that his inclination towards the monumental is spurious; it is the genuine, exasperated outcome of his expressive force; it is a genuine cry, not a self-imposed idiom. Sironi has never been a cold neo-Classical painter.

His best works have an advantage over those of other painters in that the subjects themselves—city outskirts, gasometers, factory chimneys, railways and buses—are not merely illustrative, but new and expressive, and give his painting a feeling of contemporary compulsion. His output has been enormous, often consisting of studies and sketches, like pages in a diary. In what follows we will try to pick out his best achievements.

His early formation can be seen in the *Autoritratto* (Self-Portrait), painted in 1908. Though born (1885) and brought up in Sassari, Sardinia, his mother was Tuscan and his father Lombard. He began his career in Rome as a student of engineering but abandoned this after a year to take up painting. He joined the life class at the Academy of Fine Arts and, like Boccioni and Severini, was constantly to be found in Giacomo Balla's studio. But Balla could give him little except contact with the Divisionists; their temperament had nothing in common. The *Self-Portrait* already shows Sironi's tendency to summary, rather metallic colouring, far indeed from the Impressionists. The rough wall in the background gives relief to the mass of the head with remarkable psychological

Mario Sironi *Composition with Horse 1953*

Mario Sironi *Mural Painting 1938*

effect. We can detect an affinity with some of Boccioni's pre-Futurist painting. Sironi's contact with Futurism took the form not of splitting up the object nor of interpenetration of the object and its surroundings by means of lines and planes of energy, but of an increased freedom of invention and expression as regards the real, the rejection of representation and a new sense of rhythm which was also suggested by the Cubists. Futurism also encouraged him to turn to typically modern motifs such as factories, cranes, chimneys and engines. He never actually turned his back on Futurism, like some of the painters who had signed the manifesto, but he never at any time felt tied to a programme; he was always consistent with himself. *Camion* (Lorry) (1914) is typical of Sironi with its metallic masses, its unexpected contrasts of light, and the monumental composition. He came nearest to Cubism with *Atelier delle Meraviglie* (Magic Workshop) and *Elica* (Propeller) (1918). His *Cavallo Bianco* (White Horse) (1919) marks the end of his experiment with Futurism and shows Meta-physical influence.

In 1920 he started his famous series of paintings of city outskirts. In that year he painted *Paesaggio Urbano* (Townscape) in the Cacciabue Collection. The picture expresses the squalor of modern loneliness. A dark sky shot with pale lights, a sombre wall, a crane, a few isolated houses in the distance, and in the foreground a van on grey asphalt. The angle of vision is from above, and the subdued lights evoke a feeling of the infinite. Other examples of the best of this series are *Periferia* (City Outskirts) (1922) in the Foa Collection, *Paesaggio Urbano* (Townscape) in the Rome Gallery of Modern Art, *Strada Ferrata* (Railway Lines) (1924) and the well-known *Gasometro* (Gasometer) (1943) in the Jucker Collection. In all of them the areas of colour—greys, lead whites, burnt browns, purples—are in luminous contrast, and the light is harsh. There are no literary or theatrical overtones in these studies of city life, such as we find in De Chirico's *Città d'Italia* (Italian Cities). They are born of Sironi's deep need for expression and his intense participation in the scenes depicted.

Pica has pointed out that "obviously Nordic Expressionism had some influence on Sironi", but, he goes on, "it would be difficult to assess how far these echoes of Expressionism are deliberate and cultivated and how far they spring from a spontaneous community of feeling".

Sironi spent some time in Paris with Boccioni and was in Germany in the period just before the first World War. In France he felt no attraction to Impressionism, but was influenced by some of the Cubist ideas and by the general spirit of European revival current in Paris at the time. His affinities with Permeke became clear only at a later stage, some years after his own idiom was defined. What he chiefly admired in the German Expressionists and in Northern painters generally was their force of expression, their freedom from the model and their principles of moral and even social order. Distortion in the interests of vivid, immediate expression appealed to him enormously. On the other hand, we can see by his preference for sombre colours, tonal paintings and unexpected lighting that neither the Fauves nor the painters of the Brücke or Blaue Reiter movements had much meaning for him.

By 1922 the "museum" influence had got the upper hand. In 1922, as has been said, Sironi became a foundation-member of the Milanese "group of Seven Modern Painters" which was subsequently called the *Novecento* movement, and we find contrasts of light being chilled by the requirements of grandiose form—as in *Modella dello Scultore* (Sculptor's Model), *Architetto* (Architect) and various monumental nudes.

His series of *Multiple Compositions* that extend from the time of his large murals down to a recent date tend to rigidity in rhythm but are brought to life by the colour, which is more varied than usual, and by overtones of the archaic. His latest paintings show freedom of invention and the achievement of new harmonies in architectonic metre. Unlike other painters of his age who have entangled themselves in their so-called "return to order", Sironi has continued to develop his idiom coherently and in a more and more European way. His style has become purified with the years, and even today the cycle of his work cannot be said to be closed.

CAMPIGLI

Massimo Campigli felt the call of Paris as early as 1919 and it became his home despite frequent returns to Italy. "In those days Cubism was passing through its period of abstraction, precision and austere discipline," he wrote. "My own inclination at that time was towards psychological complica-tion, and yet I longed to achieve order and serenity and felt that dedication to painting of that kind

Massimo Campigli *Dancers 1938*

would give direction to my life." His earliest compositions reflect not only Cubism but the "monu-mental" Picasso, and he had an eye, too, for remote civilizations of the past. The images he chose to paint derive from the contemplation of remote worlds, fragments corroded by the dust of time—and he treats them with subtle irony. Even the subjects he culled from the present are projected into the past or even outside time. Gestures, smiles, girls with urns and huge bewitched eyes, hang in a buried past.

This gives Campigli's pictures Metaphysical overtones. Etruscan tombs, the Korai, the Fayum, Egyptian ideographs, Pompeian frescoes and Ravenna mosaics are not, of course, seen by Campigli as examples to be imitated; they are pretexts for subtle and ironical interpretation in terms of a fully self-conscious culture.

So Campigli is not neo-Classical. He projects the present into the past only to make it more fabulous and to load it more suggestively with symbols. In the abstract space of his delicate decora-tion there is full freedom for rhythm. As all correspondence with nature has been removed, the objects in the composition are linked by subtle analogies, by harmonies of voids and masses, of browns and greys, warm or cold tones.

In his early stages we find Campigli inclined towards the rhythms of volumes which stand out in relief against backgrounds of subdued grey. As Raffaele Carrieri put it in his penetrating remarks about Campigli: "His beginnings as a painter were laborious and slow and bound by a rigid system . . . it was a time of enormous immobility before venturing forth into the fresh world of games and dreams, into that paradise for sophisticated adults that is his memory. . . ."

Le Amazzoni (The Amazons) (1924) in the Mattioli Collection shows a new departure in idiom and increased freedom. The few colours are based on terracottas, browns and yellows. The white dominates, and the black modulates, the grey. The other colours are in accord with the terracotta that set the key. Here and there we find a little green and blue, and there is an occasional touch of pink.

But as the years pass we find the volumes being reduced to two dimensions. The colour is rough, as in frescoes, and absorbs the light, making it opaque. The rhythm is expressed in hiero-glyphs, the symbols recall lost ages and buried civilizations. We find a multiplication of heads, busts, emblematic gestures, spaces whose rhythms have a grace born of the intellect.

After these experiments Campigli returned once more to a feeling for volumes, but this is less clear cut than in the earlier stages. The Cubist influence was still there, as we see by the reversal of the planes, the arrangement and the inlay effect of the profiles. The key in which the picture is set moves through the interplay of space and colour and the objects are not detached from the back-ground. The more subtle, imperceptible passages are created by colour.

Of course Campigli varied his motifs with time, but he always remained faithful to themes born of culture and history—and this is both the limitation and the essence of his style.

DE PISIS

Filippo De Pisis also exhibited in the first exhibition of the *Novecento Italiano* in 1926; but after his period in Ferrara and Rome he abandoned monumental themes and closed forms and the other tenets of that group's creed.

De Pisis was ardently imaginative. He could transform anything into paint—flowers, clouds, houses, fishes, feathers, skies, street corners, moths, fans. As the years passed, his painting was achieved with ever lighter strokes, with swift and penetrating vibrations. He saw the world in terms of light, colour and breaths of wind. His tones are exact; each vibration of colour has its accurate

Massimo Campigli *Figures on a Couch 1952*

Filippo De Pisis *Still Life 1953*

value and is confident and instinctive. His critical control is straightforward—there was never any conflict between mental control and instinct. Nothing in his pictures has repose. All the elements seem to be vibrant with emotion. His delicate and nervous grace makes him one of the most vital painters of our time.

There is of course a dark side to the moon. His ease and felicity sometimes involved him in rather repetitive *tours de force*. His output was enormous, but we will deal only with the best. His high standing as an artist was confirmed by the two comprehensive exhibitions of his work in 1951, one in Ferrara and the other at the Gallery of Modern Art in Milan. In his paintings we find sensuality and feeling, abandon, lucid mental control and free fancy. Even at moments of diminished tension there is no trace of self-conscious effort. De Pisis never had time for theories, wars of words, groups or group-arguments about whether painting should be up to date or not. With a painter so instinc-tively gifted, so delicate and imaginative and given to short intense lyrics, it is difficult to make any detailed study of his relationship with the pictorial climate around him. The important thing is to establish the various elements in his formation, the indirect influences and his own preferences.

De Pisis was born in Ferrara in 1896. There he came into contact with Carrà and De Chirico at the time of their Metaphysical experiments. As Pallucchini puts it: "His literary spirit and his birth in Ferrara were both conducive to an understanding of the elegant intellectualism and pure rhythm of shapes in space that were expressed and liberated by the Metaphysical painters." But the compositions of the Metaphysical painters were not really suited to De Pisis's temperament, for with him angles, squares and circles lose their definite geometry; his expression is always a state of becom-ing. When still very young he adapted Metaphysical influence to his playful fancy which knew nothing of precise measurements or stage-set effects. He felt colour in a sensual way and with an emotional involvement that excluded calculation; his compositions were the fruit of inner compul-sion. Even the specimens of his Metaphysical paintings exhibited in 1951 show how mobile were his rhythms; and his cursive idiom was later to become abbreviated into swift essential painting that has been called "shorthand".

But though his Metaphysical period contributed little to the formation of his idiom, nevertheless it left its mark on him, for it appeared later though in a different form. Pallucchini defines it as "a sense of apprehension, an extreme lucidity of feeling that has given his art such a singular accent of spiritual tension". And De Pisis himself wrote: "Some pictures done in 1926 and 1927—fishes hanging in the sun outside a window, melancholy red wine in an old carafe set on a pensive table within the empty parallelepiped of a macabre room—are works that could be called *metaphysical* even in the ordinary historical sense." But here he is writing of a metaphysics of expression that lies

Filippo De Pisis
Flowers 1927

in allusions of colour rather than the detached nature of the vision. In other words, we are dealing with something nearer to Guardi or Magnasco than to De Chirico.

The fact that in 1919 De Pisis adopted certain Dadaist mannerisms only confirmed his need for complete freedom from all theory; but he soon tired of Dadaism with its disputes about the arbitrary and the absurd. The arbitrary and irrational for him became incentives to further imaginative poetry.

De Pisis tells us that his stay in Rome from 1919 to 1925 taught him to admire Spadini, and further encounters that played their part in the development of his painting took place in Paris, where he spent many years, though frequently returning to Italy. We must not forget that De Pisis was already definitely formed when he went to Paris—he was anything but provincial. He already knew all about the general trends through Carrà and De Chirico, his contact with the Dadaists, and *La Ronda* and *Valori Plastici*. In Paris he gave his feeling for colour freer rein. Manet, Sisley, Pissarro, Utrillo and Matisse helped to define his taste. His palette became lighter with a new luminosity. Contact with the Impressionists brought him back in a new way to the eighteenth-century Venetian painters, and above all to Guardi: here lay the living precedent for his idiom. After periods of residence in London, Rome and Milan, he decided that Venice was his favourite city—its lights and colours and secrets were a constant joy to his poetic temperament and his love of sudden surprise, mystery, unexpected light, and the miracle of the present moment perpetually destroyed and reborn. De Pisis's debt to Manet, Degas and Cézanne has been analysed by Giuseppe Raimondi. It was Umbro Apollonio who pointed out his debt to Tintoretto, Guercino and Tiepolo, while Cesare Brandi, as early as 1932, in analysing his success in terms of the richness of the quality of his colour, noticed similarities with Guardi.

We have already said that still lifes, landscapes, figures and the seaside become poetry at De Pisis's light touch. He himself said: "Even in the views or landscapes of Paris (sad streets, leafy or bare, blank walls, age-old courtyards) there is always an overlying lyrical motif which in no way detracts from reality." The object, whether a flower, a landscape or a figure, is subsumed into the artist's subjective consciousness.

De Pisis is an outstandingly pure painter. Even in his black-and-white drawings—portraits, nudes, still lifes and landscapes—we can see how highly he values light, atmosphere and intensity

Filippo De Pisis *Still Life with Bread 1925*

of expression in his quick gossamer touches. The greys, greens and pinks, the liquid blacks, the blues and browns, put on with extremely agile brushwork in dabs of pure colour, give him a high place in lyrical painting. He is a rare and happy example of a painter who "naturally" and without effort obtains painterly results.

Filippo De Pisis *Street in Paris 1928*

Mino Maccari *Women 1952*

STRAPAESE

At this time a movement was growing in Italy in sharp reaction to the *avant-garde* spirit and the prevailing international idioms. It was prompted by various "recalls to order" and by those public activities that put a high price on Italian traditions. There was a glorification of nationalism, provincial feeling and provincial dialect.

This movement, which was known as *Strapaese*, was encouraged by two reviews, *Il Selvaggio*, founded and edited by Mino Maccari in 1924, and Leo Longanesi's *L'Italiano*. The movement in Tuscany and Emilia was based on local popular tradition and advocated a living and spontaneous idiom suitable for depicting lively scenes of local life and the popular grotesque.

Today it is easy to see the fallacies of the *Strapaese* movement with its glorification of a closed nationalist spirit and reactionary opposition to the international scene. And yet the movement had a certain value which, in the field of painting, it owed principally to the personality of Rosai. The ideal of "dialect" painting, withdrawn from contact with European culture, obviously entails exclusion from the vital developments in the history of art and in this way is negative, leading to anecdote, illustration or the frank Primitivism of Sunday painters. On the other hand, local movements, as we know from previous experience—of Ensor, Daumier, Futurism, Cubism, Cézanne and Corot —can bring about new and valid idioms; they can promote deeper penetration into a given milieu, into the painter himself, and hence tend towards an elimination of hypocrisy. Whether such a movement falls into decadent and self-satisfied aestheticism, or whether it produces great painting, depends on the inventiveness and poetic energy of individual artists.

Unfortunately *Strapaese* played a mainly negative part in the development of Italian art, and the final result was the breeding of a reactionary atmosphere of querulous and equivocal returns to the past which merely delayed the development of fresh idioms.

One of the names associated with *Strapaese* is Mino Maccari, but though his idiom gave the impression of being simple and primitive and characteristic of the common people, it was really the product of a complex cultural background, as critics such as Roberto Longhi, Pallucchini, Marchiori and Apollonio recognized at an early date. Maccari was not only an expressive and caustic illustrator with a taste for satire and the grotesque, but in some of his paintings he was a genuine artist, and it would be a grave mistake to relegate him to the outer fringes of the achievement of his time.

From *Strapaese* he inherited the frank vitality of his subject-matter that suited his personal and capricious inventiveness and his ability to hit the target. It gave him the moral stimulus for his richly funny and grotesque satire against the prejudices, beliefs, clichés and privileges of certain sections of society. But behind his satire we find something else. Maccari can turn from mere caprice to images redolent of the allusive atmosphere of dreams. These two tendencies within him reflect basic moods in his character which can blend and achieve coherence through their common origin.

Maccari's idiom was not born of provincial or local influences. His early formation was academic; after which it was Ensor and Grosz who taught him the urgency of the Expressionist line, and Daumier and Rouault who introduced him to the French tradition. The resonant colours of the Fauves were not entirely foreign to his own anti-Naturalistic colour-schemes, and he learnt from the luminous colours that he found in post-Impressionism to tone down the harsh and strident disharmonies of the Expressionists. His caustic, satirical and incisive line becomes gentler, lighter and more extended when the image is a fanciful caprice in the neo-Baroque spirit, just as the loud colours of his "grotesques" soften into luminous pinks, purples, greens and azures. As Umbro Apollonio put it: "Maccari is unable to think outside figurative terms." There is no question of dualism in Maccari but of successive moments reflecting the fancy of a personality indifferent to programmes and endowed with a wealth of inventive imagination.

Any material—from exercise books to copper—gave Maccari the opportunity for creating his figures—figures that often transcend illustration and attain a mood of deep lyricism even when at first sight they seem no more than grotesque jokes.

ROSAI

"For the first time an Italian painter has put himself not at the centre of the universe but in its most hidden corner"—a phrase of Argan's that is as good an introduction as any to Rosai's art. Some critics have misunderstood Rosai's inclination to tell stories "about hooligans and street urchins", and this has led to a false distinction being made between the idiom he uses for typical street scenes and the clearer more lyrical language of his landscapes. But in fact Rosai's personality cannot be explained in terms of two different types of painting, for even his seemingly detached landscapes reveal an emphasis on expression.

The experiences that helped to form Rosai were various. He himself tells us that the masters he most admired were Daumier, Corot, Courbet and Cézanne. "My favourite is Corot," he wrote.

Ottone Rosai *Still Life 1919*

"His closed sonorous tones in forms which are real and yet invented—creating an atmosphere of dream-like magic and drama—carry my mind to the past . . . and I see how everyone has been modern in his own time. Masaccio, Giorgione and Tintoretto were, as it were, the Corots of their day. I find Cézanne in the great Tuscan painters—he is the Giotto of today. He is the most classical and the most modern of modern painters."

In his detailed analysis of Rosai's formation Parronchi brings forward Ensor as a decisive influence in his life—as having taught him "the existence of a sort of caricature which is not caricature but painting of character raised to the level of fantasy". And then, according to this theory, between 1912 and 1914 his idiom moved on from the twists and distortions of Ensorian satire to the Futurist breaking-up of the object.

Ottone Rosai *Little Concert* 1920

We agree that Ensor's name cannot be excluded—not for any influence over style but over subject-matter—the haunting, nightmare quality. But Daumier, mentioned by Rosai himself, surely played a bigger part in the development of his caustic and grotesque outline—more, however, through his drawings than through his paintings. For we must not forget that Rosai himself began as a draughts-man rather than a colourist, and his drawing had immediate impact, incisively fixing gestures, people, milieux in a few direct strokes.

Rosai's participation in the Futurist movement was merely incidental. It was a necessary experience and a process of liberation that set him on the way towards rhythms in composition and a new Primitivism of expression. *Bottiglia+Zantuntun* (Bottle+Zantuntun) (1912), *Bar San Marco* (The San Marco Bar) and *Scomposizione di Strada* (Breaking-up of a Street)—both done in 1914—and the *Natura Morta* (Still Life) (1916, Mattioli Collection) show how emotion is condensed in thick colour and charged with allusions, with a certain hardness of line in the dashes and curves. *Banco di Falegname* (Carpenter's Bench) (1914) has an almost Metaphysical air about it with its sharp contrast of shadows. But *Paesaggio* (Landscape) (Jucker Collection) of the same year shows the influence of the strict Cubist formulas inherited from Braque. (In these years Soffici was struggling to re-establish contact with Europe and to make Cubism known in Italy.)

Rosai had a very fruitful period between 1919 and 1922. In *Interno con Suonatori* (Interior with Musicians) (1919), *Partita a Briscola* (Card-Game), *Giocatori di Toppa* (Card Players), and the still lifes, all of 1920, and in the small intense portrait of his father (1921) and the well-known *Via*

Ottone Rosai *Evening Card-Game*

Ottone Rosai *Tuscan Village 1947*

Toscanella (1922), Rosai established the limits of his expression. His colour is clear and bright and the browns, greys, purples and cold blues vie in fixing the expressive force of the drawing, while the drawing itself sustains the structure of the painting. The "hidden corners" of Rosai's universe, referred to above, lie in the quarters across the Arno with the poor and the homeless, street musicians, card players, workmen's wineshops, barrow men, scavengers.

After 1930 he began to develop a rough *Macchiaiolo* chiaroscuro style but, as others have pointed out, this was not an inheritance from the Tuscan *Macchiaioli* of the nineteenth century: the palette of Signorini and Fattori was based on traditional earth colours, whereas Rosai began by making use of blues, turquoises, terracottas, dark greens, greys and purples, and his texture has a rough and corrosive quality.

In the early years after the first World War Cézanne's influence was steadily growing and in Italy he became a symbol of "the recall to order". But it appears that it was not until 1920 that Rosai first saw reproductions of his work, whereupon he, too, came under his influence both as to form and colour. Some critics have mentioned Seurat as yet another influence on Rosai, and others Douanier Rousseau, but if we go on naming names we shall get bogged down in a world of generalizations.

In recent years Rosai has lightened his palette and his landscapes have become sunnier. By and large it can certainly be said of his paintings that they are a notable contribution to Europe from a province.

The same cannot be said of another Tuscan painter, Lorenzo Viani. His scenes depicting pathos, squalor and despair seldom rise above description. His use of paint has nothing remarkable about it. He is perhaps at his best and freest in his drawings.

Viani's early years were influenced by the "art nouveau" style then in vogue, but on his travels in 1908 and 1910 he got to know Toulouse-Lautrec's work and was influenced by that painter's

Lorenzo Viani
Woman of Paris 1909

incisive and powerful lines. Nordic Expressionism, especially that of Munch, also left its mark on him. But nevertheless his taste for the pathetic and the violent-grotesque is communicated primarily on the literary plane.

After experiments with Cubism, Viani's vision became more serene and in his latter years he has painted landscapes with less sting in them.

CASORATI

Conscious self-criticism and cerebration have been factors in the work of nearly all modern painters, but in the case of Felice Casorati they definitely came first. His colours have always been filtered by his intellect, and his intellect has set emotion and sensuality apart against a cold, lunar background. Casorati also manifests a continual pervading sense of disquiet which he carries beyond the object to the allusive significance of the symbols which, in their turn, merge with the objects in the ghostly

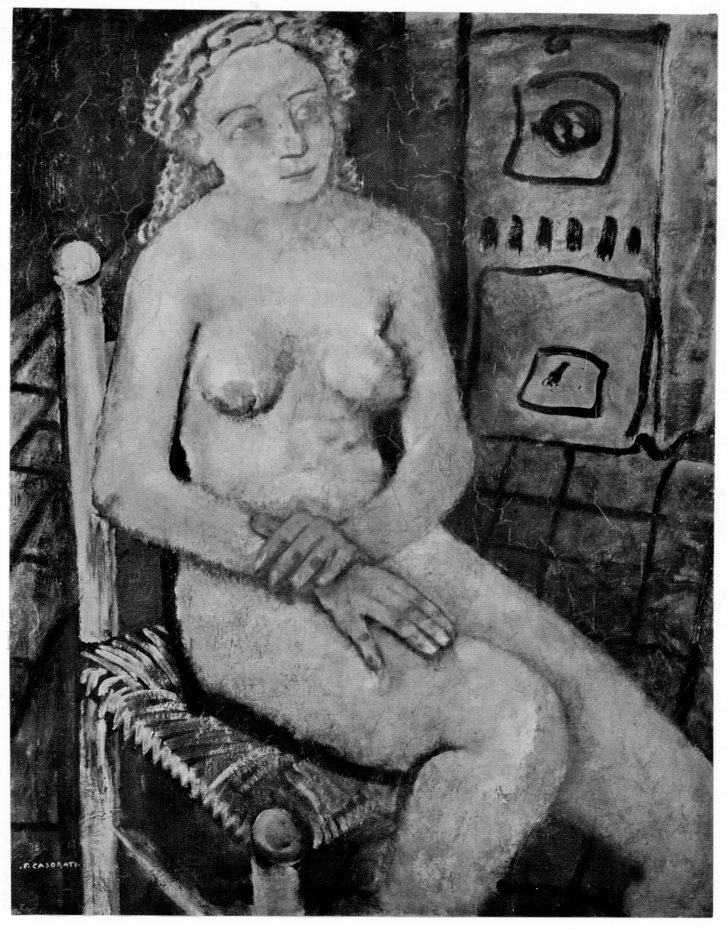

Felice Casorati *Seated Nude 1933*

Felice Casorati *Reclining Nude 1951*

light produced by the insistent prevalence of cold tones. The result is a solid, strictly disciplined world, but a world suspended over an invisible abyss and with a vague sense of guilt and anguish.

We find this ghostliness even in his earliest works, when he was learning clarity of composition from Piero della Francesca, the neo-Platonic Mannerists and the Cubists: we sense the continual pull to the north, to Klimt, to the Munich Secessionists and to German Symbolism. This has isolated him to a certain extent even though, as Albino Galvano puts it, "he is of first-rate importance to many of his generation, as regards formation of taste and orientation of culture—not only in the figurative field". A comment of Umbro Apollonio's would seem to throw light on his isolation: "In Turin, where Casorati lived and taught at the academy, there were a number of painters whose work was the very antithesis of his own. The orientation of their art—inherited from the Impressionists and post-Impressionists—was totally opposed to that of Casorati."

In *Ritratto della Sorella* (Portrait of my Sister)—which was accepted by the jury for the Seventh Venice Biennale—and *Le Figlie dell'Attrice* (Daughters of the Actress), *Le Vecchie* (The Old Women) and *La Cugina* (My Cousin)—all done in 1910—we can already detect acute psychological insight, a pre-established system of composition and vague literary feeling. By 1912 we find the cerebral sense of line emphasized with elegant detachment under the influence of Symbolism —*Le Signorine* (The Young Ladies)—and by 1914 there are marks of Klimt's influence—*Una Donna* (A Woman). Under the influence of Kandinsky he set about seeking a reality in drawing and painting that transcended the motif. One of his most significant paintings is *Tiro a Bersaglio* (Target Practice) done in 1918; and there ended the experiments of all that period. From then onwards Casorati felt free to move on to space values by means of perspective from above and the search for pure tone; he had come to the end of his links with Naturalism and his efforts at psychology. The results had certain Metaphysical overtones—but were none the less very different from Carrà and De Chirico. Casorati's Metaphysical painting had the staticness of silence, desolate and icily lonely. He was stimulated by the neo-Platonic Tuscan Mannerists of the sixteenth century, and yet in the treatment of detail and the reversal of planes we see something that reminds us of the reconstructions of the Cubists.

From flat designs we find him moving on to volumes which he composed with subtlety and great care in the modelling. He tended to simplify his forms so as to be more generous with colour, but the cylinders and cones are rounded with subtle tonal sensibility. He caused the light to divide the forms into two clearly contrasting zones, giving an architectural effect. And yet the plastic forms have "appearance rather than reality" as Giacomo De Benedetti put it. "Of true, direct plastic feeling all we find is the idealized re-evocation."

For long years—from his *Uova sulla Tavola* (Eggs on the Table) to his various still lifes, figures and nudes—he continued along this same path of lucid and penetrating Mannerism. The *Nudo* (Nude) of 1933 and *Venere Bionda* (Blonde Venus) of 1934 are evocative of arabesque rhythms.

But even paintings which are obviously the outcome of intense rational analysis have an air—in the cadences of their composition—of suspended uneasiness, of not belonging to the world. According to Luigi Carluccio, Casorati's art is one of "conscious detachment and calculated silence. The emotion is one of infinite probability. In his rigorous search for quintessential purity all feelings have been peeled away, and human symbols are put aside in favour of his habitual iconography. . . ."

To sum up then, most of Casorati's paintings lie within the limits imposed by craftsmanship dominated by the intellect; a few display a search for idiom; and others—most notably *Tiro a Bersaglio, Uova sulla Tavola*, the *Nude* of 1933 and various other figures of that period—attain a personal idiom always dominated by the search for lucid and formal purity.

SEMEGHINI

Pio Semeghini is another artist who kept out of group programmes. In Venice he belonged to the "Pleiade" of the island of Burano with Moggioli, Gino Rossi and Scopinich, but on the whole his meditative and solitary temperament made him fight shy of polemics and experimentation. He has a definite if subdued talent. Apollonio points out that it took a long time for him to establish his place in the history of Italian art; but by now Lamberto Vitali, Ragghianti, Pallucchini, Marchiori as well as Apollonio himself have all come to realize that the place is well deserved. It is hardly surprising that at the time when everyone was admiring the monumental compositions of *Novecento* art, a poetry that was less spectacular should be overlooked. Misunderstanding placed Semeghini among the lesser post-Impressionists, as "a painter of reality who was ready to make use of any kind of picturesque subject". But his one-man show at the Fifteenth Biennale in Venice confirmed that he was endowed with original gifts.

His youth was tempestuous. The year 1899 found him in Paris at the age of twenty-one. He stayed there on and off until 1914. He came into contact with Soffici and exhibited in company

Pio Semeghini *Landscape 1927*

with Picasso. But in Semeghini the influence of French post-Impressionism—of Cézanne, Pissarro and Matisse—was crossed with the traditional background of meditation and observation of the early Venetian colourists and fifteenth-century frescoes by Piero della Francesca and the Lombard masters. Hence though his painting echoes the French idiom of the end of the nineteenth century, it would be erroneous to consider him merely as a post-Impressionist.

"The lagoons of Venice", says Pallucchini, "played a fundamental part in Semeghini's formation." Cézanne's influence is obvious in his work until about 1919, after which he turned to an idiom that was controlled and whittled down to the very minimum of what was essential. During the period when *Novecento* taste held sway, Semeghini stood aside and went on painting his minor harmonies in light tints, with outlines either clear cut or almost dissolving in morning light: pale rain-washed greens, tenuous pinks and violets and lilacs, ochres, very light blues. There is subtle counterpoint in his chords and discords of colour with no use of chiaroscuro. The light, as Apollonio points out, is not Impressionist but "constant and abstract"—a clean shadowless morning light. The spaces and colours in his compositions are calculated with barely perceptible asymmetries and rhythmic disharmonies in movement. Semeghini's grace and charm are subtly strident.

The subject of his pictures comes from the observation of real nature. His Burano girls have a melancholy which has psychological insight in the background, and yet in his better works the result is not merely descriptive. The poetry is reduced to a few essential elements mastered on a minor scale. His incisive lines show long experience of engraving. His early activities as a sculptor were never entirely forgotten.

As the years passed his colour became more transparent and his images took on an elegiac grace. But this must not make us confuse him with the decadence of the twilight. There is a subdued but

82

Pio Semeghini *Figure 1934*

original lyrical value in his landscapes of the Venetian lagoon, the canals, the bridges of Burano, the lace-makers and the countryside. With Semeghini French culture once more finds a place in Venetian tradition.

Semeghini's idiom has no great breadth nor clamorous appeal, nor is it particularly new. But within its well-defined limits it is sharp and clear.

GUIDI

The retrospective exhibition of Virgilio Guidi's work at the Seventeenth Venice Biennale which included fifty of his paintings from 1919 to 1954, showed to what extent this painter's idiom was a sustained effort to reach sheer essentiality, a continual jettisoning of what had gone before. It showed his passage from the humanistic conception of space, to space seen as something limitless and cosmic in movement. It also showed how his restless adventurous questing finally became the motif of his best pictures. As Alfonso Gatto puts it, we feel that Guidi "found his expression in the form of questions, not answers, concerning the mystery of his art". Guidi's world is always

Virgilio Guidi *Figures in Space 1947*

Virgilio Guidi *Figure 1952*

in a state of suspense outside time, which the slant of his figures emphasizes. His limitless and lucid spatiality suggests a new kind of Metaphysical painting to our minds—a Metaphysical painting of light which, by its transparency and movement, becomes cosmic in "a single breath". As Guidi himself has put it: "At the hour of midday reality is immense; light shines down from the heights of the sky and illumines everything impartially; all things have their being in an extreme purity and clarity, responsible for their aspects of form and colour, and yet they are gathered together in a single breath. . . ."

His early formation took place in Rome in the circles round Spadini. At this time there was a tendency to enclose Impressionism within solemn classical compositions with a nostalgia for the past. We can trace Guidi's development through *Modella* (Model) of 1913, *Maternità* (Maternity) (1919), *Madre che si leva* (Mother getting up) and the copy of Correggio's *Danae* of 1921 to the *Tram* of 1924. We can see how the neo-Classical formula is used as a defence against the sensitive diffuseness of Impressionist origin. This early work gives an overall impression of compromise which nevertheless corresponds to the general aims of the *Novecento* movement. And yet, as Sergio Solmi points out, we can detect even at this early stage "an accent of suspense in the quiet vibration of colour and in the diffusion of the soft, light, even tones that immediately calls to mind a way of painting that is open and personal to an extreme degree".

Thenceforward, from his Roman landscapes with their trace of Cézanne in the lyrical solidity of composition, down to the Venetian landscapes and figures of the late twenties, we find colour becoming more and more limpid, bright and transparent, and the colour-light relationship tending to eliminate all chiaroscuro. Space becomes increasingly rarified, shadows lose their substance and become pure and luminous colour. A brooding melancholy strips the world bare. The browns, pinks, ochres and blues become harsh. Obviously there is no room for illustration in this kind of vision. Landscapes, figures and portraits are pretexts for evoking the subjective image. There is less and less interest in the individual object. The pink of drapery, the blue or yellow of a scarf, the curve of an arm or the slant of a figure disclose the huge luminosity of his vision of Venice and the transparency of his sky.

Guidi's detachment from the object is typically modern. Some writers have mentioned Modigliani and Picasso as inspiring freedom from the model, but the bigger part was played by the whole modern artistic climate. Hence Guidi's "stubborn asceticism" which, according to Cecchi, made him reject "all the graces and surprises of reality", was not a defect but an outcome of his temperament and critical conscience. We should look for his shortcomings rather in a failure—in some pictures—to achieve his purpose: the image is perceived but not always stylistically realized; his intuition shades off into refinement of taste and his effort to reduce the image to essentiality leaves his formula too obvious. *Marina attraverso la Grata* (Seascape seen through a Wire Fence) (1953) is a good example of this. The wire fence, and the space occupied by the light of the water and the sky, are two parallel abstractions superimposed on one another; they are never really brought together. Guidi, we feel, wanted to eliminate all conventionality, but the wire belongs to a geometric, abstract formula while the light of the space, even though rarefied to a maximum degree, is still evocative and bound up with nature. And we must bear in mind that all light in Guidi's paintings is born of a sensitive assimilation of the natural light of Venice and the lagoon, so that in origin it corresponds to something in nature even when he tries to make it cosmic or abstract.

In any case the indecision between sensitive evocation and abstract symbol, between intention, taste and the search for lyricism, was born of a clearly defined personality that shunned modern experiences with the uneasiness of a restless solitary.

His greatest paintings, those entitling him to a high place for their originality and lyricism are his Venetian *Marine* (Shores), *Incontri* (Meetings) and several *Figure nello Spazio* (Figures in Space).

Roberto Melli *Smiling Woman 1932*

MELLI

Argan has described Roberto Melli's function in the Italian artistic landscape thus: "While others were challenging the Futurist frenzy of speed with Metaphysical staticness, it was Melli who opened the way to *Valori Plastici* and the effort to identify space and colour that finally led to the Roman School." Yet it was not until the end of the second World War that the critics gave this painter the recognition that was his due.

Melli was both a sculptor and a painter in his early years, and on the whole his sculpture was more interesting than his painting as can be seen when we compare *La Fantesca* (The Servant Girl) (1911) with bronzes such as *La Signora dal Cappello Nero* (Lady in a Black Hat) and *Mia Moglie* (My Wife) of the same period. Though one of Melli's freest paintings of that time, *La Fantesca* betrays a certain contrivance in the composition. His taste has more in common with the Expressionists than with the

Fauves, but the impetus of his imagination is checked by critical control and intellectualism. His tone values are carefully calculated and have a subtle brightness, but his colour seems as it were frozen by mind. It is this constant slowing-down process on the part of the mind that makes Melli's painting "difficult".

In the sculptures mentioned above, however, the expression shows freedom and complete mastery of technique. It has been said that these sculptures lie somewhere between Boccioni and Medardo Rosso, and certainly Melli was familiar with those two artists, and yet the idiom is different: different from Boccioni owing to his more static, less dynamic, effort at expression through the breaking-down of form; different from Rosso owing to his greater formalism and the strong rhythms created by his "negative volumes". The colour derives not from his impetuous touch that makes the material vibrate, but from the alternation of the hollows which get tonal value from the thickening of the shadows. We find attempts at similar effects in some of the paintings done at this period, such as *Studio di Testa* (Study of a Head) (1916) and various other studies and portraits down to 1919. But the outlines become increasingly contrived so as finally to verge on calligraphy, and freedom of expression is reduced by over-control. His sensitive craftsmanship and love for pure materials in the service of space-colour identification are incontestable—but to the detriment of fancy.

Yet when Melli overcomes the limits imposed by analytical abstraction and the conflict between criticism and free imagination, the results are as good as in his early sculpture. In *La Sorridente* (Smiling Woman) (1932) we find perfect harmony between colour, space and outline. Some of his paintings of the banks of the Tiber and some of his still lifes disclose a Melli free from preoccupation and achieving the authentic accents of poetry—for instance, *Autunno* (Autumn) in the Natale Collection, or *Sul Tevere* (On the Tiber) done in 1947. In these space, light and colour are harmoniously resolved and the principles expounded in *Valori Plastici* are worked out in practice.

THE ROMAN SCHOOL

The first manifestation of what was later to be known as the Roman School took place as early as the winter of 1928 with an exhibition in two corridors of the Doria Gallery: it consisted of a small selection of works by Scipione and Mafai and a few by Di Cocco, Ceracchini and Capogrossi. The contrast between the two first-named painters and the officially sponsored *Novecento* art was obvious. Mafai exhibited a self-portrait and some early views of Rome, including *Colosseo* (Colosseum); Scipione exhibited *Colazione del Lupo di Mare* (The Sea-Dog's Meal) and *Il Sogno di Giacomino* (Giacomino's Dream). I do not know whether Raphael exhibited her *Passaggiata al Palatino* (Walk on the Palatine), also of 1928. But in any case it was certainly no easy task to decide which of these three painters was responsible for inventing the idiom which they so largely shared.

But the Roman School only really attracted attention after a larger exhibition in November 1930. This was organized by P. M. Bardi at the Galleria di Roma in the Via Veneto, following on a posthumous exhibition of Spadini. This time there were twenty works by Scipione and another twenty by Mafai. The event, in De Libero's words, constituted "a real hurricane in the artistic sky of Rome". But the enthusiasm it aroused in fact was limited to a few critics such as Ungaretti, Longhi, Cecchi, Cardarelli, Barilli and Oppo. Other Roman circles and the official critics remained indifferent.

But it was plain that a new tendency—in a European direction—was beginning to take shape. Readers must remember that in those days the drama of the younger generation of painters lay in their being cut off from the life and culture of the rest of the Continent, and this gave them a feeling of tortured inferiority. It was also plain that whereas Italian painters of the previous generation had fastened on all that was most formal and lucid in European art in their advocacy of a return to order

Scipione *The Prophet in Sight of Jerusalem 1930*

and tradition, the new generation had a weather eye open for all that was most restless and tormented —from Van Gogh to the Fauves and the Expressionists. As Argan put it: "They want to make the world's grief and suffering their own." It was this sense of anguish that emphasized the need for lyricism on a closed as distinct from a discursive plane. The younger generation opposed the *Novecento* movement by means of freer and more penetrating colour and intensity of expression. Post-Impressionism, the Fauves and above all Expressionism were to be their means for proclaiming their feeling of revolt against rhetoric and academic art.

After Scipione's death the critics were much exercised as to whether it was he or Mafai who had originated their common language. Argan tried to shed light on the problem by comparing their cultural backgrounds. "Scipione reached his conception of Europe across Catholic and Counter-Reformation Rome—itself a deep root of the modern crisis; Europe whose eternal spirituality is paid for in guilt. . . . It is a one-sided conception but terrifyingly penetrating. Scipione's position was religious; Mafai's moral." In his antithesis of form and colour Mafai was protesting against the fullness and knowledge of life towards which the Roman tone-painters around *Valori Plastici* had been striving: so Mafai's position was a defence "against any possible rhetoric".

Mario Mafai
Self-Portrait
1929

But for Cesare Brandi the fundamental distinction between the two is expressed in the phrase "Scipione's torment, Mafai's ascent". Brandi finds in Scipione the deep drama of a man who wishes to attain, without ever succeeding, an "autonomy of culture". In Mafai he traces the assured process whereby he managed to take up, through Morandi, "the purest strain of Italian painting".

De Libero, who was a personal friend of both painters, is more forthright. "Scipione and Mafai were absolutely different even though they were both furiously involved in looking for newer and more flagrant alibis to distinguish themselves from the tired and often discredited *Novecento* movement. I cannot understand why critics always lump them together—at Mafai's expense of course—say that one is better than the other, and represent the one intent on developing an idiom that the other has dictated from on high. . . . They were friends, that's all—and very odd it is that they were. They discussed together by the hour their problems, choices, loves and hates. Together they pulled various epochs of art to pieces, and together they scoured the libraries, though Scipione did this more than Mafai. . . . And they wandered around together in the long Roman nights which affected them in different ways because of their different natures."

On the occasion of the comprehensive exhibition of the works of Raphael, Alfredo Mezio weighed in with his own theory. In trying to assess the exact place of this exuberant woman-painter of the Roman School he hinted that it was she, perhaps, who had originated the idiom. Scipione and Mafai were bound together "solely through their being irregulars and rebels . . . yet there was a point on which these 'separated brothers' of the Roman School met in true community of feeling during the first (often decisive) stage of their careers—and this point was the work of Raphael."

How right was Mezio? Raphael's painting between 1928 and 1930 assuredly helps to throw light on the climate of the Roman School. We are thinking of a few portraits and scenes of Rome—the

Raphael *Walk on the Palatine 1928*

one with the arch of Constantine under snow, the Colosseum, the Forum, the corner of the Palatine. We see Rome in red or black, but with the evocation of space entrusted to colour. They are little views in an Oriental key. Raphael's painting in no way stems from *Valori Plastici* or from thought-out principles; it puts its trust in impulse and the urgency of the moment. She was born in Lithuania. We find her in Paris in 1924, having already been to London, where she had made friends with Epstein (later in her life she devoted herself to sculpture). She arrived in Rome in 1925, frequented the circles of Mafai and Scipione and set up as a painter. Perhaps it was partly her Slav character that led her to put value in symbols. Even when she is painting the Rome that lies before her eyes, her vision extends beyond immediate contact with the object. There is a lyrical dimension in memory, in the translation of physical data into the realm of fantasy, and in the resonance of colour which transcends imitation. There are sometimes echoes of Douanier Rousseau and Chagall in her work, and of course a close proximity in spirit to Scipione and Mafai. Mezio says that her part "in the story of that group was not that of an inferior, but a rival". Perhaps, but it is difficult to claim that she had any priority in the idiom over the other two.

SCIPIONE

The two post-war comprehensive exhibitions—one at the Venice Biennale of 1948 and the other at the Gallery of Modern Art in Rome in 1954—proved beyond any question that Gino Bonichi, better known as Scipione, was one of the key figures in the artistic life of Italy.

Scipione, like Modigliani, has become a legend. His imposing physique, his tuberculosis, his death when only twenty-nine, his religious torment, his lack of restraint, his visions in squalid surroundings, and his few short years of unremitting and intense work, have created a legend—and not a particularly helpful one for the understanding of his art.

Much has been written about him, especially since his death in 1933. But even today, despite attempts at clarification by various critics, he still has the reputation of being a "literary" painter. Scipione was, of course, a friend of poets and writers—and these were the first to admire him, above all for the visionary quality of his painting: indeed Palma Bucarelli has pointed out that "critics find his peaceful paintings the most praiseworthy, the rare lulls in the tempest", whereas "poets prefer his visionary and dramatic work". One thing is certain: that the majority of his paintings never won their reputation purely as paintings, but also as a revelation of hallucinating visions whose torment was rooted in the intellect. Scipione's "culture" was formed not only in the museums but also through reading the Bible, André Breton, Mallarmé, Rimbaud, D'Annunzio, Barilli, Ungaretti and Gongora: it was certainly not solely figurative. The mainspring of his symbols, especially in the first period, lay in an escape from history and from immediate contact with the life around him, and it was this that caused the myth that his paintings were a kind of literature, that they did not correspond with an inner, compulsive poetic idiom. But in fact the visions and "revelations" that he painted were achieved by a pure painter's medium, and this brings us back to the usual time-worn problem about the relationship between representational content and pure painterly values. These two ends can be antithetic, but they can also fuse together and produce two different aspects of one and the same poetry, as happened in the past from the Primitives to El Greco and Goya. Thus, though the visionary content of Scipione's work was of intellectual origin it was worked out coherently in the figurative medium.

In Scipione we find every Romantic influence including that of extreme decadence. Decadent elements in his pictures lie in his very subtle sensuality of touch and smell, in the disquieting ups and downs of mood, and in the piercing anguish. His sense of guilt was ceaselessly fanned by the conflict between the flesh and liberation—in order, or so it seemed, to excite the flesh still more. We

Scipione *The Roman Prostitute 1930*

also find the decadent influence in his love for museum culture and the atmosphere of old libraries. Scipione's formation took place in museums.

But here we come to another myth—that Scipione's work derives entirely from museums. This is really another facet of the "literary" myth. It insists on Scipione's lack of expressive compulsion. But we must bear in mind that when Scipione burst on to the scene everyone in Italy had their eyes on museums and the old masters of the fourteenth and fifteenth centuries. Scipione's preferences were against the tide, and narrower; they came from his personal vision of the world. He was attracted by El Greco, and he tells us why in one of his private notebooks. "His figures are phantasms that become concrete with terrible, palpable, reality. . . . The intangible beauty of the divine personalities is distorted, corrupted. . . ."

This comment would be more applicable to Scipione himself than to El Greco. Palpability is precisely a feature of his work, deployed with an almost morbid sensuality. El Greco's exaltation of colour was different from Scipione's—neo-Byzantine in origin and still more so after his stay in Venice. In my opinion Scipione's knowledge of El Greco was not confined to pictures in the Corsini Gallery and other Italian collections; he had also meditated at length over black-and-white reproductions, and he did the same with Soutine and Rouault and other modern painters whom he was unable to see in the original. A certain high-lighting in his painting—rather than in the palette itself —may well derive from El Greco seen in black-and-white, also passages that are palpably luminous and the slant of the rhythms of composition.

One thing is certain: that Scipione saw El Greco in Expressionist terms and hence as an example of freedom from the laws of composition and with an emphasis on particular details in an inner and hallucinating light. He was also attracted to El Greco by his feelings of religious torment in a Counter-Reformation climate.

Scipione *Piazza Navona (sketch)* 1930

If Scipione did turn outwards and look around him, his keen decadent eye fell on a bright and pompous Rome, heir to the Counter-Reformation and now grown old. The Cardinal Inquisitor De Juvara, rigid as a new Byzantine *Pantocrator*, became the romantic ninety-year-old *Cardinale Decano*—in other words, was Scipione influenced by Velasquez' *Cardinal* in the Doria Pamphili Gallery? Perhaps, but Scipione's spirit was very different. Against the background of the great domes or on the bridges of the Tiber he always saw the decaying flesh of the prostitute; everywhere he found uneasiness, the sense of sin and damnation, the need for redemption. His accent was on the symbol rather than on the outward aspect of things; hence the hallucinating high-lighting, the dark disturbing backgrounds, the diffused red-and-black light that makes everything phantom-like.

Scipione had something of the neo-Baroque in him. The irrationality of his visionary and expressive impulse made him avoid straight lines and angles. Even in the *Piazzale del Laterano*, which at first sight seems straight and rectangular, the lines move, the colour is diffused, and the emptiness of the piazza and the street with the obelisk create an intensely subtle brooding uneasiness. The imperceptible disharmonies break up any kind of fixed geometry. It has been said that Scipione had studied De Chirico's piazzas, but the pictorial substance of the *Piazzale del Laterano* is utterly different. What he must have liked in De Chirico was not the substance of the painting but the evocation of silence and brooding death. And what about the theory that he was attracted by the drawings of Rubens, Tiepolo and Jordaens? He studied them, yes, as he studied Ingres—whom he approached through Picasso—and as he studied the symbolic illustrations of Gustave Doré,

Magnasco and the more visionary works of Tintoretto. But it seems certain that when old masters excited his interest it was in so far as their works were expressive and anti-formal.

El Greco apart, one of his strongest feelings of fascination was for the large, free expression of Goya. We find Goya's influence not only in *La Meticcia* (The Half-Caste) and in *La Madre* (The Mother) but in the general texture of the paint, which is luminous and palpable, despite the fact that Goya's paint is deep—we feel the blood in the bodies and the weight of the draperies—whereas Scipione's is more on the surface, like a thin rind, anti-formal and shot with light.

But Scipione's knowledge was not confined to old masters. We have already said that he studied Soutine and Rouault in reproduction. He was probably also familiar with Ensor, and knew the drawings of Grosz and Pascin. As Sinisgalli puts it: "Scipione entered modernity—which is neither progress nor technics, but a deeper sense of original sin—with the urgency of a man crying aloud for help."

His Expressionism remained tortured and obsessed with guilt. He never seemed able to find heaven nor console himself with the peace of God. Doubts and torments of the flesh caused him continual mortification and continual excitement of the senses. The balance between lucidity of mind and irrational impulse was not always achieved—and all this is reflected in his art. He aimed at being a European but, as Argan points out, there is "no common ground between Italian Expressionism and German Expressionism, whose religious theme is still by and large Lutheran —salvation by faith and heaven thrown wide open over the abyss"; while for Catholics, death— which is the slow, deep corrosion of every corporeal appearance—condemns them to live in the obsession of guilt.

Scipione approached painting through drawing. When he first attended the Rome Academy of Fine Arts with Mafai and Mazzacurati he showed ability as a draughtsman. But his line and subtle chiaroscuro variations show an inclination to colour as well as a tendency to react against form. In some of his drawings we find an element of illustration, but his studies for the portrait of the Cardinal, the portraits of Ungaretti and Barilli and various drawings of the Apocalypse and the Zodiac have a style in harmony with the development of his painting. This harmony enables him to transcend any conflict between colour and line. Before he began a painting he made a large number of drawings, but in the final result the light, lines and colour are worked out in painterly coherence —always anti-formal and neo-Baroque.

Even when the simplification of the masses seems conducive to formalism, as in his first *Autoritratto* (Self-Portrait) of 1928, the effect is anti-formal owing to the softness and luminosity of the colour. This tendency is emphasized still more in *Piovra* (Octopus), and we find it at full strength in the paintings of 1930. His *Natura Morta con Tubino* (Still Life with Hat) in the Tosi Collection must be ranked among the most lyrical achievements in the Italian art of the time: the purples and lunar greens echo one another with subtle modulations in arabesque-like rhythms. In *Il Cavallino* (The Pony) in the Mattioli Collection, the stressed brush strokes of the deep greens, browns and flaming reds give the picture a phantom-like feeling with unity of style. Visionary exaltation is even more marked in the study for the *Piazza Navona* (Bottai Collection), which is unquestionably more lyrical than the final painting. Scipione's imagination is inflamed in the intuition of the moment, and cannot be sustained.

One might be tempted to say that precisely here lies his limitation, that he finds it difficult to surpass the efficacity of his sketches—but it must be understood that his "sketches" are pictures of burning poetic intensity. When Scipione tries to paint the same image in a more ample and final way, his creative process is hampered by excessive criticism. We find the same thing with the portrait of the *Cardinale Decano*. Cardinal Vannutelli exercised on Scipione a deep and subtle fascination connected with the decay of Baroque, but the two studies in the Jesi and Mattioli Collections are altogether more living than the final portrait (1930) that we can see in the Galleria

Comunale in Rome. The final painting is colder and the colour has somehow extinguished his expressive fire; it is a display of technical skill rather than a great picture, whereas *Il Cardinale sul Letto di Morte* (The Cardinal on his Death Bed) in the Jesi Collection is a work of intense and unified lyricism.

Various works done in 1930 achieve great purity of expression, including *Profeta in Vista di Gerusalemme* (The Prophet in sight of Jerusalem), *Apocalisse* (Apocalypse), the caustic *Ritratto di Ungaretti* (Portrait of Ungaretti), *La Cortigiana* (The Prostitute) and *Piazzale del Laterano*, in the Jucker Collection. The images with their sensuality, mysticism, abandon and delirium suggest the last stages of Baroque Rome, full of sin and life. The backgrounds are dark and deep in greens, purples or reds, with flaming yellows, blues, greys, browns, and always a preponderance of reds.

MAFAI

The myth that came into existence after Scipione's death—that it was he who had had the ascendency over Mafai—has now almost been reversed; not in the sense that anyone thinks that Mafai had an ascendency over Scipione, but because Mafai's prolonged period of activity since that time has enabled people to acquire a more detailed knowledge of his gifts. Though brought to maturity by European culture, these had links with a new taste in Italy through his admiration for Morandi.

Mafai's essential idiom seems to have been already defined in the early years of the Roman School. Two examples show this, *Autoritratto* (Self-Portrait) (Guido Ballo Collection) and *Ponte Garibaldi*

Mario Mafai *Ponte Sisto 1943*

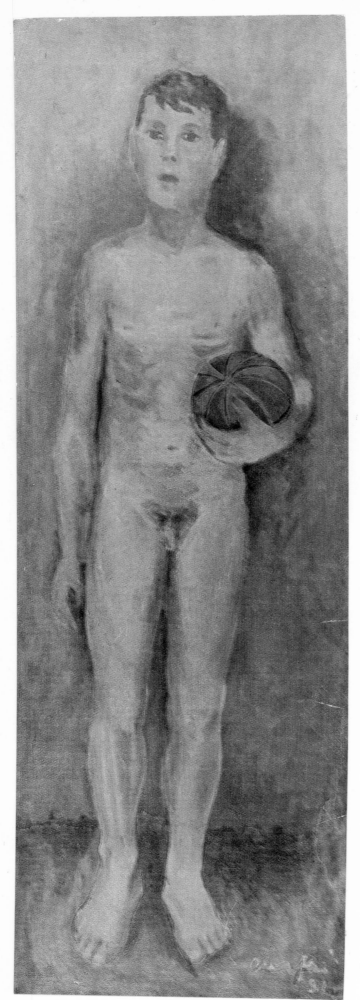

Mario Mafai *Boy with Ball 1934*

Mario Mafai *Flowers 1936*

(Bassiano Collection), both painted in 1929. In the *Self-Portrait* we find that the colour has not yet caught up with the limpidity of the tones—the browns predominate with sheeny high-lighting suggestive of "museum" influence. But the expression is strong and direct; it does not veer off into symbols and allusions. The painting has bodily substance and we instinctively feel that there is total knowledge and possession of the object. Several later self-portraits, for example the one in the Gallery of Modern Art in Rome, echo the 1929 one, but the colour is sharper and free from muddy passages. In *Ponte Garibaldi* we see the other aspect of Mafai's personality—his ability to transfigure familiar sights with heightened fantasy and create a structure not Expressionist but architectural through a process of contemplative vision.

With Mafai we often find these two moods—namely Expressionist participation and Impressionist contemplation—side by side or fused together. The structure of *Ponte Garibaldi* is altogether different from Scipione's neo-Baroque spirit. The composition, though seemingly top-heavy, achieves an equilibrium of forces from the dynamic *élan* of the rampart on the left and through the balanced distribution of clouds, of reflections in the water, of voids and masses, of dark shadows and warmer colours. *Ponte Garibaldi* foreshadows the later series of views with their more vibrant colours.

Unlike Scipione, Mafai always had both feet on the ground. He was no mystic; the play of his imagination was confined within the limits of the ordinary world. He felt no dualism between heaven and earth, no sense of sin or guilt or mortification, but found fulfilment in the here and now and in participation with the human lot here on earth. Endowed with an exceptionally vivid imagination, he shunned pedantic systems. His sympathetic participation in all forms of life made him make flowers, draperies, still lifes and landscapes human. He moved effortlessly from portraits and nudes to interiors of houses, demolitions, flowers and red peppers. Everything was kindled into life at the touch of his fancy. Mafai himself confessed that his fading flowers and gutted houses reflect no lament or regret for things past, but "the certainty of a stable existence henceforth, of an ultimately ineffaceable residue of life".

It is not difficult to outline the influences and preferences in the development of his idiom. It was towards 1926 that he began to oppose the *Novecento* movement. It has been said that Kokoschka influenced him in the early stages—the Expressionist phase—of the Roman School, before 1929. But as Santangelo has pointed out, Kokoschka's distortions are rendered pitiless by the strident and violently dissonant colour, whereas with Mafai "they are regenerated by a vivid feeling for the spirituality of light", and this cancels out their horror. But we should talk less of Expressionism than of the burning imagination that distorts, accentuates and transfigures the images, and sometimes attains a candid simplicity suggestive of Douanier Rousseau.

By 1931 every trace of Expressionism was over and done with—and indeed the Expressionist tendency of the early period of the Roman School was accidental rather than integral to the idiom. In *I Fiori* (Flowers) in the Scialoja Collection the harmony of spaces seems to recall Metaphysical painting. Mafai had studied Metaphysical painting, especially in Carrà and Morandi, but despite his strictness of metre and the brooding melancholy of the images which seem outside time, he was really far removed from that idiom owing to his predilection for daily life and homely objects and his dislike of exaggerated geometry. His composition was measured but this was the fruit of intuition rather than of calculation. Morandi appealed to him not as a Metaphysical painter but for his compositions of flowers, landscapes and still lifes of a later period.

Mafai began to paint his series of *Demolizioni* (Demolitions) round about 1935 at a period of urban replanning in Rome. The result is not a protest so much as an evocation of dream atmospheres and the uncovering of remote civilizations. During this period, too, we find Mafai painting nude women dressing or spreading out clothes, in or out of doors. Outstanding for its breadth and severe construction among these paintings is *Donne che stendono i Panni* (Women hanging out Clothes) where the sensuality of the colour finds scope in the areas of weary flesh, though there is a basis of drawing in the structure. Later on, cold harmonies—azures, purples, lilacs—were used for their pure resonance of colour regardless of reference to the surroundings, and the severity of the construction became accentuated and less atmospheric: *Omaggio a Vermeer* (Homage to Vermeer) and *Camera di Bambini* (Nursery) (1941) show this tendency.

Since the war Mafai has turned to a more narrative idiom. We often find a loss of his subtle tones in the interests of a more immediate effect. Post-Cubism has had some influence as we can see in *Trattoria Romana* (Roman Inn) done in 1949, but most of all a concern for clear, plain communication. *La Strada* (The Street), also done in 1949, has reached the stage of anecdote.

It is obvious that the shock of war had its effect on Mafai's way of seeing things. His private vision and subtle lyricism—Morandi's legacy—no longer satisfied him. On the other hand, the best among his most recent works show that he need not be narrative: an occasional aggressive selfportrait and, still more, his flowers and still lifes—for instance, *Peperoncini Rossi* (Red Peppers) —show that Mafai is by no means finished as a painter. He stands in the first rank of contemporary Italian artists.

PIRANDELLO

Fausto Pirandello, son of Luigi Pirandello the Sicilian dramatist, developed his idiom by overhauling his rough southern Expressionism in terms of general European trends.

Though he was born and lives in Rome, we nevertheless see Sicily in the sundrenched and dusty light of his pictures, and we can detect the influence of his father. By "southern Expressionism", as applied to Pirandello, we mean a personal direction in which Naturalism, realistic compulsion, obsessive southern sensuality, preoccupation with drawing rather than colour, and finally Cubism are blended together with noisy expressive effect. For even when Cubism seems to have taken control of his idiom, we find that becoming "southern" in its turn; that is to say, we find it charged with obsessive accents of expression and retaining a Naturalistic point of view. Hence we see that Pirandello's idiom has been first and foremost the South, and only secondly Braque, Picasso or the German Expressionists. His problem has been to integrate these influences into a single personal language.

This basic southernness is not only a matter of aesthetics and taste but also of moral coherence, as we can trace from his early more academic works to his latest Cubist ones. Moral preoccupation is typically southern, as is the love for paradox, the need to push everything to extremes, to exaggerate, to pursue absolute intransigeance. Man and nature are felt with a physical "panic" sense. Pirandello needs vast spaces for his synthesis of masses. He dislikes the small canvas and light tonal passages. He is rough and impetuous in his work, though he has meditated deeply beforehand.

Pirandello's work has run parallel to that of the Roman School, though he was never a member of it and his idiom is different. On rare occasions a picture of his may show affinity with Mafai as regards experiment with tone, but basically his palette is different from that of the Roman School, with its browns, whites, ochres, greys, greens and blues. His colour is sharp and loud, yet he never entirely renounces local tone of Naturalist origin, nor a physical feeling for things, for air and for light.

In his early stages he studied the work of Carena, Carrà and possibly Spadini. This was the period of his early attempts at large female nudes which inevitably savoured of academicism and Realism. Later he went to Paris and came into contact with the works of Cézanne, Braque and Picasso, and this set him on the path towards a new spacecolour synthesis. *Oggetti* (Objects) (1928) in the Gallery of Modern Art in Rome, *Le Bottigliette* (The Little Bottles) in the Laudisa Collection and *Il Lume* (The Light) in the Natale Collection—both of 1929—are examples of exceptional discipline. The colour is set in a low key, and we feel that Braque has aroused our painter's interest. Yet he has not abandoned Naturalist renderings, and in a way his Cubism reminds us of Meta-physical painting; yet there is no idea of putting heterogeneous objects side by side. His still lifes are disciplined and spatial and altogether his idiom is very different from that of the Roman School at the same period.

Donna e Bambino (Woman and Child) (1931) shows a more discursive and Naturalistic emphasis: Pirandello was back again at a compromise with provincialism. For more than ten years, to put it in his own words, he "searched for content". Yet his crowded beaches, his bathers with their sensual rough flesh, his typically southern feeling for summer heat, have a fascination that is not only

Fausto Pirandello *Trees at Grottaferrata 1955*

Fausto Pirandello *Nudes 1954*

Fausto Pirandello *Still Life 1928*

illustrative. I would go so far as to say that if we compare *Antonio in Viola* (Antonio in Violet) (1947) with the earlier *Spiaggia* (Beach) or *Ombrelloni* (Beach Umbrellas) (1939), the latter are the more intense. Naturalism has not disappeared in *Antonio in Viola*; it has merely become more cerebral and programmatic.

But this 1947 picture is not a particularly good example of his return to Cubism and Expressionism, and other recent works show a clear clean idiom. We feel Cézanne and Picasso behind him, urging him to break up the object so as to set colour free, leading him back to his first compositions in space, but with a sharpened feeling for colour and a freer invention. *Natura Morta con Flauto* (Still Life with Flute), *Paesaggio* (Landscape), *Figure Femminili* (Female Figures) and *Tavolino da Tè* (The Tea Table) are good examples of free idiom, though here as elsewhere there is the danger of an imperfect fusion between Naturalism and Cubism. This danger has always been Pirandello's limitation, only overcome when his expression is particularly intense and derives from a deep inner compulsion, as with a few recent landscapes.

DEVELOPMENTS IN THE ROMAN SCHOOL

In the years before the last war there was a trend towards expressiveness of colour with tonal variations. Roman tone-painters either tried to achieve the third dimension by a synthesis of space, light and colour (following the *Valori Plastici* tradition) or else fell into Expressionistic attitudes and trusted the emotive impulse. In Roman circles after 1930 inspiration came not only from Melli, Scipione and Mafai, but also from Soutine, Kokoschka and even Ensor, as we shall see in the case of Gentilini. Cagli, Cavalli and Capogrossi exhibited at the Milione Gallery in 1933 under Bardi's auspices as typifying the "new Roman School of painting". Others who joined this so-called school included Tamburi, Omiccioli, Stradone and Scialoja. Since the war, however, the scene has changed; Capogrossi has rejected his earlier idiom in favour of non-figurative ideograms in accordance with international taste; Corrado Cagli has been so intent on discovering new ways of seeing things, and new creeds, and has changed his idiom so often that his importance is confined to taste-formation; Emanuele Cavalli, having started off with tender elegies of colour—for instance, *Il Pittore* (The Painter) exhibited at the Milione Gallery in 1933—soon showed his limitations by turning to fables and literary myths; Orfeo Tamburi went back to Paris, and his painting became

Giovanni Omiccioli *Suburb 1944*

Orfeo Tamburi *Houses at Neuilly 1951*

so subdued that there was hardly anything left in it of the Roman School; Scialoja, one of the youngest of them, after experiments at the expense of colour under post-Cubist influence, has recently come back to glorifying it; while Stradone tried to integrate Expressionism and Cubism without any clear or conclusive results, bringing "humility to both"—to use Apollonio's metaphor.

The painter who most obviously justified his early promise was Giovanni Omiccioli. At an early stage he was influenced by the heightened colours of Scipione and Mafai, especially Mafai, but these colours have become more and more strident with variations of mainly cold tones—so that some of his greens and blues, alternating with browns and violets, look as if they were under neon lighting. His images sometimes suggest local dialect, but a dialect so full of expressive humour that it can take its place in a non-provincial idiom. His pungent, sometimes melancholy, elegies echo a kind of Expressionism with simplified tonal gradations.

It could be held against Omiccioli that sometimes a certain sketchiness, at other times a feeling of popular illustration, enter into his work. Yet some of his pictures, especially the series called *Orti* (Gardens) and *Feste Campestri* (Fêtes Champêtres) achieve true and coherent accents of poetry.

When Giuseppe Capogrossi painted *Le Due Chitarre* (The Two Guitars) in 1948—a figurative work in a tonal three-dimensional key—it contained nothing to foreshadow the ideograms which he has painted with imperceptible variations ever since 1949. Will he pursue these variations, one wonders, or will he try to forge some link with his early experiments? As it is there has been a complete break in the development of his idiom. Compared with *The Two Guitars*, his abstract paintings are unquestionably cleaner and more disciplined, for in his tonal painting there was an element of professional compromise. And yet some of the work that he did during his Roman tone-painting period has remarkable subtlety. Good examples of this period are to be found among his *Ballerine* (Ballet Dancers) which, as Carrieri points out, "are redolent of a delicate and luminous Impressionism superimposed on tonal rhythms". There is delicacy in the severe tones of some of his portraits of women, for example *Contadina* (The Peasant Girl) (1939) in the Gallery of Modern Art in Rome. But his decision to adopt an international idiom has caused him to repudiate all links with his artistic past.

Orfeo Tamburi, however, despite his break-away from the Roman School mentioned above, has always developed coherently. He has gone back, with severer taste and cleaner palette, to his first compositions based on greys. He was a draughtsman before he was a painter. As Carrieri puts it: "Tamburi plays the part of a descant for Scipione and Mafai: he takes the top notes and plays them as a nervous and delicate cadenza." His drawing shows a quick and cursive calligraphy; his work has an elegant grace and a tendency to virtuosity. Some of his works of the Roman period, such as *Gigantomachia* (Giant-killing) (1938) and various landscapes, show a clear evocative spirit which has grown subtler in recent years since his return to Paris. *Case a Neuilly* (Houses in Neuilly) is a good example, in which his painterly wariness brings out the essentials in greys, violets and deep blues. And other paintings of Paris, in which the various greys predominate, also show his personal and cultivated accent. It is clean painting and has its own quiet grace.

Orfeo Tamburi *Garden 1951*

THE "SIX" OF TURIN

At this time other groups of painters in Italy, besides the Roman School, were seeking to make contact with the European tradition in the teeth of *Novecento* domination. In Turin the spear-head of this tendency was Lionello Venturi as "idea-man", and Edoardo Persico as "man of action".

Persico spent his short life as a tireless and unremitting champion of European and international ideas in the field of art. From 1920 to 1925 he lived in Paris. On his return to Italy he settled in Turin, where he had to sell furniture, books and even paintings so that he and his wife could avoid starvation in a garret. He took a job in the Fiat works and started his own publishing house which produced the first edition of Venturi's *Pretesti di Critica*, but soon had to close down through lack of funds. By 1928 Persico had made friends with all the best artists in Turin, gathered them together in a group known as the "Six", and organized several exhibitions.

As Menzio put it: "Without any formulated programme or manifesto, these 'Six' opened their first exhibition in January 1929, in a small room in the Galleria Guglielmi in Turin—which at that time was the store room of a carpet shop. Of the "Six" only Carlo Levi and Gigi Chessa were actually Turinese: Jessie Boswell was English by origin, though she had lived for years in Italy and studied with Casorati; Nicola Galante was from the Abruzzi, Francesco Menzio from Sardinia, and Enrico Paulucci from Genoa, but they had all lived in Turin for some time. As Persico put it: "These painters may seem completely different from, and even contradictory to, one another; but the connoisseur will see that they form a cultural group that is anything but provincial: the outstanding thing about them is that they are Europeans." The group had come together under the banner of Manet's *Olympia*, which seems exaggeratedly traditional nowadays, but at that time was taken to epitomize French Impressionism, so ardently championed by Persico. As Menzio admitted, the first exhibition contained "no really important work", yet it made its mark on both critics and public, and about half the fifty-three paintings shown were sold immediately. Various critics saw the link between the "Six" and French Impressionism and realized that the group was opposed—not to Casorati, who encouraged the exhibition with his presence—but to provincialism. When the group exhibited in Milan it was praised, if with qualifications, by Sironi, Carrà and Oppo.

Of course opposition was not lacking. Various critics who had seemed friendly at the time of the first exhibition became more guarded later. Persico continued to insist that "this group, with its strictly European spirit, deserves to be given careful attention by the new generation". Menzio tells us that they were accused "of copying the French and of bringing from Paris vague and inaccurate information about the painting of Modigliani, Matisse, Picasso and Marquet". Nevertheless the "Six" were undaunted and went on painting and exhibiting in Italy. After their exhibition in Milan the personalities of the artists became more defined and three of the group withdrew, leaving only Levi, Menzio and Paulucci. A few years later these exhibited in London and Paris under the auspices of Lionello Venturi.

The most exciting personality in the group was Carlo Levi, who was also the most uncompromisingly hostile to all forms of *Novecento* art. His paintings exhibited in Turin and Genoa in 1929 showed an arabesque line modulated without disturbing the colour with chiaroscuro—that hall-mark of the *Novecento*. By the time of the Milan exhibition he had abandoned line values and in *Le Vele* (Sails), *Palme* (Palms), *Il Letto* (The Bed), and most noticeably of all in *Aria* (Air) we

Francesco Menzio *Figure 1929*

find post-Impressionist tendencies clearly defined. Persico likened his paintings to the lyrics of Baudelaire and Valéry. Levi's paintings at this period seemed to be born of a contemplative vision based on memory and acute sensibility combined with mental lucidity. In the years that followed, Levi put his emphasis on intimate participation with objects, and dimension ceased to be post-Impressionist but became Expressionist with biting humour. This tendency, already noticeable in *L'Eroe Cinese* (The Chinese Hero), became more apparent in the series of portraits of his mother. But Levi's developments and his increasing emphasis on "content"—producing effects of rough Naturalistic story-telling with the immediacy of dialect—were partly explained by his political exile in Lucania. *Christ Stopped at Eboli* has revealed his narrative gifts, and in painting too he has tried to portray the people and landscapes of Lucania, choosing dialect as his means of expression. His one-man show at the Twenty-seventh Biennale in Venice contained a series of portraits and land-scapes of Lucania in which he avoided any stylistic self-indulgence so as to concentrate on immediacy of expression with accents of popular oratory. From this latter point of view the paintings were effective, but from the point of view of painting as such, Levi was returning to illustrative and

Enrico Paulucci *Still Life 1929*

story-telling Naturalism of a deliberately provincial kind. Occasionally, in a portrait of a boy or in a small landscape, we find more luminous and cleaner colours and greater clarity of style.

Menzio, like Chessa, was indebted to Casorati for strictness of composition, and he rounded off his first period with *Le Signorine* (The Young Ladies) (1927). Prompted by Lionello Venturi, he then turned his attention to the main European tradition. "This melancholy Orpheus," wrote Persico, "with the pale face and bowed shoulders of a refugee, obeyed the dictates of his conscience and set out to seek his own inner harmony in the world of colour." He went to Paris to see the Impressionists and the latest painters of the *avant-garde*. On his return his painting was transformed. In *Ragazza con Cappello* (Girl with Hat), *Portofino* and *Nudo* (Nude)—all done in 1929—we find him using colour in a different way. But the old problem of harmony is still there and so is his subtle melancholy with its tendency to delicate lyricism. Menzio was indebted to Manet, the Fauves, Derain, Modigliani and Matisse, though the ideas he received from them were sometimes in conflict. But throughout we can trace his own inner vision, elegiac and melancholy.

In his early days, when he first came back from Paris, Enrico Paulucci differed from the other members of the group by the full-blooded warmth of his pictures, apparently easily achieved, but in fact subtle and refined. He rejected Cézanne's sense of structure in favour of a tasteful and pleasing drawing in the manner of Dufy with hints of Marquet and Matisse. He broke away from provincialism and joined the European current inspired by Lionello Venturi and promoted by Persico, but his type of painting brought him the reputation of a facile decorator. Persico, however, though noting "the rather literary grace of certain gouaches and canvases", affirmed that "Enrico Paulucci's art is neither decorative nor trivial. He is perfectly aware of the value of a line

Luigi Spazzapan *The Hermit* (tempera) *1953*

or a tone, and this gives expertness to his work in spite of its light grace; it moves us in spite of its simplicity."

Persico's words are foundational in any effort at a critical estimate of Paulucci's work, and they apply equally to his most recent paintings. His graceful fancy, his confident mastery of his means and the subtlety of his vision have remained constant throughout his changes of taste, and it is these that give an individual note to his work—a note that is there even in his less good pictures when his calligraphy seems almost mechanical. *Chiesa di Portofino* (Church at Portofino)—a gouache of 1929 —is fresh and luminous, light and tasteful, with post-Impressionist overtones. Marchiori has pointed out that, compared with the meditated compositions of Casorati, this picture seems to be "tossed off at a stroke". *Natura Morta con Fruttiera* (Still Life with Fruit Bowl)—also 1929—must be ranked among his best paintings. He has assimilated French taste, and the tones and the drawing recall Braque as well as Marquet. Paulucci's inclination is always for the cursive outline, for the moment of intensity, and for immediacy—all, as it were, at a stroke. His best post-war pictures are those born of inner compulsion. In *Porto* (Harbour) (1953), *Passeggiata* (Walk) (1954) and the recent *Castello* (Castle) we find all traces of calligraphy have been transcended. The surface dimension is extended and the subtle rhythms give bright and unified resonance to the colour.

Luigi Spazzapan was not one of the "Six". He went to Turin from his native Istria in 1928 to do decorating work at the International Exhibition of that year. His formation had already been completed in Central Europe, where he had lived in Munich, Trieste and Vienna—"in the full flush of Freudian doctrines" which, according to Persico, led him "to represent the world in a

Enrico Paulucci *Castle 1955*

demoniac light". He had also been to Paris and exhibited there with Chessa, Levi, Menzio and Paulucci—the nucleus of the "Six"—under Lionello Venturi's auspices in 1930. Before painting, he had been immensely active as a draughtsman, and behind his paintings we always find draughtsmanship and even his palette seems to echo draughtsman's inks.

Persico has written about Spazzapan "the draughtsman", while Luigi Carluccio, introducing his one-man show at the Twenty-seventh Biennale in Venice, surveyed the whole range of his activities. Influences in his early formation included Klimt and Slevogt, Kandinsky and Dufy. But in Spazzapan we always find an urge towards fantastic expression which has "the speed, violence and yet the lightness of a firework" (Carluccio).

Spazzapan's coherence lies in his "inexhaustible capacity for producing images", an attribute which goes beyond any idiom to which he may have been thought to adhere—such as Impressionism, Expressionism or Abstraction. He himself has confessed "I believe only in inspiration . . ." and goes on to explain that by inspiration he means something closely linked to intelligence rather than to instinct.

Spazzapan's inspired freedom has produced the liveliest images which give an impression of immediacy but are in fact the fruit of long premeditation. The images are charged with symbols and flow impetuously within the outline. But when—as with *Paesaggio Amalfitano* (Landscape around Amalfi) (1954) or the series of gouaches called *Cavalli e Cavalieri* (Horses and Horsemen) or *Figuri con Gatti* (Figures with Cats) or some of his still lifes and flowers—the colour vibrations are not spread within calligraphic outlines but move with their own inner rhythms, then Spazzapan achieves his best work. It does not matter about draughtsman's inks, and it does not matter about his being a draughtsman endowed with inspiration and invention rather than a painter—for the means are transcended by the vitality of the pure image.

THE LOMBARD PAINTERS

In the ebb and flow of idioms, each region of Italy, with its ancient painting tradition, has had an influence on the orientation of colour. Thus we can say that Tosi is a typically Lombard painter not only because he knows at first hand the light and colours of Lombardy, but because he has assimilated the light and colours of the Lombard masters—by which I do not mean to say that there is any "provincialism" in his painting. More recently Del Bon, Breveglieri, Morlotti and Meloni have preserved their Lombard colours within an idiom quite free from any kind of descriptive local tone.

The influence of Aldo Carpi, senior professor of painting at the Brera Academy since 1931, over some of the younger generation of painters in Milan—especially, perhaps, Morlotti—is undeniable, and could be likened to that of Gustave Moreau whose school helped to form Matisse and other French painters.

Carpi is an heir to the Lombard *Scapigliatura* movement; he loves the light of greys, browns and half-shadows; he clings to his story-telling and often gives it good-tempered metaphorical irony. Though he took part in some *Novecento* exhibitions, his idiom is in conflict with the formal requirements of *Novecento* art. Some of his self-portraits seem to echo Cézanne, but the colour is gently Lombard and bathed in a light not very different from that of his elegiac landscapes. His painting is a sort of story-telling of a popular kind—allusive and literary, melancholy and ironical.

Ennio Morlotti *Woman Washing Herself 1943–45*

MILAN IN 1930

Artistic circles in the Lombard capital around 1930 were full of contrasts and efforts to find new idioms. Carrà and Soffici were exhibiting at the Bardi Gallery. Sironi was art critic for the *Popolo d'Italia*, and Carrà for *L'Ambrosiana*. Tosi was still painting his quiet landscapes. At the Milano Gallery an exhibition of Zandomeneghi followed one of Funi. But the younger generation was moving towards a sharp break-away of some kind. We have seen how the Roman School rose up

Aligi Sassu *The Cyclists 1931*

in revolt in a whirl of neo-Baroque high-lighting, and how, in Turin, with its more liberal and Jansenist traditions and its enlightened critical intelligence, the restless spirit of the younger generation led to the French experiences of the "Six". Similar feelings of unrest were at work in Milan, where the impact of the Fauves' colour orgies, Van Gogh's dazzling colour system, Ensor's skeletons and Expressionist exasperation was beginning to have its effect.

Later the Milanese revolt was to go much farther and culminate in the group known as *Corrente*. But already in 1930 some of the young painters of that group, such as Sassu and Birolli—and the sculptors Manzù and Grosso—were forming a nucleus of opposition to all other groups. What distinguished them most of all was their uncompromising demand for contact with Europe. In 1931 Birolli was painting his *San Zeno*, worked out in terms of flat surfaces with colour coherence, and a year later his *Ritratto del Padre* (Portrait of my Father) which had marked Expressionist tension. Sassu, who had joined the Futurists when only eighteen, was painting *Il Concerto* (The Concert) and his series of *Ciclisti* (Cyclists). By now reproductions of the work of the new French painters had begun to circulate in Italy, not only in black and white but in colours. Artists as well as poets and writers foregathered in the cafés and talked until dawn. Their haunts were the Savini, the newly opened Craja beside the Scala, and some of the little cafés round the gallerys. During those ten years up to the outbreak of war in 1940 the artistic life of Milan was lived in those cafés, mostly at night. And also in the Mokador, where, according to Persico, the most dramatic discussions of all took place. "For a year it has been the meeting-place of all the young painters"—these included Ghiringhelli, De Amicis, Lilloni, Bogliardi, Spilimbergo and Del Bon—"it was here that the Milione Gallery was founded and that the first concrete and dignified reaction took place against the decadence of Lombard painting."

Their exhibition of 1929 at the Pesaro Gallery revealed that the Futurists of the second generation had taken a decisive step towards Abstraction. This was particularly true of Prampolini, with his *Immagini Astratte* (Abstract Images), of Munari and of Fillia. Meanwhile the School of the Decorative Arts at Monza, near Milan, was taking the new artists on to its staff—the sculptor Arturo Martini (who was succeeded by Marini), Persico, Nizzoli, and the painters Semeghini and Raffaele De Grada. Interest was shown in the Bauhaus movement, international culture and the demands of contemporary society. But it was Persico, arriving in Milan from Turin in 1929, who was the real animator of Milanese activities, with his tireless championship of the European outlook. He became assistant editor of *Belvedere*, Bardi's review, and joined the editorial board of *Casabella*, which he subsequently edited with Giuseppe Pagano. Finally he founded the Milione Gallery, which started its career with an exhibition of Rosai.

Meanwhile collections of pictures, destined to become the most important in Italy in this century, were beginning to be formed. In December 1933 the Milione Gallery exhibited Pietro Feroldi's collection, and since the war Achille Cavellini has built up in Brescia a remarkable collection of Italian and foreign non-figurative works.

THE *CHIARISTI*

In Milanese circles around 1930 there were a number of painters with no programme or cohesion as a group and yet having one important aim in common which could loosely be defined as: opposition to official *Novecento* art. As time passed, they came to be known as the *Chiaristi* because of the light, pale backgrounds to their pictures—a reaction against the chiaroscuro of academic art with its monumental masses.

Reforging links with post-Impressionism and the Fauves—above all Matisse—might have meant acquiring that European outlook so strongly advocated by Persico. And yet this did not happen in Milan, as it had in Turin with the "Six". In Milan, Persico was content to uphold all forms of art which were in opposition to the official idiom, whether the painter was Rosai, Garbari, Birolli, Sassu, Del Bon, Spilimbergo or Lilloni. But though the absence of pre-established formulas helped the *Chiaristi* to avoid theorizing, their results, especially after Persico's death, were not always clear, and as the years passed moved increasingly towards provincialism. But the need at the outset was to put up decisive opposition to late nineteenth-century traditions in Lombardy, to eliminate local tone and to transcend all superficial and Romantic sentimentality.

While Birolli with his *San Zeno* linked up with the Primitives of Verona, some of the *Chiaristi* sought inspiration in the Lombard Primitives, Foppa and the frescoes of Luini. The early Lombard painters, before Leonardo da Vinci, had used delicate colours—violets, rain-washed greens, pale

Angelo Del Bon *Still Life 1947*

blues and greys—and as Lombard painting had never based itself on monumental forms but on colour and light, it naturally offered inspiration as to colour rather than form.

Angelo Del Bon has kept a coherent idiom throughout the years. Though he helped to create the *Chiaristi* climate, he himself was not always a *Chiarista*. The other principal painters of this tendency were Adriano Spilimbergo, Francesco De Rocchi and Umberto Lilloni. In the early days of the *Chiaristi* Cristofero De Amicis had an abstract idiom; it was only later that his painting moved towards light tones.

In 1938 Mario Tinti defined Francesco De Rocchi's draughtsmanship as "primitive". By this he meant that De Rocchi had a kind of innocence uncontaminated by academic preconceptions. He also said that his method of painting "belongs to the Romantic tradition of Lombardy". Later Alfonso Gatto described De Rocchi's painting as being "far from Impressionism, however rarefied". Recently Sergio Solmi has noted "the chaste and almost timid gentleness" of De Rocchi's art. Some of his delicate atmospheres of spring-time dawns, graded in colour from the extremely light to the light and the less light, on reddish-white and golden-grey tone schemes, have accents of subdued elegies. On other occasions, however, we find sentimentality predominating, and we can see Carrà's influence in some of his denuded landscapes. Altogether De Rocchi's language is typically Lombard and seems almost afraid to venture beyond the plain around Milan.

Spilimbergo's *Chiarismo* was in its early stages turned dogmatically towards Europe. Argan tells us that "there was a decisive and happy crisis in both the personal and artistic life of Spilimbergo —his meeting with Persico". Persico not only helped him generously with credit but also inspired him to find an idiom free from the chiaroscuro elements of the *Novecento* movement.

In Lilloni's paintings we find a lightness like the shafts of light in Lombard miniatures, a gentleness that sometimes reaches lyrical description. In its light transparencies his painting tends to lose all weight. There is a prevailing literary motif in his work that comes from a sort of reiterated Arcadia.

Angelo Del Bon *Nude on Rocks 1932*

Yet some of his landscapes of the valley of the Po between Lecco and Mantua, with their damp greens, subdued greys and pale colours are not easily forgotten. They are delicate elegies in a low key and the dialogue with nature is filtered through memory.

"Primitive painting", Sironi called it, "in its pale tone schemes, absence of shadow and chiaroscuro contrasts." In his early stages Lilloni was influenced by Cesare Tallone and the woman-painter, Alciati. His personal idiom became crystallized round about 1927. Some of his landscapes of this period still reflected Gola in style of composition and light values, but they had a lightness of colour that was to become typical of his style. The landscape *Monterosso* with its high horizon and *Burrasca* (Storm) done in 1929 show his new direction. From the *Novecento* he inherited nothing but balanced and controlled composition; his greys, greens, sky blues, yellows and pale reds were never heavy with shadows. His various landscapes of *Entella*, his lakeland paintings and disembodied trees have made some critics suggest the influence of reproductions of Chinese art.

Cristofero De Amicis began with experiments in chiaroscuro in the *Novecento* manner, and then turned to pure abstract forms in geometric rhythms. In 1935 he exhibited in Rome with the abstract painters, and he also took part in the first exhibition of Italian abstract art which was held in the studio of Casorati and Paulucci in Turin. In his next period De Amicis concentrated on subtly decorative line drawing. His inclinations towards *Chiarismo* only matured later and owed more to Lombard influences than to Morandi or Cézanne. Even some of his recent landscapes show Romantic Lombard overtones in their diffused and subdued radiance.

The really outstanding personality among the *Chiaristi* was Angelo Del Bon. Indeed he has not yet been given the place he deserves in Italian painting. Alfonso Gatto and Giulia Veronesi have

Umberto Lilloni *The Wood 1954*

Angelo Del Bon *The Island of San Giorgio 1936*

tried to explain his art, but even on the occasion of the exhibition at the Venice Biennale of 1954—
two years after his sudden death—only a few critics really seemed to recognize his importance.

Angelo Del Bon was richly endowed with painterly instincts. We can find the germ of his
typical idiom in *Piazzale Asso*, one of his very early paintings. It is in pale tones with Lombard
light, and almost gives the impression of a sketch. We can feel Gola's influence, but the flavour is
more bitter. At this time, of course, he lacked any contact with Europe. Next we find him picking
up the thread of his early chiaroscuro experiments—even paying tribute to the monumentalism of
the *Novecento*: yet the final results were never formal. They remind us more of Douanier Rousseau
than of the *Novecento*. *Signora allo Specchio* (Lady at her Mirror), exhibited at the Sixteenth Biennale
in Venice, is a sombre picture done entirely in purplish-browns with an effort to attain a synthesis
by means of ample volumes. Even so, we can see that it is by a colourist who has no feeling for
closed monumental form.

The next stage came with his meeting with Persico in 1929. Persico encouraged his interest in
the post-Impressionists, the Fauves and Matisse—in a word, in Paris. Yet he noted that Del Bon's
sympathy for European taste manifested itself in an independence from any kind of bourgeois
system and a jealous regard for individual standards.

When Del Bon gave his instinct as a painter full rein he cast off all traces of preoccupation with
form as suggested by the *Novecento* movement. He put his trust in the autonomous expressiveness of
colour and in immediate and inspired brush strokes. In *Due Nudi Femminili* (Two Female Nudes)
in the Giovanni Romana Collection, the figures are light in tone after the manner of Matisse, and
there is subtle line-drawing. From this Del Bon moved on to his *Lo Schermidore* (The Fencer)
of 1934 in the P. Ruffini Collection. Here we see how the piercing severity of his earlier *Ritratto di
mio Padre* (Portrait of my Father) (1928) with its emphasis on brown is finally worked out in light

colours which eliminate all traces of formal emphasis. The seated figure is two-dimensional, tense and without any chiaroscuro. His *Nudo Rosa* (Nude in Rose) done a year later has a clear painterly lyricism. The greys of the rocks, the greens of the sea, and the nude suspended in light, have a primitive purity of a new kind.

Del Bon's colouring has Lombard accents in the greens, greys, light purples and burnt siennas, but we find neither the atmospheric tone nor the chiaroscuro of the Lombard tradition. His contacts are not with the nineteenth century but with the Primitives and, still more, with Foppa and Luini. His colours are clean, without half shades, based on cold tones though alternated with others unexpectedly warmer. There is a radiance undimmed, a Lombardy seen cleanly with the help of ancient frescoes and post-Impressionism. Del Bon had learnt from Bonnard's colouring, but his palette, though luminous, was harsher with subtle dissonances.

After that Del Bon's idiom developed coherently. Some of his best work was done in his maturity, after he had withdrawn from the world. This includes *San Giorgio* (The Island of San Giorgio) of 1936, *Fiori Gialli* (Yellow Flowers) of 1945 in the Rossetti Collection, which is joyous in its intensely emotional flights of colour, his series of still lifes, and his *Fiori* (Flowers) of 1952.

BREVEGLIERI

Cesare Breveglieri *The Races at San Siro 1941*

Cesare Breveglieri, a Milanese, has given new life to Lombard colour, with the help of Douanier Rousseau and Utrillo.

He has often been confused with the "naïf" painters or seen in terms of story-telling content—for, in spite of Guido Piovene's book written in 1943, and Valsecchi's essay which appeared two years after the artist's premature death in 1948, there is still some critical ground to cover as regards the origin of his idiom and the process of his formation. Carrà, as early as 1935, when writing in praise of *La Gabbia delle Aquile* (The Eagles' Cage), noted "the realistic and poetic sense that gives substance to this painter's vision and is achieved by relations of tone and space rarely to be found in one so young". A few years later he pointed out that in Breveglieri's work we "do not need to seek

Cesare Breveglieri *The Hunter at Lambrate 1936*

the so-called 'natural' which deceives the eye, but the 'idea of nature' that the artist is trying to express, the thoughts and sensations that the real has aroused in his spirit".

Despite the differences in idiom, it is not difficult to see that Breveglieri had given deep consideration to Carrà's work. His structure of composition is different, but there is the zeal for balance adopted—after the Metaphysical period—by Carrà himself. The damp radiance of the colour recalls Carrà's *Sesia* landscapes and *Circo* (Circus) or *Mattino al Mare* (Morning by the Sea). Of course we are speaking only very generally, but the red of the ground in *La Fine del Terzo Atto* (The End of the Third Act) (1941) and even the tree-trunks in the background recall Carrà, though Breveglieri's colour is gentler and more luminous. Yet his taste for the lyrical story of daily life, which is his speciality, does not come from Carrà but rather from Utrillo and the Douanier.

In 1930 Breveglieri was in Paris, where he studied the colours of the Impressionists. What attracted him to the Douanier was not so much the escape into an exotic world of tropical forests as the paintings nearer to daily life, the banks of the Seine and the suburbs of Paris, works like *Family Reunion, Country Wedding, The Footballers,* and *Papa Juniet's Cart*. Breveglieri got his light irony, his subtly innocent eye and his bewitched simplification in the popular sense from the Douanier. We even find an occasional picture with a Douanier title, such as *Lo Sposalizio in*

Cesare Breveglieri *Terrace at Ischia 1940*

Campagna (Country Wedding) (1938). He also got from the Douanier (and, indirectly, from Oriental prints) his tendency to simplify his planes with precise outlines. But Breveglieri's colour, with its subtle vibrations and evocative and luminous texture, is Lombard. He was attracted to Utrillo for his lyrical story-telling in which the images of daily life are bathed in radiant colour. But Breveglieri's colours have something strikingly original about them. The blues, the greens, the fresh sky blues, the light—almost white—colours, the greys, the blacks, the pinks and the reds have tones that help to express his humble, tender and un-rhetorical poetry. There has been talk of the anecdote and the twilight story in connexion with Breveglieri, and also of Sunday painting, but in fact there are absolute painterly values in his work and the visual image is autonomous. His medium is not literary but figurative, depending on space and colour. The geometry of his compositions is sub-merged, implicit, moving with the colour.

Some of his best works are *Il Ponte* (The Bridge) in the Hintermann Collection, *Terrazzo a Ischia* (Terrace at Ischia), *Il Cacciatore* (Hunter), *Palchetto* (Box at the Theatre), *Giardini* (Gardens) and *Il Piccolo Campo* (The Little Field). In all these the fire of composition is hot, and his expressive distortions—only apparently naïf—and the particular quality of his colour are born of lyrical compulsion and give his images a concreteness which is all his own.

Meanwhile in other cities there were painters who, while belonging to no specific group, were busy overthrowing the last remnants of late nineteenth-century tradition—and by means other than those of the *Novecento*. I shall name the most outstanding among them: Giovanni Brancaccio from Naples, Bruno Saetti from Venice, Enzo Morelli from Romagna, Fiorenzo Tomea from Cadore and Domenico Cantatore from Apulia.

Giovanni Brancaccio is a typical exponent of southern art, where it is more difficult than elsewhere to cast off influences deeply rooted in tradition. Even when drawn to international idioms he could not renounce chiaroscuro and rather massive, theatrical representation. Behind the candelabras, figures and still lifes, we can feel ancient Pompeii, but we can also feel Salvator Rosa and even Mancini. In short, when we consider Brancaccio as a whole we see him as the typical Neapolitan painter for whom Cubism, change of expression, measure, Pompeii and fifteenth-century monumentalism are, as it were, stirred in with instinctive Naturalism and the need for direct representation: in fact, we are reminded of that constant in Italian life—the Baroque.

Giovanni Brancaccio *Composition with Figure* (tempera) 1955

Bruno Saetti *Landscape with the Sun 1954*

When we look at the range of Saetti's paintings up to *Fanciullo con la Corazza* (Child in Armour) and *Madre Veneziana* (Venetian Mother) (1951) and his most recent landscapes, we see how he has transcended his Bolognese beginnings and arrived at the radiance of Venice, how he has broken away more and more from the object in favour of the free autonomy of colour.

Saetti has achieved a mastery over the technique of fresco-painting which corresponds to his feeling for construction. He works like the early masters, slowly preparing the structure of his composition in a series of studies and sketches, followed by rapid execution. In this way his basic subjects—maternity, quayside scenes of Venice, still lifes—are firmly constructed; and the greens, pinks and reds are thrown into relief by the greys and browns, and there are occasional dashes of cobalt and white.

We can follow his development from the frescoes in the University of Padua and in the new church of Sant' Eugenio in Rome, and the mosaics in the Romanesque church of the American College, also in Rome, up to his fresco *Paesaggio col Sole* (Sunny Landscape) done in 1955. His danger lies in an over-stylization of the elements of the composition, but recently he has shown greater freedom and his idiom has become more inventive.

When he was invited to participate in the first exhibition of *Novecento* art in 1926, Enzo Morelli tended towards paintings with a lot of drawing in them based on obvious formulas and weighed down with chiaroscuro, but his colour has grown increasingly limpid with the years. He is a solitary painter though always keenly aware of the innovations taking place in the rest of Europe.

126

His *Composizione Murale* (Mural Composition) in the Palazzo Comunale at Assisi (1927-30) has something in common with the Italian fourteenth century—the tribute he paid to the *Novecento* spirit of seeing traditional art with a fresh eye—but his wide colour areas are now free from chiaroscuro contrasts. His idiom consists in the value he gives to spaces as vehicles for colour. He found Hodler a useful example for the structural design of his shapes, while Sironi and Carrà have helped him both with his closed compositions and his warm peaceful Lombard light. His urge towards caustic or grotesque representation with Expressionist tendencies became increasingly softened down in warm colours of evocative emotion, and it is in this sense that he comes nearest to post-Impressionism and French painting in general, from Bonnard to Matisse. His series of landscapes round Lake Garda and his native Romagna are based on memory and depend on the warm emotive movement of the colour and the inner measure. On the other hand, his six recent stained-glass windows for the church of Maria Bambina in Milan display his decorative gifts. It is a kind of decoration that sets out from the architectonic value of space, suggestive colour, and essential storytelling, and carries them on to an abstract plane.

Fiorenzo Tomea's first exhibition was organized by Persico in 1931 at the Milione Gallery. Tomea spent some time in Paris and studied the modern painters from Cézanne to Derain and from Tosi

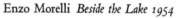

Enzo Morelli *Beside the Lake 1954*

127

to Carrà. The low skies of mountain landscapes, still lifes with candles and other sacristy furnishings, the grotesque masks of peasant processions—these are his themes and they sometimes digress into literature. We can feel the appeal of Ensor and Goya, but Tomea's colour is nearer to that of Tosi and Carrà. He also recalls Morandi, though his transparencies are more waxy and his lighting more diffuse. Sometimes his vivid reds and blacks seem reminiscent of Metaphysical painting or suggestive of Surrealism.

Some of his recent landscapes are outstanding for their metre of composition and their special clean light, while some of his still lifes with candles and lanterns or with fruits—such as *Fichi*

Fiorenzo Tomea *Wild Flowers 1951*

Domenico Cantatore *Girl in Grey 1954*

(Figs) in the Gallery of Modern Art in Rome—unquestionably overcome the literary danger and any sort of naïveté. But we see Tomea at his most limpid in his series of *Fiori di Campo* (Wild Flowers), which are humble and in a low key. De Pisis was quick to observe the freshness of these paintings and has written an excellent appreciation of this painter's genius.

Domenico Cantatore went to Paris in 1932, where he made hundreds of drawings and learnt about modern European painting. He was especially interested in Modigliani, who had died in 1920, Cézanne and Picasso. After successfully exhibiting his drawings at the Milione Gallery, he spent some years quietly in Milan trying to clarify his idiom in his own mind. Cézanne's construction

Enzo Morelli
Summer at Garda 1954

Domenico Cantatore
Still Life 1954

Domenico Cantatore *Woman Indoors 1943*

of shapes in colour awoke his deepest interest—"he was fanatical about Cézanne", as Carrieri put it. But he also admired Carrà and Morandi.

In his series called *Donne nelle Stanze* (Women Indoors) the atmosphere is homely and rather subdued. The tones are low and the colours have thick shadows. In these paintings his basic Romanticism finds a balance between "pathetic" expression and the metre of the composition, which is achieved in the plastic weight of the light as well as in the plastic weight of the bodies. The light is gentle like a rather misty twilight, and though it is in the Lombard tradition we see echoes of Roman tonalism.

His *Contadini* (Peasants) and *Cucitrici* (Sempstresses), and other figures done since the war, show that he has learnt not only from Giotto and Rembrandt but also from the line rhythms of Modigliani and the broad structures of Cézanne. We also feel the influence of the monumentalism of Picasso's women and the plastic quality of Matisse's colour.

"Since 1950," Carrieri writes, "Cantatore's figures seem to have emerged from a bath of coloured crystals. . . . The light lies within the bodies, spread out in broad, bright, plastic harmonies. . . ."

131

Enrico Prampolini *Geological Metamorphosis 1933*

FROM FUTURISM TOWARDS ABSTRACTION

As early as 1929, at the time of the exhibition in the Pesaro Gallery in Milan, it was obvious that Futurism was moving towards Abstraction. Outstanding examples of this trend were Prampolini with his *Immagini Astratte* (Abstract Images), Munari and Fillia. A tendency towards Abstraction had already been discernible in the work of the first generation of Futurists: though the object had not been eliminated, colour had had a plastic value of its own independent of representation and every kind of local tone had been abandoned. At the *Lacerba* exhibition in Florence in 1914 not only had Boccioni exhibited *Dimensioni Astratte* (Abstract Dimensions), but Balla had also shown abstract tendencies, while Prampolini's *Le Linee-Forza nello Spazio* (Energy-Lines in Space), suggested by the speed of a car, had displayed a decidedly autonomous use of colour.

Prampolini joined the Futurists as early as 1913 when he was still a young man and had been expelled for "non-conformity" from the Academy of Fine Arts in Rome. He is usually classed with the second generation of Futurists, for whereas most of the first generation abandoned the idiom fairly soon, he always followed his own coherent line and became the liveliest personality of the second phase, though tending towards Abstraction. The nucleus of the second generation consisted

Enrico Prampolini *Concrete Anatomies 1951*

of Munari, Tato, Depero, Fillia and Dottori. Bruno Munari, with his inexhaustible supply of imaginative invention, became one of the inspirers of Abstraction; Fortunato Depero's mechanical stylizations tended towards description, while Fillia, a polemist and theoretician, rarely rose above pre-established formulas. Gerardo Dottori, lyrical and contemplative in temperament, original and

Atanasio Soldati *Interior with Red Bust 1933*

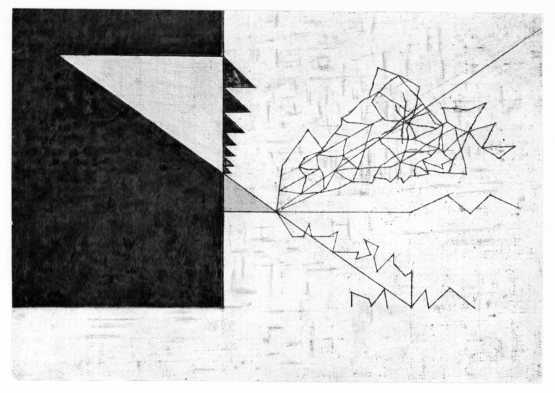

Osvaldo Licini *The Dragon 1933*

tireless in his search for rhythms in space, painted his *Incendio di Città* (City Fire) in 1925—a work highly representative of the second Futurist phase.

But by far the most outstanding personality on a European level was Prampolini. Ungaretti wrote a perceptive article about him for the exhibition at the Twenty-seventh Venice Biennale. "Whoever meets Enrico Prampolini and is the object of his searching, inspired gaze, must inevitably feel in the presence of someone destined to have his say at all costs. . . ."

This will "to have his say" prompted Prampolini to write a whole series of manifestoes and to develop some of the original principles of Futurism in the direction of "absolute synthesis". Ungaretti sees Prampolini's images as "poetry". Perhaps we should give this word its original meaning of "making" or "producing", for in Prampolini there is a constant inventive compulsion; the image is in a continual state of becoming; the Futurist creed which he developed so coherently has kept him in a state of continual invention and pure production. The traditional idea of certain things being "beautiful" is a myth for Prampolini because anything can be made "beautiful" by the interaction of relationships. Space does not exist in itself but is a relationship which is transformed into the fourth dimension. Though first and foremost a painter, Prampolini is one of the most original scenographers of our time, and also a sculptor.

So we find him moving on from Futurism to the contemporary problem of abstract art. His paintings become "objects" in themselves: they are not drawn from nature—they are "Nature". Yet Prampolini was against Kandinsky: he believed not in "pure" painting but in "absolute" painting.

Prampolini has contributed something new to the concept of decoration and the applied arts. For him decoration is not mere ornamentation but a part of everyday life, something active, not merely aesthetic but practical. Here we see one of the Futurist tenets—that works of art are not only to be looked at, but to be lived—pushed to the extreme. All this represents the most modern and living aspect of Prampolini—the one that drove him to produce work in many different media, whether porous, rough or shiny and in colours like sulphur: it is not to be looked at; it is life. The artist has become a demiurge with outstanding craftsmanship constantly refreshed on the intellectual side. The works of his last bioplastic series are a clear example of this tendency.

135

But Prampolini had another more traditional aspect, typified by his series of *Metamorfosi Biologiche* (Biological Metamorphoses) and *Maternita Cosmiche* (Cosmic Maternities)—emblematic images under Metaphysical influence, at times showing signs of compromise and extraneous stylization. It was his decisive break with the contemplated image that marked his return to Futurist principles and the branching out into functional Abstraction, not as a result of decadence—as was the case with the Dadaists—but as a further outlet for his idiom and his new materials.

Prampolini was at all times a European. Up to his sudden death in 1956 he consistently sought and invented new idioms suited to the character of modern society.

In any account of abstract art in Italy it is necessary to distinguish between two trends—the one towards absolute lyricism and the pursuit of form; the other, which is nearer to the neo-Plastic artists of the Bauhaus movement, towards what Argan calls "the art of pure perception". No clear-cut division can be made between the two trends, as often they stem from the same international roots and have undergone the same influences.

Behind the first tendency lie our early traditions—the fourteenth century, Piero della Francesca, Paolo Uccello—but considered exclusively in terms of rhythm and colour. This involves no creation of "objects" nor any tendency to applied art, but has Cubist and Metaphysical undertones. This

Osvaldo Licini *Amalasunta 1950*

Alberto Magnelli *Composition 1944*

sort of Abstraction, as we shall see, is capable of being figurative, and sooner or later its Italian exponents—Soldati, Licini and Magnelli—had to come into contact with Kandinsky and Klee.

The second group owes much more to Van Doesburg, Mondrian and Dutch neo-Plasticism in general, as well as to the experiments in industrial art made by the Bauhaus movement. Here the emphasis is not so much on lyricism as on the detached creation of pure autonomous rhythms to be perceived independently of any sort of representation whatsoever. Besides Prampolini, Munari was a Futurist who took this line. Interest lies not in the image but in the relationship of rhythms with their environment. There is no distinction between drawing, painting, functional rhythms and lines, and art as applied to industry. We find Bruno Munari, for instance, turning to applied graphic art, and Luigi Veronesi—one of the first painters to follow this current—seeking answers to the vital problems of modern society along Bauhaus lines, while Mauro Reggiani, Mario Radice and Manlio Rho pursue, in architecture as elsewhere, that absolute strictness of composition that can be grasped with pure perception.

Since the war the new abstract group of the *Libreria Salto* in Milan has adopted for its own kind of painting the name *Concrete Art*—already used by Kandinsky, Van Doesburg, Mondrian, Max Bill and the Swiss and Argentine schools. They felt the distinction to be necessary "owing to the fact that Italian critics had taken to using the term 'abstract art' to designate either purely imaginative work, or neo-Cubist breaking-down of the object, or neo-Expressionist distortion" (from the notes in the fourth catalogue of the *Concrete Art* series published by the *Libreria Salto*, October 1949).

Thus, in 1948 Soldati, Gillo Dorfles, Monnet, Munari and Veronesi founded the *Movimento di Arte Concreta* (Movement of Concrete Art), commonly known as *MAC*, which subsequently became the Italian end of the French *Espace*.

And now we must clear up another difficulty. There has been too much insistence on the distinction between "abstract" art and "figurative" art—a distinction which is in fact superficial. The object, as remembered, can be present and yet be worked out in an anti-Romantic and abstract way, as happens in many pictures by Soldati or Licini; just as a non-figurative work can have Naturalist origins.

So if a dualism does exist, it is not between "abstract" and "figurative" painting but between attitudes of mind and sensibility. On the one side we find the detached painter, objective, mathematical, intellectual, interested in pure relationships, setting out from rational principles, insulating his work from emotion and avoiding any intensity of expression. Whether he be "abstract" or "figurative" he is always in danger of falling for the mechanical pre-established formula.

On the other side we find the more restless painters who feel rhythm with cursive compulsion. Here the impulse, more or less filtered by the intellect, loses none of its immediacy and the effective charge can lead to intense expression. Whether "figurative" or not, the limitation of these painters may lie in the very fleetingness of the moment of inspiration—however intense; the limitation, in short, of the Romantic principle as such.

But between these two extremes there is scope for infinite variety—just as there is also scope for a "phoney" type of "modernism", whether abstract or figurative. By this I mean that certain forms can seem "modern" but, owing to the lack of true personal participation on the part of the painter, they are merely academic in a new way; or again a formula may be "modern" while the contents are traditional and Naturalistic.

In the history of abstract art in Italy the Milione Gallery in Milan has been the most active cultural centre. It exhibited gouaches and drawings by Léger in 1932, and the first exhibition of abstract art in the whole country took place there a year later with a one-man show of Atanasio Soldati. In 1934 the Milione Gallery exhibited works by Kandinsky for the first time, and there followed an exhibition of Vordemberge-Gildewart presented by Grohman. At the end of that year Bogliardi, Ghiringhelli and Reggiani exhibited their abstract work and issued a declaration that can be viewed as the first manifesto of Italian abstract art. "We are favourably disposed towards the classical cycle, but obviously there can be no question of arches or columns now. . . . We are particularly concerned with technics and science because they clear the ground . . . formidable collaborators, they bring us face to face with a wonderfully exact reality. . . ."

The next year, 1935, Josef Albers and Luigi Veronesi exhibited wood engravings, Lucio Fontana abstract sculpture, Soldati and then Osvaldo Licini abstract painting.

On the occasion of his exhibition Licini wrote: "Until four years ago I did my best to produce good pictures from reality, but then I began to have doubts. . . . Painting is the art of colour and form freely conceived; it is also an act of creation; and, unlike architecture, it is an irrational art governed by the imagination. In other words, it is poetry. So, four years ago, I began inventing my pictures." He concluded with the words: "We intend to prove that geometry can become feeling."

Meanwhile Soldati declared at his exhibition: "Abstract painting—even if the adjective isn't exactly right—loves analysis, order, the harmonious relationships of geometry, the clarity that goes

Alberto Magnelli *Composition No. 6 1950*

with every work of art. . . . Each line, each shape, is a miracle. That is the mystery of art. Lines love space, they create rhythms logically, functionally. . . ."

Magnelli made his final submission to abstract painting in Paris in 1935. In the same year came the first "Collective Exhibition of Italian Abstract Art" in the studio of Casorati and Paulucci in Turin. The exhibitors were Bogliardi, Cristofero De Amicis (who had become abstract), Ezio D'Errico, the sculptor Fontana, Ghiringhelli, Licini, Melotti, Reggiani, Soldati and Veronesi. In the following year Soldati exhibited at the Bragaglia Gallery in Rome, while at Como another group of abstract painters—Mario Radice, Manlio Rho and Carla Badiali—were forging links with the Milione group. The new architect, Terragni, lived at Como and there was a strong feeling there for the relation between abstract art and rational architecture. From 1935 onwards the work of all these artists was reproduced in the principal reviews, both Italian and foreign.

It is important to bear in mind that before the war it was possible for the abstract and figurative idioms to be in some way fused—the meeting-point being the fourteenth century and Piero della Francesca, in other words the anti-Romantic tradition of the past. This produced in some painters, and notably in Pompeo Borra, a figurative-abstract idiom—extremely near to Abstraction while not totally renouncing representation and story-telling.

We admire Atanasio Soldati for his orderly composition and the subtle luminosity of his paint. He is always a painter even when we feel that the formula of his composition is pre-established and hence anti-colouristic. He was a product of training in architectonics and always struggled after absolutely pure relationships. With him instinct was tempered by lucidity of mind. Memory relegated feeling to distant secret zones, and yet both memory and extremely subtle feeling have their part in his painting. His "dialogue with the object" was not entirely eliminated until a few years before his untimely death.

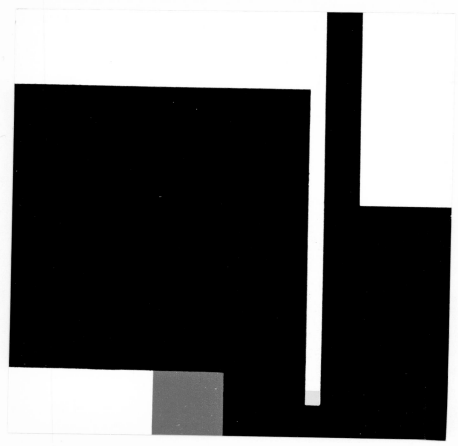

Bruno Munari
Negative-Positive 1954

Atanasio Soldati *Horizontal Image 1952*

Soldati learnt his strictness of style from Carrà and Morandi in their Metaphysical period. But Soldati has a moral and aesthetic intransigeance all his own. He makes use of bright, shrill relationships in his colour areas. His *Composizione col Busto* (Composition with the Bust) reminds us of Carrà, as do *Interno* (Interior) and other paintings of 1933. But Soldati's real emphasis is quite different and is to be found in his strict treatment of space and outline and above all in the absence of tones or chiaroscuro. We can trace other influences in the formation of Soldati's idiom—some of his browns, and green skies round the edges of houses, remind us of the Metaphysical De Chirico. Yet Soldati entirely lacks De Chirico's theatricality, and his colour harmonies and assonances are more subtle. Picasso encouraged his tendency towards an uncompromising autonomy of form, while Ozenfant suggested his purist elements. Kandinsky, Klee and Mondrian were also in his general background. Yet despite all this Soldati's manner is utterly personal. Sometimes he is too formulistic—and this is his limitation. But more often his sense of order gives his colours increased scope precisely because they are enhanced by rhythm. In the upsetting of planes, inherited in part from Cubism, the surfaces seem to form a sort of mosaic and are hermetically sealed in. The third dimension is abolished; a foreshortened perspective suddenly has a flattening effect which seems almost a trick of magic. We feel a sense of stupefaction derived from distant emotions and recollections filtered and purified in the luminous paint. Light causes no shadow. There is neither space nor time for abandon—all is suspended in terms of static relationships. The violets, reds, pale blues, lemon yellows, whites and blacks all seem like subtle and perfect enamel work. We should make no distinction between his paintings that have not erased the memory of distant objects, and those of his last years which are definitely non-figurative. His rhythms of colour in space show us that he always sought for the absolute purity of poetry with an inflexible moral and aesthetic coherence.

Alberto Magnelli first came across *avant-garde* ideas in Florence, where he used to frequent the *Lacerba* circle, Boccioni, Carrà and Soffici. Thus his formation took place in an atmosphere of

Mauro Reggiani *Composition No. 9 1939*

Futurist theories. Yet for him the discovery of forms was independent of anything revealed to him by Nature, and his paintings showed no signs of being suggested by Futurism.

He moved to Paris as early as 1913. There he became a friend of Picasso, Léger, Apollinaire, Max Jacob and Juan Gris. His first abstract picture, *Composizione* (Composition), dates from 1914. Earlier in that year he had painted his last figure—*Donna Seduta* (Seated Woman)—a painting enclosed within a system of lines which, as Roberto Longhi pointed out in the first number of *Paragone*, foreshadowed both Modigliani and Matisse. In the *Composition* we can detect a hint of Futurism in the movement of the rhythms, but nevertheless it owes a great deal more to Cubism with its disciplined spaces and an emphasis on forms of plastic origin worked out with a careful sense of balance.

Picasso's influence is not entirely absent from the two pictures called *Pittura* (Painting) done in 1915. As Carrieri says: "In the flowing, transparent, triangular construction we find a certain rhythmic feeling that comes from Picasso (see *Le Modèle*, 1912, in the Chrysler Collection, New York, and *L'Afficionado*, 1912)—a rhythmic feeling that Magnelli employs for anti-figurative purposes. . . ." But the works done during his first period in Paris in fact come nearer to the Cubism of Juan Gris.

With *Esplosione Lirica, N.1 e N.2* (Lyrical Explosion, Nos. 1 and 2) which he did in 1918 a sudden impulse made him abandon disciplined geometrical relationships in favour of free rhythms in which colour became more autonomous. Then came his figurative parenthesis which lasted a considerable time and coincided almost exactly with his return to Italy. At that period he was doing Naturalistic landscapes under the influence of Cézanne or allusive figures in which we can see Metaphysical undertones. Magnelli returned to Paris in 1933. In his series of pictures of rocks, the rocks "are treated as pure forms and as motives for plastic experiment, while the colour arranged around them is often of dazzling intensity" (Umbro Apollonio). Three years later he acquired an international reputation when he took to painting in a definitely abstract idiom. In 1947, on the occasion of his exhibition at the Drouin Gallery in Paris, a monograph on him was published with a preface by Jean Arp.

He is nowadays known as "the brilliant disciple of Kandinsky", but Kandinsky's vision was more Oriental. Magnelli defines his forms in such a way as to bring into sharp relief the colour quality of his surfaces.

Sometimes Magnelli's imagination still plays around natural forms as the titles of his paintings show. *Punti di Ostilità* (Points of Hostility) done in 1944, and *Ore del Mattino* (Morning Hours) (1948) suggest emotion. Yet this emotion is subjected to a geometric discipline that at times acts as a brake on his imagination. On these occasions we can see that he is painting to a formula—the intellectual control has led to such detachment that only skilled professionalism remains.

The most subtle and imaginative lyricist among the Italian abstract painters is Osvaldo Licini. He has indeed shown, to use his own words, that "geometry can become feeling". Though he has

Luigi Veronesi *Composition 1954*

undergone neo-Plastic influence, his direct line of descent is from Klee. We can follow his development from his early more geometrical compositions to the series of images of *Amalasunta*, where the use of outline on almost monochrome surfaces reminds us of Matisse.

Licini's decisive break with the figurative tradition came from his need to explore the bare essence of what he had to say. The purity of his images is born in a moment of soaring imagination, sudden as an illumination. Neither is he absolutely non-figurative. *Il Drago* (The Dragon) and *Amalasunta*, as well as many other geometrical compositions, derive from a figurative idea. Though some of his secondary paintings are over-formulistic, taken as a whole Licini is a poet. No one can deny him an outstanding place not only in abstract, but in Italian painting as a whole. And this judgment stands despite the fact that for some years he has been living in solitude and no one knows about his recent work.

Pompeo Borra *Composition 1938*

Mauro Reggiani began as a figurative painter in the tradition of Cézanne, Carrà and the *Novecento* movement. After 1932 he turned to Abstraction and has often been called "the Italian neo-Plastic painter, *par excellence*".

In his early non-figurative days, while working out the laws of proportion—the golden number, the golden section, and so on—as expounded in the writings of Ghyka, his compositions bore some resemblance to Van Doesburg, whose work, however, he did not yet know. But he also favoured elaborate media. Even when his forms became freer, Reggiani "always kept very much in mind the tone relationships between the various colours of the picture, their bearing on one another, their subordination or their predominance. . . ." One of the best examples is *Composizione N.9* (Composition No. 9) in which the Cubist and purist influence is worked out not only in balance of spaces but also in subtle colour assonances of browns and greys in rich paint of marked plastic significance.

Giuseppe Capogrossi *Composition 1953*

Among the abstract painters who have come into their own since the war, the most outstanding is Giuseppe Capogrossi. In his early stages he was an exponent of the figurative tradition of the Roman School from which he finally broke away in 1949 and began a series of compositions that resemble ideograms. Their rhythm is broken up in counterpoint and they have strict arabesque surface movement. At first sight each picture seems the same as the one before, because the constituents, taken from examples of remote civilizations, are unchanging: the variation in fact lies in the rhythms, and hence in the space and the colour.

After the clear poetic invention of his early images, we find Capogrossi moving on to new media, new dimensions and a new sense of decoration. His compositions are not lyrical images calling for pure contemplation: they are more like archetypes for something that can be mass produced *ad infinitum*. Nor is this a limitation; for the point precisely is that they should be applicable to new media and in new spaces—in industrial art, for instance—along Bauhaus lines. This can be seen in Capogrossi's ceiling decorations for the Tenth Triennale of Milan. For the fundamental aspiration of the abstract idiom at its most authentic is that it should find new applications, be active in society, establish new relationships. The real novelty of Capogrossi's surfaces lies in the fact that the image does not seem necessarily finite, in the sense that it is ineluctably defined by its rhythm. In other words, we feel that the image could well extend beyond the actual picture.

Another painter who has a special place today is Pompeo Borra. As we said above, his idiom could be called figurative-abstract. His beginnings are to be found not so much in the *Novecento* movement as in his love of the past which drew him to Piero della Francesca of whose harmonies and laws of measurement he wanted to make a critical study. His abstract invention lies in the consistency of the colour relationships even if the surfaces become volumes. His vision still remains two-dimensional. Like Léger in France, Borra has made use of decisive colour relationships that he himself has invented and which are increasingly anti-Naturalistic. His best compositions are those which, whether they contain figurative elements or not, achieve rhythms with loud colour harmonies without literary inclinations or surviving traces of Metaphysical influence. *Composizione Astratta* (Abstract Composition) of 1938 and *Figure* (Figures) of 1955 are two examples of Borra at his best.

Mario Radice *Composition 1950*

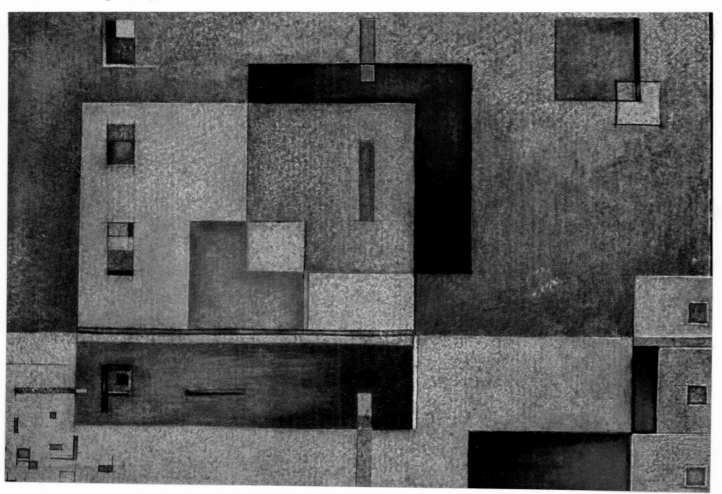

CORRENTE

Neither the second phase of Futurism nor the strict demands of Abstraction seemed able to appease the uneasiness by which a certain group of young painters was beset in the years immediately before the second World War.

Corrente was a movement that developed in Milan from Romantic premises but without a definite programme. The artists who belonged to it, though differing as to temperament and idiom, had one fundamental belief in common—that modern art, in contact with Europe as it was, should express the ferments and unrest of the time, which were not only aesthetic but also moral. "In art as in other things," declared the review *Vita Giovanile*, which later became *Corrente*, "intelligence and sensibility are not enough to form a man if he lacks character: in art as in other things the problem is ethical. We must give new value to the human personality. . . ."

Their attitude towards moral activity turned the artists of this group against all forms of neo-Classicism and rhetoric. The group emphasized the value of colour as a constituent element of form and rejected all survivals of Naturalism. We must not forget that at this period—that is, towards 1939—only a few artists were painting according to Futurist or abstract principles; the majority belonged to the *Novecento* movement with its superficial and illustrative Naturalism, its rhetoric and its provincial clichés—all eminently suited to the political background. This *Novecento* spirit was

Renato Birolli *San Zeno
the Fisherman* 1931

Aligi Sassu *Horses at Fontemara 1954*

epitomized in the Cremona Prize—to counterbalance which the Bergamo Prize was founded to encourage new and freer forms of art. *Corrente* stood for "the defence of modern art" at a time when the campaign against *entärtete Kunst* or "degenerate art" was spreading even to Italy. Hence for some members of the *Corrente* group, moral opposition involved political opposition. And here lay *Corrente*'s cultural importance.

And yet the group had no common idiom—indeed there was even a conflict of tendencies which later, after *Corrente* had ceased to exist, caused an open breach among its former members.

Raffaele De Grada, one of its most fiery exponents, explained the group in terms of "neo-Realism". But when we look at the work produced by painters in those years it seems to us that their aspiration was rather in the direction of Personalism—coupled, of course, with intransigent opposition to facile Naturalism and academicism. They did not believe that the "content" need be moralistic; what was moralistic was the fervour with which they believed that the new idiom should arise from deep within each artist's personality. In this sense the origins of the movement were Romantic. The term "Realism" which was occasionally used in the review *Corrente* was given an anti-Naturalistic twist: it meant the need to express the human personality. Colour was exalted after the manner of the Fauves and the post-Impressionists, and there was persistent distortion of the object. Delacroix, Ensor, Kokoschka, Soutine and Van Gogh all had their influence on the images, which were charged with hallucination and unease. By and large these sculptors and painters had much in common with the Italian "hermetic" poets of the same period and, indeed, collaborated with them.

In 1938 Badodi painted his phantom-like *La Battaglia di Milazzo* (Battle of Milazzo), which is as light and visionary as a dream. The following year he attempted to evoke a bewitched and brooding atmosphere, with Metaphysical undertones, in *Sartoria* (The Tailor's Shop). Birolli, from 1931 when he painted *San Zeno the Fisherman* up to the present, has never suffered from neo-Realistic preoccupations; he represented all that was most European in *Corrente*. For him the "real" was never antithetical to the "abstract"; abstraction, when born of a concrete emotion, was always an imaginative process. In *Maschere Vaganti* (Strolling Players) (1937), *Il Caos* (Chaos) (1936), *I Funamboli* (The Rope-Dancers) and *Maschera Gialla* (The Yellow Mask) (1940) and *Una Domenica in Periferia* (Sunday in the Suburbs), the "real" is overlaid with the infinite. Here Birolli uses allusions and associations; he puts his trust in the autonomous expressiveness of colour, and his culture is always present. He and Sassu had a decisive influence on the formation of the *Corrente* group. They shaped its fundamental tendency which led not to neo-Realism but to moral opposition to programmes as such. Migneco, for example, who developed a Realist emphasis after 1950, was also painting bewitched figures in the *Corrente* period, with a colour in which intensity of expression was heightened by tortuous brush-work and assumed visionary emphasis with its seaweed greens, blues and yellows. *La Fossa dei Lebbrosi* (The Lepers' Ditch), *Le Massaie Ubriache* (The Drunken Peasant Women) (1939) and *Sedile al Parco* (The Seat in the Park) (1940) are paintings in which there is no attempt to present objective reality: all is state of mind, a more or less tortured dream and panic hallucination—sometimes self-satisfied, withal. As for Cassinari, his chief aim was not detached Realism either, but the subjective lyrical effect, a flight from realistic detail in favour of suggestive, allusive resonances.

Valenti, another typical exponent of the group, at that time stood for escape into the land of fable and enchantment by means of suggestive associations and allusions and freedom of colour along Fauve lines—all passing through childhood memories transfigured by the imagination. Typical examples are: *L'Uomo Albero* (The Man-Tree), *La Maga* (The Witch), *L'Isola delle Fanciulle* (The Island of Little Girls) and *I Bicicli Incantati* (The Enchanted Bicycles). Aligi Sassu painted *Il Concerto* (The Concert)—with its broad harmonies in red—as early as 1931. At the *Corrente* period he was painting pictures in which the real and the mythical were blended, and the highlights of fantasy were suggested by the sheer expressiveness of colour in which Delacroix, the Fauves, Renoir, the Nabis and the Expressionists had a part. In the group Sassu stood for painterly immediacy with motifs at times inspired by the real and at times invented under literary influences. Typical examples are *Grande Caffè* (The Big Café) (1936–9), *Orlando* (1942), *Postribolo* (The Brothel) (1939) and his flaming landscapes with mythical Baroque horses.

Guttuso, who was living in Milan in 1935 and 1936, joined forces with the *Corrente* group in his urgent desire for a fully European culture. For Guttuso, Cubism and Expressionism were necessary experiences in the life of figurative art. *Donna che piange* (The Woman who weeps) (1939) has a typically Expressionist exasperation. *La Crocifissione* (The Crucifixion) (1942)—Expressionist with influences deriving from Picasso's Cubism—aroused fierce discussion at the Bergamo Prize exhibition. In those days Guttuso's theories were exactly opposite to the ones he has had since the war. He was open to wide European influences and was deeply aware that Realism, Cubism, Abstraction and Expressionism need not be antithetic to one another. His Realism at that time (because Guttuso has always had an undeniably realistic background) was at the opposite pole to the spirit of the Cremona Prize: to begin with, it was anti-Naturalistic. At that time he was not preoccupied with direct and illustrative communication; all that came later and quite independently of *Corrente* views.

At the time when Guttuso was far indeed from De Chirico's "reactionary" painting, there was an exhibition of eight *Novecento* painters at the Barbaroux Gallery. In Raffaele De Grada's words: "The three still lifes exhibited at the Barbaroux Gallery (they were by De Chirico) reveal to what depths of realistic boredom the converts to reaction would have us reduced. Will not the new men (we won't say the 'young' men about whom we have heard *ad nauseam*)—that is to say the really alive men—take this opportunity of declaring that chapter of contemporary art closed?" De Grada

Aligi Sassu *Concert 1931*

concluded: "To sum up, the basic conviction of *Corrente* has always been that the Romantic revolution is not yet at an end; that the freedom that animated it is not yet exhausted; that the revolution must go a full circle before reaching a conclusion: abstract art is part of that circle; Realism is its end. This conviction is the basis of the whole *Corrente* movement."

This was Raffaele De Grada's view. But his affirmations do not take into account the paintings of all the members. Neither Birolli, Cassinari, Valenti, Cherchi nor Migneco—at that period—

Bruno Cassinari *Green Landscape 1943*

would have agreed with this. On the contrary, they believed that the problem of Realism could only be understood in terms of inner lyrical necessity; as the truth of the anti-Naturalistic image; as the coherence of man and artist independent of "content".

The time has come to give some facts about the origins of *Corrente*, the review, and about the development of the movement. *Vita Giovanile*, a periodical of politics, literature and the arts, first appeared in January 1938. In October of the same year it changed its name to *Corrente di Vita Giovanile* and was edited by Ernesto Treccani, then still in his teens. Outstanding among the painters and sculptors who wrote for the review were Birolli, Migneco, Valenti, Cassinari, Cherchi, Guttuso, Manzù, Broggini and Badodi (Sassu, who had been particularly active in directing the spirit of *Corrente*, had been arrested in 1937 for political activities).

The first exhibition of *Corrente* took place in Milan in March 1939. Although confined to artists of the Milanese circle, it represented many trends. I quote from the catalogue: "For a year now *Corrente* has been discussing certain artists—and it is those artists who are exhibiting today." They included "the most typical modern painters of the Milanese tradition"—Carrà, Marussig, Tosi, De Grada, Bernasconi and Cesare Monti "invited to exhibit out of homage to our elders"; various painters and sculptors of the "mature younger generation", including Cantatore, Tomea and Mucchi; and the principal *Corrente* exponents—Birolli, Valenti, Migneco, Badodi, Cherchi, Dino Lanaro, Cassinari, Giuseppe Mantica and Luigi Grosso.

More important was the second *Corrente* exhibition in December of that same year. This time only artists of the younger generation were included. The most prevalent note among the various painters was an emphasis on colour opposed both to the formal demands of the *Novecento* movement and to the strict metre of Abstraction. Besides the principal members of the *Corrente* group exhibitors included Santomaso, Mafai, Afro, Fazzini, Franchina, Mirko and Pirandello.

Italo Valenti *The Island of Little Girls 1939*

By now the group had a huge programme of exhibitions prepared, including another twelve in Milan alone. But six months later, on 10 June, 1940 (the eve of Italy's entry into the war), the review *Corrente* was suppressed. The movement continued with the help of art publications and essays and the tireless activity of a small but enterprising gallery, Bottega, where Birolli, Migneco, Cassinari, Badodi, Lanaro and Valenti exhibited. Later Bottega became the Galleria della Spiga e Corrente, with the help of Stefano Cairola, and here Cassinari, Morlotti and Treccani exhibited in 1943.

As we have seen, Aligi Sassu was one of the most active painters of the movement. His singular personality as an artist has been discussed most fully by Enrico Emanuelli, but Carrà, Anceschi and Carrieri have also written on him.

Sassu began to play an active part in *avant-garde* exhibitions when still in his teens. In 1927, when only fifteen, he joined the Futurist movement. But this constituted no more than his initiation as a painter, an adventure opposed to the academic tradition; soon he was painting balanced spaces reminiscent of Carrà. But already we can recognize his own bewitched evocation of things, with much colour activity. *Paesaggio Urbano* (City Landscape) (1930) shows a palette in which the reds, blues, greens and purples are harsh and sharply dissonant. Next came Picasso's influence, of the Blue, Pink and Harlequin periods, as seen in reproductions. In his series of *Nudi Atletici* (Nude Athletes) and *Uomini Rossi* (Red Men) the drawing gives a spectral intensity to the very narrow range of colours.

We can already see which way Sassu is going—not to pure painting but to painting as narration, by means of one colour which, while its animation recalls Delacroix, also draws on Renoir (but without the Impressionist light) and still more on the Expressionists. His shapes have their being in the nervous movement of the brushwork, and the fire of the composition is always controlled by the mind. He can switch from his *Interni di Caffè* (Café Interiors) to mythical horses with neo-Baroque attitudes, the *Dioscuri* landscapes, crucifixions, pictures of councils and the most varied kinds of portrait. His variety of motifs derives from the need to express himself in the freest possible way, and transcend any kind of distinction between illustrative and formal values. We can see Sassu's distinctive voice in various works dating from as early as 1930. On other occasions clever crafts-manship gets the upper hand, and detail sometimes has pride of place in the picture. Among his best works we can list his *Concerto* (Concert) of 1931, which is one of the most lyrical achievements of the period, some of his early paintings of cyclists, some of his café interiors, *Orlando* (1942), some scenes of horses, including his *Cavalli a Fontemara* (Horses at Fontemara) (1954) and *Concilio Ecumenico* (Oecumenical Council), grotesque and vast in its masses.

Arnaldo Badodi *The Circus 1939*

Giuseppe Migneco *The Lepers' Ditch 1939*

A painter who was influenced by Sassu in the vividness of his reds was Arnaldo Badodi, but his lyricism was more melancholy. His idiom was Expressionist accents which often shade off, at least in his early period, into memories of Lombard tone. His freest period as a painter coincided with *Corrente*. His premature death (he was reported missing in Russia in 1942 when not yet thirty) brought his experiments with colour to an end.

At the first *Corrente* exhibition his *Le Pettegole* (The Gossips) already showed his gift for irony. "The irony of the distortion reflects the characters of the figures, real in their own absurd and fantastic world," wrote Sandro Bini in the catalogue. It is the colour, somewhat shrill in its harmonies though with undertones of Lombard light, that creates the shapes. Both the phantom-like *Armadio Aperto* (Open Wardrobe) and *La Battaglia di Milazzo* (Battle of Milazzo) date from this period. At the second *Corrente* exhibition *I Saltimbanchi* (The Acrobats)—painted at the same period as *Sartoria*

(The Tailor's Shop) (1939)—shows links with Ensor in the melancholy state of mind and with the Metaphysicals in the brooding, static atmosphere. But in *Il Veglione* (The Old Man) we find the Metaphysical undertone totally eliminated in rhythms based on a grotesque intensity of colour. We find Badodi at his most coherent in *Il Circo* (The Circus) in which the evocative colour is in harmony with the spaces and with the spirit of the story he is telling.

Giuseppe Migneco *Boy Removing a Thorn 1952*

The image, with Giuseppe Migneco, derives from a compulsion that is moral as well as imaginative. The search for effective truth has been his task since the early years when he left his native Sicily and began painting in Milan. His particular idiom in the general *Corrente* background showed links with the Expressionists. Names such as Soutine, Rouault and De Groux occur to mind—and above all Van Gogh. But these painters served him as examples of method rather than for their stylistic results. As Anceschi has pointed out in his penetrating essay on Migneco, "not even in Van Gogh do we find such obsessed feeling, such secret recesses of humiliation, such a feeling of desolation and the continual presence of death". Migneco felt his colour with a sensuality heightened by his intellect, with an "anguished and writhing Baroque spirit". With his tortuous brush strokes, form was entrusted exclusively to colour and the third dimension was eliminated or reduced to merely allusive echoes.

Behind a world in which everything is undefined, a world in which earth, eyes, hair and hands are blended in the liquid quality of harsh greens, lay the Romantic myth which exalted the state of mind; it is as if a diary had become colour. *Le Massaie Ubriache* (The Drunken Peasant Women) and *La Fossa dei Lebbrosi* (The Lepers' Ditch)—both of 1939—*Sedile al Parco* (The Seat in the Park) and *L'Uomo dal Dito Fasciato* (The Man with the Bandaged Finger)—both of 1940—must be listed

Italo Valenti *Flying Fish 1955*

Italo Valenti *At the Gardens 1954*

among the most original works of this period in which colour is the element in which the expression consists. *Cacciatori di Lucertole* (The Lizard Chasers) (1942) marks his gradual change-over to a kind of drawing that gives the colour more body, while with *Bevitori* (Drinkers) (1944) we see Migneco increasing his emphasis on drawing in circular rhythms which stress the principal centres of relief. He is beginning to feel the object dramatically yet in a way more and more detached from the spirit of subjective confession. Surrounding humanity has made itself felt—with force rather than weight. We can detect a need in Migneco to clarify himself by means of others. A certain Cubist influence prevents him from being Naturalistic and seals in the figures. The sensuality is now more controlled, for Migneco's temperament is passionate but reserved—he is the headstrong, silent kind of Sicilian. The Sicilian landscape with its fishermen, prickly pears and donkeys—which he recaptures in memory and hence with free invention—take on a hallucinating reality that reminds us of the Metaphysical painters. But Migneco's aim is the opposite of theirs, for they loved escape and intellectual games, whereas Migneco wants to reconstruct reality as absolutely and lucidly as possible—even though, judging by results, the Baroque spirit remains. The pictures he painted immediately after the war—*Pigiatori d'Uva* (The Grape Treaders), *Asinello Siciliano* (Sicilian Donkey), *Venditore di Pesce* (Fishmonger), *Asinaio* (Donkey Driver) and *Lavandaia* (Washer Woman)—show his obsession with drawing, but drawing which sets the colour free and gives it the quality of pure enamel.

Italo Valenti was another outstanding painter of the *Corrente* movement, but to give a fair estimate of his work we must first clear up one or two misunderstandings. His images derive from the impact of childhood memories on his imagination. He presents, by means of colour, a reality which is entirely enchanted—fantastic animals, men who turn into trees, kites, sailing boats in garden ponds, paper fishes, stations with toy trains. There are subtle associations and fantastic absurdities, though he makes no use of Surrealism or the mechanics of the unconscious. Some people have viewed the whole thing as a game with a literary background—but this is a mistake. Valenti's figures (I am referring to his best pictures, from *Isola delle Fanciulle* (The Island of Little Girls) to *L'Uomo Albero* (The Man-Tree) and his recent compositions of fishes) are given concrete form in colour and rhythm values with visual purity.

His motifs are dreams, memories transfigured by the imagination, and images that are only apparently escapist. There is, in fact, nothing escapist in the way they are given concrete form. His personality is expressed in a contemplative lyricism far removed from any shock of the external world, and his acute sensibility is filtered by his intellect without any inclination towards rhetoric or objective representation.

If it took some time for him to establish his reputation, this was due to his silences and periods of diminished creative tension. But the retrospective exhibition of his work at the Milione Gallery in 1955 gave ample proof of his lyrical qualities. His latest paintings, quite apart from his luminous lithographs, have shown a return, though in a more limpid and lucid way, to the *Corrente* period, when he was considered one of the group's most outstanding artists.

Ernesto Treccani, the founder and editor of the review *Corrente*, was not at first a painter, but a writer of poems, plays and articles. His *Autoritratto* (Self-Portrait) (1941) shows him when still adolescent. Since then his painting has developed under the influences of post-Impressionism, Picasso and Expressionism. He is inclined to melancholic elegy, the fragment of the state of mind, rather than to detached representation. The myth of neo-Realism by which he has become fascinated since the war has led him astray from his true path. He reaches his peak when he puts his trust in elegiac and cultivated inspiration.

THE NEW ARTISTIC FRONT

It was natural that the war, with all its destruction and political and social upheavals, should have produced various crises among artists: natural, too, that after the years of cultural isolation each country should reach out once more towards contact with the rest of Europe and a free and genuine international interchange. The works of artists condemned by the Nazis were again in circulation from the Expressionists to the Bauhaus group, and a lively critical interest in the whole of modern art immediately made itself felt. Italy was quick to react to this situation—especially in so far as it concerned all that had been done, and was being done, in Paris. When Lionello Venturi resumed his place in the life of Italian painting he played his characteristic part in establishing contact with the rest of Europe.

A need was felt to make up for lost time. The Venetian Biennale reopened in 1948 under the auspices of Rodolfo Pallucchini, and again became a means through which new demands could be met. It exhibited selected works of the French Impressionists, Seurat, the Fauves, the Cubists, the Futurists, the Metaphysical painters and the Surrealists. There were exhibitions of Kandinsky, the Expressionists, the Blaue Reiter, the Brücke group, Ensor, Nolde, the Dutch neo-Plastic painters, the De Stijl movement and Douanier Rousseau. Works by Matisse, Picasso and Bonnard were exhibited in Milan, works by Picasso in Rome and by Chagall at the Palazzo Madama in Turin. Everything possible was done to show Italians the achievements of modern European art.

But in the post-war period it was Picasso who was the main inspiration for Italian painters. *Guernica* seemed a basis from which they could advance: its idiom seemed typical of the spirit of the age. During this period Guttuso in Rome was working at his *Cucitrici* (Sempstresses) with its Cubist echoes, while a group of young painters in Milan wrote a manifesto called "After *Guernica*".

Subsequently it was Abstraction, rather than Cubism or Expressionism, that was looked to as the tendency that could finally eliminate any possible residue of romantic or sentimental painting and bring about a spirit of objective detachment. The change-over from values of tone to values of timbre in colour, and the effect this had on rhythm and space relationships, seemed to many artists a basis for a new international language—following the line of the later Kandinsky and the neo-Plastic painters.

The *Fronte Nuovo delle Arti* (The New Artistic Front) sponsored an exhibition in June 1947 at the Spiga Gallery in Milan which brought together various artists of the generation following that of the *Novecento* movement, not with much in common in terms of idiom, but all ardently desiring freedom.

Giuseppe Marchiori, the critic who backed this group, gives us a clear idea of its general direction in his introduction to the exhibition at the Twenty-fourth Venice Biennale. "In the months following the end of the war the achievement of freedom in Italy brought about a search for understanding between man and man that rose above division and suspicion; it was as if everyone wanted to start again, without a past, and find the motive for his work in the human solidarity that had been denied or betrayed for so many years. . . ."

Among the first to break down the isolation and state these new requirements were the artists promoting the movement that came finally to be known as the New Artistic Front. Originated by Birolli, the idea was taken up by Santomaso, Pizzinato and Vedova, and discussed in Rome as well as in Milan. Finally it took concrete form in a manifesto signed 1 October, 1946, in a room in the Palazzo Volpi in Venice. This manifesto, whatever its shortcomings, has real importance in that it epitomized the feelings of obligation and conviction. It was not a "group" manifesto but a united front of the most representative Italian artists of the post-*Novecento* generation who were at one in their demand for confidence in their work and in their determination to rise above the pessimism and general spiritual disintegration of their time.

The manifesto was signed by the painters Birolli, Cassinari, Guttuso, Morlotti, Pizzinato, Santomaso and Vedova, and by the sculptors Leoncillo and Viani. At the first exhibition at the Spiga Gallery in Milan the painters Corpora and Turcato and the sculptors Fazzini and Franchina also exhibited, while Cassinari withdrew his support.

But a few years later these artists had subdivided into two different groups. Eight of them—known as the "Eight"—had turned to the kind of painting that Lionello Venturi has called "abstract-concrete", and cultivated a definitely European vision; while the second group, the "neo-Realists", were primarily concerned with the immediate communicability of motif and laid special stress on moral attitudes and "content" without bothering much about inventing new forms nor the snares of provincialism.

GUTTUSO

Renato Guttuso's personality is outstanding owing to his immense vitality. From 1935 up to the present he has had a strong, not to say violent, influence on the development of Italian painting.

His moral attitude has caused him to feel an urgent need to communicate his story—not to a few initiates but to the masses: hence the orientation of his idiom in the direction of Realism. But a whole range of problems concerning Realism inevitably presented itself to Guttuso, for he was vividly aware of all the tendencies around him and yet was bent on immediacy of representation. And when

Renato Guttuso *Crucifixion 1942*

Realism became Naturalism he explained it in terms of external representation of fact in the manner of a sermon.

From his earliest days as a painter Guttuso has displayed his characteristically Sicilian inclination towards the spectacular—though always tempered by intellectual clarity. He has always tended towards contact with things, urgency of expression, and images we feel we can touch, and he has always tried to participate as fully as possible in the human drama of our time.

All the most vivid manifestations of modern art, from Expressionism to Cubism, have found their place in Guttuso's dialectic, and he has been influenced by Goya, Delacroix and Courbet. Then came his desire for direct representation of things seen, the effort to turn his back on current tendencies and express himself in the popular idiom of the man in the street, paying no heed to the obvious pitfalls. But his mistakes, such as they are, are blatant and uncompromising. What gives the poetry to his best work is its exceptionally forceful expression.

For the rest Guttuso's idiom has affinities with Sicilian Baroque, not in the sense of decoration but in the whole effect which fascinates our eye with the provocative movement of the forms, the grandiose sweep, the suggestive light—in a word the warm sensuality that comes from Sicily, sharpened and pointed by his mind.

When he began painting in Palermo his works—especially his series of female nudes, landscapes and still lifes—revealed a new accent due to the violence of their expression. Even the roughly painted flesh—with its sensuality and lack of any outward beauty—suggested that the operative element in Guttuso's idiom was drawing, modelling, perspective in all its variations, the essential outline. Even his Cubist experience was a drawing experience, while the influence of late Impressionism was merely incidental because evocation of atmosphere and nuances of tone are not part of his idiom. Hence, in spite of his strong, anti-tonal feeling for colour, his nervous, sensual feeling for line is what is most apparent in his pictures. His noisiness and stridency, which made him turn towards the Expressionists, comes from moral obligation and the need to shock.

His burning sense of the human drama is typically Sicilian. In Rome, where he went when still young, he came into conflict with the disciples of the Roman School and himself influenced various painters. And when in Milan he made his impact on the formation of the *Corrente* group, as we have seen, by urging it yet further in the direction of moral action.

Renato Guttuso *The Sleeping Fisherman 1950*

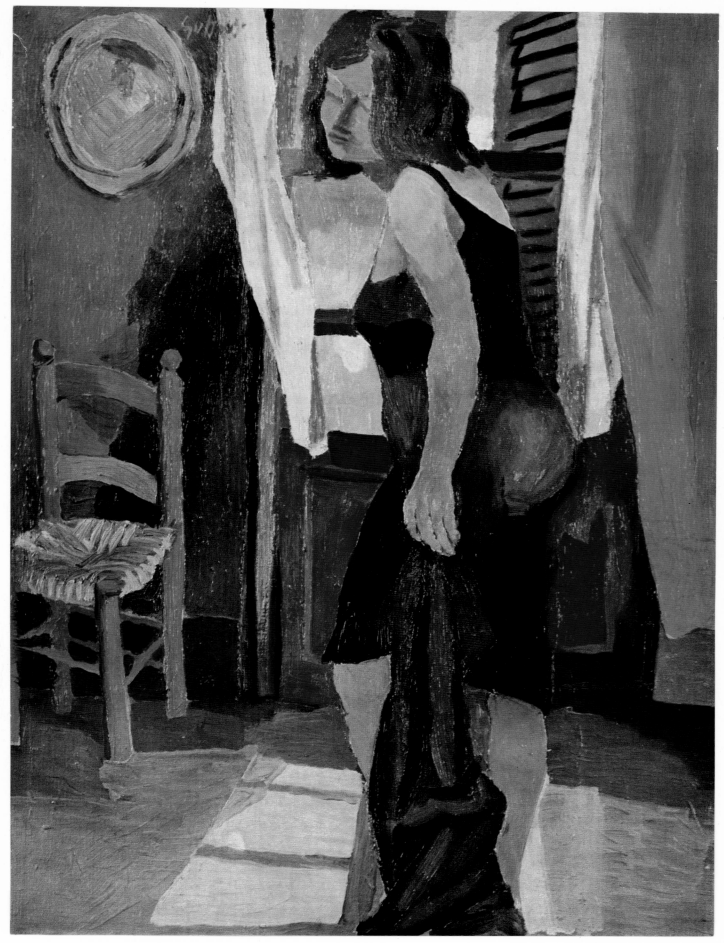

Renato Guttuso *Interior with Figure 1942*

While in *Fuga dall' Etna* (Flight from Etna) his sense of the human drama is revealed only in the agitated movement—the composition itself lacking breadth—his *Crocefissione* (Crucifixion) has broader rhythms. In this latter painting we find hallucinating Expressionist tension like a German stained-glass window, forms suggestive of Cubism and Picasso, and finally—as regards the relationship between the landscape in the background and the figures in the foreground—Giotto's early disciples. This work more than most is a statement of the crisis and predicament of modern man. But in less grandiose paintings Guttuso achieves his own special lyrical coherence: peasants, wounded horses, still lifes, windows, cages, interiors with figures such as *Fanciulla in Nero* (Girl in Black), provide motifs for plastic representation that involves no exclusion of warm evocation. In these pictures the colour, though sonorous and dissonant, is softer, though we often find the same Expressionist "shriek". The obvious Expressionist echoes of *Ragazza alla Finestra* (Girl at the Window) (1939) would appear to be a basic motif.

So Guttuso's Realism springs from the need to represent oppressed humanity. Yet until the period immediately after the war it was anti-Naturalistic: until then his tendency was broadly to reconstitute reality with an "objectivity" rendered subjective by his critical conscience. This was Guttuso's period of complete freedom of idiom. There was no conflict between invention, imagination and expressive urgency; all found integration in shapes of poetic vitality. Even in the New Artistic Front period, and at the time of the Spiga Gallery exhibition, Guttuso was in the forefront of new ideas. His *Cucitrici* (The Sempstresses) with its Cubist schema and the series of drawings and paintings of carters and his still lifes have broad and free rhythms of construction. But with *Occupazione di Terre Incolte in Sicilia* (The Taking-over of Uncultivated Land in Sicily) (1949–50)—exhibited at the Twenty-fifth Venice Biennale—we can see a break in his idiom. His new tendency was towards the immediate kind of popular appeal referred to above, with "content" predominating over any interest in the problems of form. His opposition to modern art was now decisive; for Guttuso a new art could only be born from "content" and from the possibility of immediate communication with the masses.

The emphasis on popular epic was shown more clearly in the vast *Battaglia al Ponte dell' Ammiraglio* (Battle at Ponte dell'Ammiraglio) (1951–2) in which his memories of paintings of Sicilian carts do not preclude hints of Cubism and Expressionism in the angles of vision, the upsetting of the planes and the high-lighting of the colour. The detail of the dead man, supine amid the swirl of the whole composition, exhibits the vitality of an accomplished style. And yet, in spite of all this, the work is fragmentary and superficial.

With his more recent *Spiaggia* (Beach) (1955) we find Realism and Naturalism blended together in a composition that displays outstanding skill but which cannot be said to be among the poetic works of the artist. Yet even here we still find the powerful charge of expression which shows that at any moment his idiom at its best could be resuscitated.

REALISM

At the first post-war Venetian Biennale, held in 1948, the most obvious trend was towards abstract art and the idioms generally considered international. But a few years later a group, gathered around the dominating personality of Guttuso, decided to oppose non-figurative art, and by June 1952 had founded a monthly review in Milan called *Realismo*, edited by Raffaele De Grada. Contributors to *Realismo* from different parts of Italy included Guttuso, Maria De Micheli, Ernesto Treccani, Gabriele Mucchi, Corrado Maltese, Antonello Trombadori, Carlo Levi, Paolo Ricci, Pizzinato, Zigaina, Tettamanti and Motti.

Giuseppe Migneco *Preparing Maize 1951*

The background idea was concentrated on "content" irrespective of strictness of form. There had been war, destruction and social upheaval. The new artists were to avoid the self-indulgence of formal subtleties and instead were to bring a new lay gospel to the masses. So far, so good. But in fact, and judged by its results, the neo-Realist movement failed to bring out the best in its exponents and to produce new images. It has resulted on the whole in a reactionary idiom and sometimes even in provincialism and rhetoric.

The trouble is that content, however deeply felt, is lifeless and artificial unless productive of new forms and a new language. The neo-Realist group shunned all contact with European culture in its effort to achieve immediacy of communication, and often harked back to the provincial feeling we associate with the end of the nineteenth century.

At this point we should make a distinction between Realism and Naturalism. Realism, in fact, need not be imitative. What it does is to reconstruct or invent nature according to its own laws—not imitate the surface appearances of nature. It derives from full possession and knowledge of a total reality. The trouble with the neo-Realists is that they have far too often succumbed to "Naturalism".

The case of Armando Pizzinato is typical. Before the foundation of the New Artistic Front, Pizzinato had experimented with Cubism and Expressionism, and everything in his pictures was concentrated on clarity of rhythm. The reality he was concerned with at that time was inspired by intense painterly emotion expressed in a light and clear medium, Venetian in character. At the 1950 Biennale his *Un Fantasma percorre l'Europa* (A Phantom haunts Europe), though something of a poster, still showed a keen spirit of invention and painterly impetus. Three years later, however, with *Fucilazione* (Firing Squad), he fell into the trap of pure descriptive painting: the predominance of "content" and the need for immediate communication with a wide public had precluded any invention of forms. Though Pizzinato is a painter with unusual gifts, he has produced nothing for several years; but there is every reason to believe that once he has emerged from his crisis he will paint in a different way.

Giuseppe Zigaina is a gifted artist and in some of his smaller compositions such as *Paesaggio con Falce* (Landscape with Sickle) he expresses his own fresh tonal lyricism and his drawing is flowing and alive. But in some of his recent compositions he has shown a desire to describe, to surrender himself too easily to the appeal of "content" and superficial narration. But we can still expect something from him, too, in the future.

Migneco is the most dissident element in the Realist group because of his dislike of preconceived ideas and his need to invent new forms. It is only in the last two years that he has tried to be more "objectively detached" and has lost correspondingly in intensity of expression and imaginative invention.

The Realism of Aligi Sassu, as we have seen, takes on a variety of characteristics without any clear-cut distinction between literary or mythical influences and the painterly image. His best works cannot be called neo-Realist. They go back to his early *Ciclisti* (Cyclists), his mythical horses and various café interiors and, of course, his *Concerto* (Concert) of 1931.

Franco Francese, in the exhibition in the Colonna Gallery in Milan, revealed a Realistic idiom with clearly marked accents of Expressionism. At that exhibition his Realism did not seem cut off from European culture nor over-concerned with the "legibility" of his "subject"; it showed a tendency towards broad, warm forms suggested by long contact with the life of peasants. The stature of his compositions came from line rather than colour, and his images derived not from any external imitation of nature but from his spirit of deep and loving participation. We seem to find Permeke in his work and also the more expressive side of Picasso. *Ragazzo con Vitello* (Boy with Calf) (1953) is one of his liveliest and freest compositions. But in various other works Francese, too, shows a preoccupation with "legibility". The force of expression is thus checked by clever drawing, rhetoric and the predominance of "content". It is a danger that at times results in academicism. But in spite of this Francese must certainly be ranked among the most outstanding young artists of today.

THE ABSTRACT AS IMAGE

While one group in the New Artistic Front was becoming involved in disputes about "content", eight others, known as the "Eight", were developing the background for a new idiom which was definitely European in outlook.

Lionello Venturi, in his essay called *Eight Italian Painters*, says: "Afro, Birolli, Corpora, Moreni, Morlotti, Santomaso, Turcato and Vedova belong to the generation that is now reaching maturity, that is to say they are all between thirty and forty-five. Their way of painting is actual and their works can be ranked among those most representative of Italian taste today. . . . They are not, and they do not want to be, abstract painters. They are not, and they do not want to be, 'Realist'. . . .

Franco Francese *Boy with Calf 1953*

Mattia Moreni *Return at Night 1952*

They have adopted the language born of the tradition which began around 1910 and includes Cubism, Expressionism and Abstraction. . . . It is their aim to make use of all the possibilities that painting offers them, with no preconceived ideas as to what should or should not be included in a picture—a thing that sensibility alone must dictate. If the shape of a boat or any other real object needs to be included, then they will not deprive themselves of the enrichment thereby given to their expression. If they feel delight in some unusual colour-value or tone effect then they will certainly make use of it. Unlike abstract painters, they are not Puritans; they welcome the inspiration that each individual occasion presents, and it would not enter their heads to do otherwise. . . . And yet they remain faithful to the essential principle of modern art—that a painting is valuable first and foremost for its lines, its forms, its colours, and for that coherence of vision which is the mainspring of every work of art. Delight in a particular material or in a particular experience of reality has to be subordinated to formal coherence. . . . Thus the vision of these eight painters has never lost touch with the life of the senses and the emotions, it has never become a mere imaginative sport; it always displays that moral integration which is necessary for a work of art."

These words, written on 2 May, 1952, throw important light on the general idiom—known as "abstract-concrete"—of the "Eight". As might be expected where a tendency is so broad, other painters—Bruno Cassinari is an example—though not wanting to participate in any group have obvious affinities with the "Eight". At the same time there has been divergence within the group itself, or rather a sharpening of personal accents; Morlotti, for instance, has reverted to a "dialogue", with Lombard nature, while others have shown a preference for Expressionist and Cubist formulas' or tried to make colour more autonomous. The group comprises personalities of extremely different kinds, from Afro, Corpora and Turcato who live in Rome, to Birolli and Morlotti of the Milanese milieu; from Santomaso and Vedova—both Venetians—to Moreni who broke away from the Turin circle. The idioms of Turcato and Moreni, for instance, derive from premises that are as opposite as could be—the former, broadly speaking, from Matisse and Klee, the latter from Expressionism.

Giulio Turcato began shaping his idiom in Venice—with Guidi's help. In Milan he was drawn to Expressionist innovations, and subsequently to the tonalism of the Roman School. Cubism, as interpreted by Guttuso, also made its mark on him.

But Turcato did not really find his style until after the war—with the New Artistic Front and the "Eight". One of his compositions done in 1948—*Comizio* (Public Meeting)—transcends the conflict between Realism and Abstraction, for the motif of a public rally is worked out with abstract media in an invented rhythm. His method stemmed from early Cubism, from Futurism (without its dynamism) and from experiments suggested by Matisse's use of colour and Klee's allusive rhythms. The picture's expressiveness depends entirely on the rhythm and the autonomy of the colour. There is no third dimension and the spaces are allusive and anti-Naturalistic with a subtle use of line. There are the purest suggestions of light without shadow—Matisse as seen through Venice with an Oriental touch.

Giulio Turcato *Public Meeting 1948*

Turcato's temperament is lyrical. Drama or violent clash are not for him. He is a cultivated painter, and his vision is clear and clean and contemplative. Just occasionally he falls for tasteful but rather programmatic decoration. But when his inventive imagination is at its sharpest his effects are subtle and lyrical. Besides *Comizio*, *Rovine* (Ruins) and *Insetti* (Insects)—both of 1952—should be numbered among his best works.

Mattia Moreni, the youngest of the "Eight", has an impetus that takes him to Expressionism—with the proviso that his intellect seems always to be holding his emotion in check. His first international idiom was uncompromisingly abstract, but little by little we find him moving towards the monu-mental compositions of *Porto di Antibes* (Harbour at Antibes), *Motivo Serale* (Evening Motif), and *Barche Rosse* (Red Boats) of 1951, and *Grande Cespuglio col Sole* (Clump of Bushes in the Sun) and *Festa sulla Collina* (Festival on the Hill) of 1953–4. He finally burst out into what can only be called an Expressionist "shriek" in his exhibition at the Twenty-eighth Venice Biennale. In his earlier compositions his colour was set in a low key, whereas in his recent works it is shrill and strident. His images have great vitality and he organizes his structures with freedom and breadth of composition.

The abstract-concrete idiom of the "Eight" and of other Italian painters has contributed to the establishment of new contacts with the international market. The exhibitions of their work that Catherine Viviano holds in her gallery in New York which are subsequently taken on tour through the United States, as well as the numerous articles on their work in Brazil, Germany, Belgium, Holland, Denmark, Sweden and other countries, show that this group of Italian painters has very definitely made its mark.

In Italy an outstanding new collector has made his appearance, Achille Cavellini. He has made an international collection composed exclusively of abstract-concrete art—from Birolli, who is widely represented, to Corpora, Santomaso, Afro, Guttuso in his Cubist period, Vedova, Moreni, Turcato, Cassinari, Soldati, Manessier, Hartung, Estève, Gischia, Le Moal, Bazaine, Pignon and others.

BIROLLI

From his *San Zeno Pescatore* (San Zeno the Fisherman) (1931) to his *Incendio alle Cinque Terre* (Fire in the Cinque Terre) (1956) Renato Birolli's painting has always followed a coherent line. His idiom has always been European and has always involved moral *engagement*; and his colour, of clear Venetian origin, has tended to timbre rather than tone, without any Naturalistic chiaroscuro.

His coherence rests on these bases. He has never been either a realistic or a purely abstract painter. From his Expressionist and Cubist experiments up to his abstract-concrete work, with its tense intellectual overtones, he has developed with the critical awareness that every image must be imagina-tively invented, must be a pure god-like act of creation. In Argan's words his two moral imperatives have always been: no denial of life, and no surrender to story-telling. Edoardo Persico, Argan and, more recently, Lionello Venturi have all placed Birolli high not only in the general Italian scene, but in that of Europe as a whole.

Birolli, a native of Verona, brought to Milan and the Lombard painters the example of colour without shade, allusive and lyrical (a tendency which, among others, had brought him into opposi-tion with the *Novecento* movement). *Il Tassi Rosso* (The Red Taxi) (1932) depends entirely on the charm of the colour. We find keener expression in the *Ritratto del Padre* (Portrait of my Father) of the same year, and in other compositions in which line is particularly strongly felt. From his rough

Renato Birolli *Composition in Red and Purple 1955–56*

nudes of the 1933 period he turned, in *Colombe al Tramonto* (Doves at Sundown) (1934), to a more emotive sense of colour. Van Gogh's delight in brush strokes stimulated Birolli to greater freedom of colour in which to work out the image, while always preserving the balance of the composition. Ensor, who was beginning to make his mark on Italian painters at that time, was a stimulus too, though a less direct one. *Foglie e Maschere* (Leaves and Masks) (1934) depends entirely on colour texture, while *Maschere Vaganti* (Strolling Players) (1937) has a more hallucinating quality. But by now Birolli had discovered Cézanne. *Domenica delle Palme* (Palm Sunday), *Una Domenica in Periferia* (Sunday in the Suburbs) and *Paese a Monluè* (Countryside at Monluè)—all of 1939—show assimilation of Cézanne where structure is concerned.

We have already seen the important part that Birolli played in the *Corrente* movement—always advocating contact with Europe. During the war his activity as a draughtsman was expressed not only in his portraits and landscapes but also in the series he called *Italia 1944* (Italy 1944). Horrors, massacres, struggle and bloodshed provided an incitement to moral protest, and we find Expressionist accentuation in these obsessive drawings. They are a documentation by a man truly alive.

At the end of the war, as soon as the frontiers were open, Birolli went to France—to Paris and Brittany. Cubism, Braque and Picasso now provided incentives for freedom in composition and colour, and Birolli's colour grew in the plastic significance of its timbre, the colour areas sealed off by clear and clean lines. He achieved new rhythms in his breaking-down and rearrangement of the object.

Pictures including *Molo Brettone* (Breton Jetty), *Porto con Barche* (Harbour with Boats), *Trinité sur Mer* and *Ragazza alla Finestra* (Girl at the Window) show his allusive use of colour which, while establishing contact with French painting, preserves the enchantment of Venice: the Veronese greens, blues, violets, whites, reds and above all greys have subtle modulations, but the paint is always tactile and sonorous. The colour has become freer and sharper. If some of his works of this period were studies to "consolidate" his idiom and hence formulistic in line, many other pictures, whether seascapes, still lifes or figures, are lively and painterly, as we can see if we visit the Cavellini Collection at Brescia. The sunlight casts no shade, and reference to the object, while not entirely eliminated, takes on new values of allusion.

Following along this path, Birolli has become one of the foremost exponents of the abstract-concrete idiom—from the cycle of works shown at the Twenty-fourth Venice Biennale down to his more recent paintings which mark what may perhaps be called his happiest period or at least one of his most intensely poetical periods. His intellectual fervour has become free inventive fantasy. Pictures of this period range from *La Vigna* (The Vineyard) and *Rovi e Strada* (Briars and Road) (1953)—one of the most lyrical achievements of contemporary painting with its low harmonies of greys, greens and blues, to his large *Spaccato di Mare* (Section of the Sea) also in the Cavellini Collection, his *Adriatic* series and the *Incendio alle Cinque Terre* to which we have already referred. Birolli has certainly earned his place among outstanding painters of his generation—both in Italy and in Europe as a whole.

Renato Birolli *Agricultural Machine 1955*

Renato Birolli *Hill in Summer 1955*

Bruno Cassinari *Still Life 1954*

CASSINARI

Bruno Cassinari developed his idiom in the atmosphere of the *Corrente* movement of which he was one of the foremost exponents, but he has accents all his own.

His colour is Lombard in origin and, arranged in light-filled tonal gradations, seems so luminous that it reminds us of an Eastern mosaic. Though his taste has grown out of the study of culture, past and present, he has never lost contact with the earth and earthy things. Indeed a warm sensuality, though controlled by the intellect, gives his imagery an earthy vitality, and the things themselves, even when worked out in flat surfaces, are tactile and sensual. Cassinari is a poet with acute sensibility; his invention and the verve of his imagination gain strength from his critical control of his material. He tends to make the image autonomous—something absolute that lives in and through itself and transcends illustration. Hence the strictness and balance of his compositions.

Cassinari does not like groups or programmes. He himself is a living proof of the absurdity of the abstract-figurative controversy. Even when under Cubist influence he made use of strict symbols yet without losing touch with things and life. Memory in Italian painting—as has been apparent ever since Morandi's pre-Metaphysical period—becomes evocative resonance, and Cassinari's allusions took concrete form in the rhythms of his spaces and his colour. If we sometimes find "mannerism" or "stylism" in Cassinari, it is nearly always dominated by the vitality of his expression.

In the *Corrente* period his landscapes and portraits showed the influence of Morandi, Van Gogh, Cézanne and of the Impressionists' sense of light. Expressionist accentuation was not strong in Cassinari because his compositions at that period were worked out in subdued greys, purples, greens, blues, yellows and sombre earth colours, all in a soft watery Lombard light which toned down any strong Expressionist feeling.

Bruno Cassinari *Motherhood 1953*

Bruno Cassinari *Sea at Portofino 1955*

Natura Morta con Brocca (Still Life with Jug) (1942) was an outstanding painting of its period, with unusual coherence of forms depending entirely on the colour passages, which range from the lowest tones to very light greys. *Il Ritratto di Vecchia* (Portrait of an Old Woman) (1943) is interesting for he made a preliminary series of drawings from life which became more and more archaic in structure as he proceeded; but the final picture lives by the particular concreteness of the colour based on silver greys, pinks, purples and very dark greys within a deeply suggestive atmosphere. Also in *Paesaggio Verde* (Green Landscape) (1944) there is something acutely lyrical in the subtly luminous cascade of green, in the dark purple, in the composition with its high horizon and in the painterly line. During that period, working on *Corrente* lines, Cassinari still retained something of the Lombard sense of light. But after the war he, like other painters of his generation, turned to something more European. He went to Paris and to Antibes, where he held an exhibition in the Musée Grimaldi in 1950.

Yet the change-over was gradual. We can feel he was fascinated by Chagall, Picasso, Cubism, the French emphasis on timbre, and also Klee; yet his vision of the world was the same—the need for absolute lyricism in which nature is something to be transfigured by memory. His stay in Antibes allowed him to develop along these lines still further, and we find cross-references to Cubism working in with his own personal style. *L'Atelier* (1952), in the Jesi Collection, is a clear example of this. The recumbent nude suggests Modigliani as seen through Marino rather than Cubism, and yet the whole composition presupposes Cubism. *Natura Morta* (Still Life) in the Gallery of Modern Art in Rome and *Pecora Nera* (Black Sheep) are other paintings of this period. A year later, in 1953, we find Cassinari trying to squeeze more and more light out of colour, which becomes purer and reminds us of mosaics. The head entitled *Luisa* is a positive revel of blue, pink, purple and yellow. Henceforth we find him painting variations of the idiom that led to the expansive *Maternità* (Maternities), to imaginative landscapes such as *Portofino* and to very delicate still lifes.

Cassinari must be ranked among the most coherent of modern Italian painters.

MORLOTTI

Ennio Morlotti, more than any other of the "Eight", has returned like a prodigal son to his regional origins, and is the least inclined by temperament to follow international taste. His tendency is to the burning inspiration of the moment and in this sense we could call him the last painter of the *Scapigliatura* tradition. I do not mean by this that he has no critical control, but that he sets out with intense and fiery emotion from Romantic premises. The rhythms of his pictures are not detached, but call for the participation of the spectator. More important to Morlotti than Cubism in the post-war period were certain moods of Picasso—moods not of style but of sudden burning inspiration. In other words, he followed Picasso in all that was most expressive and Romantic. Yet Morlotti is not an Expressionist except in the most indirect sense. Even in *Dona che si lava* (Woman washing herself), where the intensity of expression upsets the object and gives a feeling of exasperation and tragedy, he uses harmonies of Lombard colour and gives value to soft light. Even in the period when he came nearest to Cubism—that is to say after 1945—his paintings have a typically Lombard light. The purples and blues and above all the greens and greys have transparencies and shafts of light and harmonies originating in tone. His images are invented with quick, tense intuition, and there could be no question of going back on any picture to correct it—he prefers to do similar pictures over and over again.

Francesco Arcangeli has mentioned "Naturalism" in connexion with Morlotti. Morlotti does invent images which participate deeply in the climate of nature, yes, but in a "panic" rather than in a descriptive sense; and from this point of view his idiom is no more "Naturalistic" than that of other young painters who have kept intact their memories of natural surroundings. However we look at it, the word "Naturalism" seems to cause confusion. Memory, when translated into fantasy and imagination, creates a new synthesis and leads to monologue and state of mind. Morlotti sometimes feels the appeal of local tone, and when this happens the danger of clinging to the end of the nineteenth century—to the *Scapigliatura* movement, in fact—can be felt. Yet he always manages to overcome this danger in the end by the heat of his emotion transmuted into the lines of his excited brush strokes. The image surrenders itself to colour derived from the memory of a climate of nature

Ennio Morlotti *Hill at Imbersago 1953*

Ennio Morlotti *Evening in Brianza 1953*

that has been long assimilated and is now delivered as a sum of experience—and hence description is avoided. Sky, tree, rock, greens and browns become an emotive charge of light and colour, but in anti-natural relationships. Only taken as a whole do his pictures recall the climate of typical Lombard nature through the transparencies, echoes or suggestions of the greys, blues, greens, purples and more burnt tones.

Of all the artists whose formation took place in Milan during the *Corrente* period, Morlotti is the most opposed to programmes. At the time of the exhibition with Cassinari and Treccani at the Spiga e Corrente Gallery in 1943, his background was that of the Brera Academy. In his landscapes of the Brianza he combined a Lombard sense of light with Van Gogh's impulsiveness and

Cézanne's structures. The picture which best sums up his activities as a painter up to 1945 is *Donna che si lava*.

Immediately after the war Morlotti went to France, but although he was not happy there a new-found freedom of composition—inspired by Picasso—enabled him to paint some highly significant pictures such as *Donne di Varsavia* (Women of Warsaw) (1946). Then came *Tessitrici di Rete* (The Net Weavers) (1947), followed by a series of pictures with totem-like figures and the deep suggestive poetry of *Siesta* (1952). But Morlotti's restlessness prevented him from confining himself to pictures of Cubist inspiration. He soon returned to the landscapes of 1946—the time of the *Brianza* series—and for a long time buried himself in Lombardy, on the banks of the Adda. His colour was still that of post-Cubism with luminous transparencies and harmonies in violet, red, brown and yellow, and no sense of spatial depth. The skies, with their high horizons, were invented and transcend all local tone.

Thus he came to his finest series of landscapes done in 1953 and 1954, which are penetrating in their lyricism and show the full freedom of his poetic invention.

MELONI

The story of Gino Meloni is one of how colour turns into imagery and is communicated to us with aggressive immediacy. In colour lies the fascination of his idiom, and in his moments of experiment or diminished tension it also becomes his limitation. That is why Meloni is one of the most discussed painters of post-war Italy.

Meloni's formation was highly individual. Until his one-man show at the 15 Borgo Nuovo Gallery in 1946, which put him on the map as a painter, he had been a solitary outside all groups and creeds. He looked to Soutine, Van Gogh and Kokoschka as examples—for their attitude to painting rather than for style. From Cézanne he learnt not the strictness of construction that paved the way to Cubism, but the glorification of colour which was Expressionist before its time. He was also aware of the way in which Picasso, Modigliani or Matisse made the figurative object anti-natural. These stimuli helped him to discover his own inner voice and taught him that the image is always an invention to be achieved with purely painterly means. As with the so-called Primitives, his "dialogue with the object" was not an imitation of nature. He needed to assimilate a climate, a light, a background and then deliver them in absolute terms as a sum of experience and memories.

At the time of the 1946 exhibition he retained a Lombard tendency to use luminous greys and browns derived from his early formation in Milan—but these were broken up by new and sudden discords (a legacy of the Fauves): a vermilion roof detached from its surroundings, dissonances of purples, greys or burnt tones, or a sudden chrome yellow bursting out in lyric fire and making the whole picture abstract. These sudden highlights in Meloni came from a need suggested by the pure power of expression in colour, and later they were to develop in such a way that the whole picture became pure invention.

After his exhibition at the Camino Gallery in 1947, his palette underwent a change. He moved on from the dominant earth-colours of the period of his first exhibition to emerald and Veronese greens. Ultramarine was replaced by a bright cobalt; Venetian reds and terracottas by more sonorous vermilions, subdued Neapolitan yellows and ochres by bright chrome yellows. His vision became more hallucinating and some of his cross-references to Cubism in the upsetting of the planes were broken by sudden Expressionist accentuations.

Gino Meloni *The Church of Santa Maria della Salute 1955*

In the series called *Galli* (Cocks) we find Metaphysical overtones but these do not come from the Metaphysical outlook suggested by De Chirico or even by Carrà or Morandi—Meloni has no tailors' dummies nor any feeling for geometry; indeed his images perhaps should be called hallucinating rather than Metaphysical. Though they derive from direct experience of things, they in fact turn into phantom-like inventions of the imagination. In the *Cocks* series the painting has an absolutely clear and concrete quality that transcends anything merely literary, and there is an insistent repetition of ovoid shapes. *Gallo Assiso* (Seated Cock) (1947) has a large and splendid structure, while *Il Gallo di Mezzanotte* (The Midnight Cock) is one of the most lyrical of all his paintings. *Il Gallo Sacro* (The Sacred Cock) (1950) with its strict system of geometric rhythms shows abstract influences. It was the period when abstract art was felt by Italian painters to be the most international idiom. For Meloni it was a variant of his emblematic images, but soon after this he abandoned sealed-in shapes and geometry of every sort. In his *Gallo sui Tetti* (Cock on the Rooftops) the allusive power is provided by the limpid harmonies of blues, greys and reds. Another picture outstanding for its coherence is *Lotta dei Galli* (Cocks Fighting). Here we find expressiveness rarified to the maximum degree and depending on the impetus of colour contrasts.

Meloni began his *Venice* series in 1953. *La Salute* (The Church of Santa Maria della Salute) and *San Moisè* (The Church of San Moisè) are poems delivered by exclusively painterly methods. By now he had abandoned any emphasis on line or geometry: he was back at the expressiveness of

Gino Meloni *San Marco 1955*

Gino Meloni *Cocks Fighting 1953*

colour in movement. Even when the picture has ample stature, it is broken up in rapid brush strokes and space is evoked rather than represented in the third dimension.

From all these paintings up to Meloni's most recent non-figurative works we find a consistent line of development. There are no sharp breaks, but only an inner evolution. And can we really call his recent paintings non-figurative? In Meloni's case what is the meaning of words like figurative and abstract, when his dialogue with the object is always expressed indirectly through memory and invention? However this may be, he has always had an exalted imagination and the clear and candid voice of poetry.

GENTILINI

Franco Gentilini is a story-telling painter in the modern sense of the term. That is to say that his compositions derive from the critical attitude which sees story-telling as valid only in conjunction with the discovery of new forms, only where painting is autonomous and everything depends on rhythm, spaces and colour assonances. Hence his way of telling his story is "abstract" and "anti-Naturalistic" and with a new system of Symbolism. Here lies Gentilini's own personal language— achieved for the most part since the war. Gentilini has created pictures of Italian piazzas with

Franco Gentilini *Woman in the Café 1955*

cathedrals, towers, ice-cream sellers, children and buses, but he does it all on a basis of memory tinged with irony, and the result is a kind of cultivated and canny lyricism.

Gentilini, born in Faenza, arrived in Rome in 1929. At that time, as readers will remember, the Roman School was on the point of coming into being with Scipione and Mafai. But Gentilini was a lonely figure, drawing inspiration from Goya, Daumier and Ensor. Dolls, masks, chimney-sweeps and skulls were his favourite themes but, as Sinisgalli has pointed out, they appealed to him only in so far as they contained an element of wit. His paint became enamel-like and thick, and he did not exclude the lovely colours of post-Impressionism.

Franco Gentilini *The Cathedral* 1953

But that was long ago. As time passed he showed a marked preference for Chagall and the indirect result was a new kind of line which was purely colour. There were also cross-references to old masters—Scialoja has mentioned the Primitive painters of Rimini—but this influence too was only indirect.

In the years that followed the war and under the influence of Cubism, Gentilini's strictness of rhythm became increasingly mature, while his lines, pervaded with rhythmic colour, suggested Klee. Then Gentilini's idiom became typically personal and new: his harmonies became softer and highly *recherchés* in their echoes of browns, violets, greens, reds and greys—and a certain porousness eliminated all effects of light. The emphasis on story-telling with its subtly ironical and elegant grace has always given his work a peculiar poetry. Writers and critics including Bassani, Sinisgalli, Ulivi and Carrieri have commented on this, and Alberto Moravia has written a penetrating essay on Gentilini.

Franco Gentilini *The Table 1955*

Outstanding works include *Piazza del Popolo* in the Schettini Collection and *I Suonatori* (The Musicians) in the Tofanelli Collection—both of 1952; *Natura Morta* (Still Life) and *L'Abside* (The Apse), both of 1955. These pictures are good examples of how Gentilini brings story-telling in terms of paint into the realm of personal invention.

Antonio Corpora *Boats in the Argentario 1954–55*

CORPORA

Antonio Corpora's formation took place in Italy and Paris. Critics of European standing, including Lionello Venturi, Christian Zervos and Argan, have followed his development with especial interest. Born in Tunisia in 1909 of Sicilian parentage, he has retained Sicilian characteristics such as a violent and fiery sense of the image, mental lucidity, secret melancholy and a cosmic "panic" feeling. Tunis and Sicily have certainly given him his "Mediterranean" imagery; sailing ships and little fishing harbours reflect a landscape that he knows well and has long lived in—so much so that it has become transfigured in memory and is real though without a trace of Naturalism.

At the Ecole des Beaux Arts in Tunis he worked in the studio of the painter Armand Vergeaud who had been a pupil of Gustave Moreau and fellow-student of Matisse, Dufy, Rouault and Marquet. After his first exhibitions in Tunis he went to Florence, where he copied old masters in the Uffizi and developed an interest in Modigliani and Soutine. He exhibited at the Palazzo Bardi,

Antonio Corpora *Landscape 1954*

and by 1930 was in Paris, where he stayed on and off until 1937, returning to Tunis on a number of occasions and, in 1934, to Italy. His line of development was, broadly speaking, Bonnard-Matisse-Braque.

In 1934 he took part in the disputes of the Milione group. Until 1937 his paintings were not purely abstract. We find him using colour contrasts in a pattern of surfaces composed in rhythms almost like mosaics, and hence his paintings were variants of Cubism rather than Abstractions; they were forms corresponding with the side of his personality that was most intellectual and least urgently expressive. In his one-man show at the Milione Gallery in 1939 we find a Fauve accentuation grafted on to his experience of Cubism.

In 1946 Corpora, together with Turcato, Fazzini, Guttuso and Monachesi, founded a group that was later to be called the neo-Cubists. In their preface to the catalogue of their exhibition at the Galleria del Secolo in Rome they said that, starting out from Cézanne, they had found through Fauvism and Cubism the lost thread of the authentic Italian tradition. When a little later the New Artistic Front was founded, Corpora was an active member.

From 1949 to 1952 Corpora achieved an expressive vigour which in some of his works had been impaired by his preoccupation with linear systems. Now the lines themselves became colour. He also worked out a light-colour relationship, the fruit of his solar imagination, and this gave his pictures a stamp all their own. The relationship between movement and surroundings also preoccupied him, as it had the Futurists. Typical pictures of this period include *Moby Dick, Souvenirs de France* and *Gabbia-Canarina-Finestra* (Cage-Canary-Window), all painted in 1951. They show the inspiration of his invention when memory has become fantasy. *Moby Dick*, which consists of an abstract evocation of a journey across the Atlantic, obtained the Prix de Paris in 1951, awarded by a jury of French artists and critics presided over by Villon.

In 1952 Christian Zervos wrote an essay about Corpora in the *Cahiers d'Art*, which was also published in Paris. The essay sets out to define the relationship between nature and memory and between sensation and imagination. Its aim was to defend the validity of the image in Corpora's painting.

But between 1953 and 1954 Corpora took a further more decisive step. The sense of wonder which had previously sprung from memory was suggested by colour itself which followed its own rules. By a return to the emphasis on emotion—in the spirit of the Fauves and the Expressionists—he set space free: planes, lines, ground-plan all disappeared, and everything was kept moving by the pure expressiveness of the colour which seems to come right forward out of the picture. Emotion is not suggested by the content of the symbols but by the colour-light relationship. The image, while having no bearing on nature, is still allusive and introduces us into a world of wonder with pulsating rather than geometric rhythms.

We can see good examples of his freest idiom in paintings such as *Mediterraneo* (The Mediterranean) (1953), *Porto d'Africa* (African Port) (1954), *Laguna all'Argentario* (Lake at the Argentario) and in recent compositions exhibited at the Eighth Roman Quadriennale and at his one-man show at the Twenty-eighth Venice Biennale.

AFRO

Afro has received more recognition abroad, especially in the United States, than in Italy. Hostile critics persist in calling him "decorative" or "elegant", in spite of his international success at the Twenty-eighth Venice Biennale.

190

Afro *Scandal Sheet 1953*

Lionello Venturi, to whom we owe the most important comments on this painter, has pointed out that the concept "decorative" has no precise meaning in present-day criticism. Nevertheless it is true to say that when used in a pejorative sense the word means superficial, facile and lacking in intensity of expression. When a painter is called "decorative" he is usually also called "elegant", and these are the epithets by which certain critics have pigeon-holed Afro for all time.

But this is not borne out by the facts. Among European painters of his generation, Afro stands out for his clear unmistakable style. He is a refined painter, influenced by a complex international culture but outstandingly controlled and alive. Perhaps it could be said that he is always walking the tight-rope of intellectual control, emotion, and imaginative invention. It could also be said that at times his taste verges on over-refinement, but the authentic expressive impulse is never far away.

Afro has never entirely abandoned the Venetian tradition. This accounts for his modulated and extremely delicate stridencies of colour and the echoes and assonances of the reds, burnt siennas and blues enclosed in a system of lines of intellectually emotive colour—colour that transcends and works out in a new way the Cubist schemas suggested by Picasso. Hence also the allusiveness of the colours and spaces, inspired by Klee.

What we always find with Afro is inventiveness of line controlled by the intellect which isolates and dominates the emotion. Afro has become a rigorous stylist. He reduces harmonies to the minimum so as to obtain increased breadth and a more piercing single melody. He is a builder, keeping emotive movement under the continual surveillance of the intelligence. The focal-point of

Afro *Ballet 1953*

his compositions is always changing. The angle of vision is foreshortened, but the foreshortenings are flattened out in surfaces, and in a space allusive rather than Naturalistic; and this increases the magical effect.

Afro went to Venice from his native Udine, and his first exhibition took place in Milan in 1932 in the Milione Gallery when he was only twenty. The various murals and frescoes that he worked on until 1937 gave him the habit of feeling the value of large spaces in painting. Since then Afro has done no large-scale decorations; he has painted still lifes, portraits and landscapes, but he has always retained his feeling for the ample scope of wall-surfaces and for syntheses in structure.

In 1941 he was seeking after tonal effects. Three years later came the first big change. The influence of Picasso and, still more, of Braque, as Lionello Venturi has put it, "brought out in Afro's work a perfect balance between abstract and concrete, a need for formal architecture that in no way

Afro "Falso bordone" *1952*

impeded the representation of the real". In *Natura Morta* (Still Life) in the A. Crespi Collection we find the atmospheric tone flattened and tending to become surface timbre. Another example, *Ritratto di Maria* (Portrait of Maria), also shows how he is moving over from tone to timbre. The colour itself is a kind of delicate shell and lightly transparent.

Up to now we have been dealing with the ways of painting that foreshadowed Afro's truly personal idiom. This was revealed in a formed and concrete way in the post-war period. In 1948 *Lis Fuarpis* and *Occhio di Vetro* (Glass Eye) showed the influences of Picasso and Klee. But the style is already a law to itself; the image is the memory of an emotion and the whole is achieved in rhythms of arabesque surfaces made in delicately melodious lines. Afro colours by means of superimposition —a way of colouring that is in the Venetian tradition, as Venturi has pointed out. He describes it as "the superimposition of different tones and the juxtaposition of planes in which every local colour is in harmony with the whole. Hence the clarity of the individual colours and the complexity of the fusions of tone."

By 1949 we find that the rhythm between the background and the object has become more closely knit. A good example of this can be seen in the landscape in the Caraceni Collection. In this picture we find that the colours are still clear and well scanned, but a few years later we see his freedom in the use of colour accentuated. The strictness now lies in a more inner counterpoint. The light-surfaces of the colours are in motion. Line, instead of closing in the colour-surfaces, indicates their structure in a counterpoint between line and colour. Examples of Afro's latter period are to be found in *Villa Fleurent* in the Gallery of Modern Art in Venice, *Per non Dimenticare* (Lest we Forget) in the C. Viviano Collection, New York, *Paesaggio Rosso* (Red Landscape) in the Ralph Lamberson Collection, New Haven, *Balletto* (Ballet) and *Cronaca Nera* (Scandal Sheet) in the Cavellini Collection.

SANTOMASO

Giuseppe Santomaso's idiom has become typically international since the war. From Cubist beginnings and passing through the strictness of Mondrian, he finally achieved the freedom of expression of a painter such as Hartung. And yet no one can deny his essentially Venetian origin, for his colour and light are in the tradition of Venetian painters.

Santomaso's problem had already been experienced in another way by our medieval painters. An artist assimilates the light and colour of his particular region and gets to know them so well that they become an integral part of his personality. Then he paints, trusting to memory and to his power of inventing new relationships, and in some indirect way achieves the *summum* of all that he has known visually. Hence his painting is not an imitation of the reality of nature but an imaginative invention which still retains indirect bonds with the world that has surrounded him.

So in Santomaso's paintings we always find the presence of Venice, and yet there is nothing of the Venetian tradition in his general idiom which, as has been said, derives from Cubist and abstract sources. His space lacks the third dimension but is allusive, and his images have new symbols and rhythms that he has invented. Hence his international success. For success by and large comes to those artists who, though in outlook they are not provincial, show the unmistakable stamp of their native country.

Santomaso was born in Venice and his early formation took place in the circle of Gino Rossi and Pio Semeghini. A visit to Amsterdam in 1937 introduced him to the paintings of Van Gogh, and another to Paris to the colour of Braque's non-Cubist works and to that of Matisse and

Giuseppe Santomaso *Image in Green* 1955

Giuseppe Santomaso *Composition 1955*

Bonnard. In his paintings up to 1942 the lessons of these painters were assimilated in a style and colour which Venturi calls "primitive Baroque".

Several years later Santomaso became more constructive with a kind of pre-Cubism derived from Cézanne, but with Venetian light and colour. Towards the end of the war, and under the impact of events, Santomaso experimented with Expressionism, but the paintings of this period have little connexion with his real personality whose tendency is always towards detachment and lucidity.

196

Giuseppe Santomaso *At the Concerts of Arzignano 1953*

With the New Artistic Front his idiom became finally stabilized as abstract-concrete. His architecture is strict; the spaces, though flat, deepen in the most allusive way with the help of sonorous and evocative colour. Blues, purples, greens and greys have the shadowless light of a Venetian lagoon. The real protagonist in all his pictures is the sky, even when the rhythms are created by something else such as an agricultural machine, a vineyard or a dockyard. This accounts for windows being the recurring motif of his pictures up to 1947.

Little by little we find Santomaso's idiom becoming more rarefied. The proportions, the transparencies, the lines of the drawing which themselves are colour are more obviously balanced in the surfaces—but the result is an increased evocation of space. Klee, Kandinsky and Hartung have provided Santomaso with the bare data of a system of painting, and this he transcends in the concreteness of his colour and light. Good examples which explain his success with the critics are *Il Confine della Palude* (The Confines of the Marsh) (1953), *Ricordo Verde* (Green Memory) in the Cavellini Collection, *Ritmi Rurali* (Rural Rhythms) (1954) and various other compositions of dockyards, farm implements and windows.

VEDOVA

The premises of Emilio Vedova's idiom lie in an exalted and visionary Romanticism which made him prefer Tintoretto to all other Venetian painters for his contrasts of light and shade within his swirling rhythms. But as early as his first exhibition at the Spiga e Corrente Gallery in 1943, we find Expressionism in the swift line of his drawings. By now Tintoretto was a memory and Rouault

Emilio Vedova *Cosmic Vision 1952*

a more immediate stimulus. But Vedova's Expressionism was also influenced by Picasso of the *Guernica* period. *Gli Impiccati di Spert* (The Hanged Men at Spert) (1946) displayed Vedova's unusual faculty of assimilation and at the same time his expressively visionary temperament.

The following year, when the belief had spread in Italy that abstract art in its strictest and coldest form was the only international idiom, Vedova began to take note of Léger and the mechanics of a constructive abstract art. *Immagine* (Image) in the G. Natale Collection is a sign of this mood.

With *Esplosione* (Explosion) (1948) Vedova returned to the idea of dynamism in the Futurist sense, but his colour was cleaner and worked out in timbre with startling contrasts and juxta-positions of acid and sweet colours, and with no surviving traces of Naturalism. *L'Urto* (Crash) (1950) in the Gallerate Museum marks the end of this period; the intellect had intervened.

But Vedova was still drawn to "fantastic illuminations" and the invention of "sibylline messages" (Marchiori) and to keeping his rhythm moving with an excitement that makes the fabric of the

198

composition more and more tense. With *Immagine del Tempo* (Image of Time) (1951), his recent series called *Spazio Inquieto* (Unquiet Space) and his *Ciclo della Protesta* (Cycle of Protest) we see how his idiom has been set free from any kind of formula and how the rhythmic flight springs entirely from within.

This is his deepest achievement—a brilliant inventiveness as regards rhythm and a tense expressive charge. In this sense Vedova is in an *avant-garde* position among the young painters.

But there is one difficulty that he must face. His colour, so as to avoid a sensibility of tonal origin, has at times aimed at an effect of drawing, of ink, and to judge by results the tension is more coherent, the rhythm-contrasts more forceful, when his picture is achieved in black and white. When Vedova

Emilio Vedova *Unquiet Space No. 5 1956*

199

emphasizes his contrasts with the use of shrill colours, the effect is perhaps spectacular, but not always in keeping with the unity of the image.

The fact is that Emilio Vedova is a Venetian and his palette is a sensitive one. Some of his smaller compositions set in a minor key, such as were exhibited at the Eighth Quadriennale in Rome, show him at his subtlest with light brush strokes and gradations of subdued luminous greys. When he pushes Expressionist stridencies to extremes he is false to his nature and his palette becomes subordinate to his intellectual aims. *Viaggio in Italia* (Journey in Italy) owes its vitality to its rhythms not to the crash of colours which are extraneous to the picture. *Spazio Inquieto N.2* (Unquiet Space No. 2) is a more coherent achievement.

Emilio Vedova stands out among young painters for the intensity of his fantastic invention which reaches a visionary stature, and for his rare sense of rhythm in movement. These exceptional gifts may help to explain his success outside Italy, especially in countries where the tendency to an abstract Expressionism prevails.

THE GENERAL OUTLOOK

I hope it is clear from what I have said that since the war Italy has seen a second period of internationalism in painting (the first period having been the cycle of influence extending from the Fauves and Cubism, through Kandinsky and Klee, to Mondrian). The second period has produced both the abstract-concrete idiom and the idiom that relies on pure invention of forms. As a result the international market has opened up to the new Italian painters, and they have been invited to exhibit in many parts of the world.

As we have pointed out already, international tendencies in Italy can have two harmful effects— they can result in academicism, and they can result in the cult of mere fashion. Over-used and outworn formulas can produce truly original work only with great difficulty: the crucial factor at all times is the personal genius of the artist.

Among painters of the young or fairly young generation, the abstract-concrete tendency has been steadily developing.

The arabesque rhythms of the Dalmatian, Antonio Music, are perhaps a variant of this tendency. His paintings transcend all description and all Expressionist distortion, and their unusual colour harmonies achieve an extraordinary power of evocation. Landscapes, fishermen, nets and other motifs, achieved in surface painting with a delicate feeling for the emotion of colour, have timbre juxtapositions and spatial balances which reveal a delicate stylist.

Toti Scialoja, a Roman, came in for the end of the Roman School, and then experimented with Cubism. In 1955 he started inventing images which remind us slightly of Afro. Scialoja has a delicate critical intelligence and a sharp sensibility but he has not yet discovered the limitations of his idiom. This criticism remains true, even though his inventive power and his power of assimilation are rare and his paintings full of vitality. *Giugno in Provenza* (June in Provence) is a good example of his style.

Enzo Brunori, from Tuscany, composes rhythms whose colour-schemes, though vivid, are tight and closed in. As time goes on, he will develop more freely, but already he has a well-defined personality and moves with a sure touch.

The young Sergio Romiti, from Bologna, manages to combine neo-Cubist schemes with Morandi's light-effects. His taste is delicate and he achieves a rare balance of spaces distilled in subdued tones of greys and browns. His limitation lies in an extreme stylization, though this

Toti Scialoja *June in Provence 1955*

Antonio Music *Landscape 1955*

corresponds with his temperament, which enables him to dominate a sharp sense of feeling by intellectual detachment.

Gastone Breddo, a Venetian, inspired first by Guidi and then by Santomaso, has painted abstract/concrete pictures with luminous and clear Venetian colours and a sustained sense of self/criticism.

Giuseppe Ajmone, under the influence of *Corrente* in general and perhaps of Cassinari in parti/cular, has established a subtle painterly idiom all his own. Still lifes, figures, flowers and interiors have tones of Lombard origin, but are juxtaposed according to timbre values. Though he sometimes runs the risk of making structural compositions seen intellectually from outside, he is one of the most coherent painters among the over/thirties. His relation with the object is living while transfigured along the lines of the abstract/concrete idiom. His coloration is individual: blues, purples, browns, acid yellows and greys create almost imperceptible dissonances but we can see that they are tonal in origin, even if their main effect is one of timbre.

But the abstract/concrete tendency is not the only one. There are other international directions in Italian painting. For instance, we have already described the latest trends in the work of Vedova and Moreni, who tend to a form of Expressionism transcending fine colouring and technical niceties.

In Milan, Alfredo Chighine, a sculptor as well as a painter, has in his paintings since 1950 tried to construct compositions with wide masses of colour held in balance by incisive drawing. Little by little his idiom has increased in subtlety while developing as regards freedom of form. The counterpoint between the tonal values of the background and the timbre values of the superimposed incisive lines—which hold up the rhythms of the composition—gives his paintings new accents and a kind of dualism, at least at first sight. After long assimilation he has gone beyond neo-Cubism in the lyrical freedom of his structures; and the "dialogue with nature" (which is indirect for the reasons I have analysed with regard to other painters) has produced harmonies of tonal origin but in sharp discord with the autonomous expressiveness of the contrasting timbres of the lines. Chighine

Giuseppe Ajmone *Yellow Flowers 1955*

Alfredo Chighine
Shapes in Contrast
1954

has his own individual way of looking at the world, and tendencies and programmes are merely incidental to his unusual gifts. He is very much a painter to be watched.

Arturo Carmassi, another interesting new painter, is moving towards a break with the Cubist formula and the general line in France which he has reflected for a certain time. His own original impetus is leading him to pictures whose expressiveness, depending on the independence of colour, breaks in from all sides and seems to burst out of the frame. In the last two years Carmassi's styles have reflected a continual search. Some of his pictures are impressive, but his idiom is not yet formed.

These painters and others—from the *Spaziali* (Spatial Painters) and the *Nuclearli* (Nuclear Painters) to the more or less Surrealist and Nordic accents of Gianni Dova—would require a chapter to themselves, one which it will be easier to write in a few years' time when their work has taken more definite shape. Each generation tends to react against its predecessor; but over and above all dialectic, there are some values that have been established for ever in the course of our century.

One thing is plain. There is an Italian line of development in contemporary painting, within the international one. This lies in the architecture of space and in colours which, over and above their personal accents, recall the region of their origin and give pictures a concreteness all their own.

CHRONOLOGICAL SURVEY

1900

Milan, May—Arturo Tosi exhibits his *Head of a Girl* at the exhibition of "Lombard Painting in the Nineteenth Century".

Paris—Carlo Carrà works in the Pavilion of the Universal Exhibition. Retrospective exhibition of Seurat at the *Revue Blanche*.

Pio Semeghini in Paris on and off from 1899 to 1914. Soffici in Paris from 1900 to 1907, returning to Italy only for a brief visit in 1903. He takes active part in the cultural and artistic life of the capital.

Umberto Boccioni in Rome from 1898. Self-taught, he becomes a friend of Severini with whom he visits the studio of Giacomo Balla, a Divisionist just returned from Paris.

Piero Marussig is at Munich, and a member of the Secessionist group.

1901

Rome—Balla, having brought to Rome reproductions of the works of the French Impressionists, introduces Boccioni and Severini to Impressionism.

Reproductions of Signac, Monet, Seurat and Cézanne begin to circulate between Rome, Florence and Milan.

At the Fourth International Exhibition of Art in Venice, foreign exhibitors include Rodin, Corot (7 works), Daubigny, Millet, Böcklin. Belgium sends 13 aquatints by Ensor.

1902

22 March—At the exhibition of the "Society of Lovers and Promoters of the Fine Arts" in Rome, drawings and works in black and white by Toulouse-Lautrec, Rodin, Ensor, Munch and by the Japanese Hokusai and Utamaro.

In Rome Boccioni wins a picture competition and is able to go to Paris. At the *Salon des Indépendants*, commemorative exhibition of Toulouse-Lautrec who died the year before.

Benedetto Croce publishes the first edition of the *Aesthetics*.

1903

Paris—Soffici meets Picasso, Apollinaire and Max Jacob. At the *Salon des Indépendants*, exhibition of works by Matisse, Marquet, Dufy, Friesz; at the *Secession*, Cézanne, Gauguin, Munch, Van Gogh, Bonnard.

At the Fifth International Exhibition in Venice, works by Monet (2), Pissarro (2), Sisley (1), Renoir (1), Raffaëlli (1).

Rome—Severini gives his first exhibition.

1904

Paris—Soffici sends the first publications on Cézanne and Redon to Italy.

Big retrospective exhibition of Cézanne at the *Salon d'Automne* where retrospective exhibitions of Van Gogh and Seurat are also held and where Rouault exhibited. This is the year when Georges Braque comes to Paris. Kandinsky exhibits at the National Exhibition in Brussels. Boccioni goes for seven months to Russia, first to St. Petersburg, then to Tsaritsyn, (Stalingrad), as the guest of Russian friends he had met in Paris.

1905

Rome—Exhibition of Boccioni.

Venice—In the French room of the Sixth International Exhibition in Venice: Monet (2), Pissarro (2), Raffaëlli (3), Renoir (2), Sisley (2), Vuillard (2).

1906

Amedeo Modigliani settles in Paris where he meets Severini. Cézanne dies. Braque exhibits at the *Salon des Indépendants*.

From 1906 to 1908 Boccioni keeps a diary in which he notes his reflections on art in a way that foreshadows Futurism.

Milan—Carrà frequents the Brera Academy and becomes a disciple of Cesare Tallone.

1907

Gino Rossi in Paris. Retrospective exhibition of Gauguin at the *Salon d'Automne*; retrospective and commemorative exhibition of Cézanne a year after his death.

On 14 March, 1907, Boccioni writes in his diary: "I want to paint what is new: the fruit of our industrial age."

Seventh International Exhibition of Art in Venice—among exhibitors: Signac (1), Vuillard (1), Denis (2).

1908

Venice—Beginning of the activities of *Ca' Pesaro* Gallery. G. Rossi, Arturo Martini, Boccioni, Severini and Casorati exhibit there. Lorenzo Viani in Paris.

Boccioni settles in Milan, where he does drawings for advertisements and the illustrated reviews.

Florence—On 20 December *La Voce* makes its debut, a review of militant idealism edited by Giuseppe Prezzolini (in 1916 by Giuseppe De Robertis). Among its principal contributors: Carrà, Onofri, Papini, Apollinaire, Soffici, Pancrazi, Savinio, Ungaretti.

1909

20 February—Futurist manifesto of Filippo Tommaso Marinetti published in the *Figaro*, Paris.

Milan—Boccioni exhibits at the "Exhibition of Lombard Painters".

In February Carrà, Boccioni, Russolo and Marinetti meet in Milan for the drawing-up of the Futurist manifesto: secretary of the group—Decio Cinti. In April, second Futurist manifesto.

Rome—Exhibition of the works of Toulouse-Lautrec, Renoir and Ensor.

Trieste—First Futurist evening at the *Politeama Rossetti*—with Buzzi, Palazzeschi, Russolo and Govoni.

At the Eighth Venice Biennale one-man shows by Pellizza da Volpedo, Tito, Fattori, Pasini, Signorini and Cesare Tallone. Also pictures by Casorati (2), Tosi (1), Alberto Magnelli (1). Among the foreigners; Besnard, Zorn, Stuck, Krojer, Friescke, Miller, Ensor.

From this year until 1912, Modigliani shares a Paris studio with Brancusi.

1910

Paris—Modigliani exhibits with the *Indépendants*. Gino Rossi exhibits *Bevilacqua La Masa* at the Venetian exhibition.

11 February—First manifesto of the Futurist painters drawn up and signed by Boccioni, Carrà, Russolo, Severini and Balla. Boccioni invites Sironi to participate in the manifesto, but he refuses.

Balla shows his composition *Salutando* at the Eightieth International Exhibition of the "Society of Lovers and Promoters of the Fine Arts".

Paris—In February Marinetti speaks at the *Maison des Etudiants*, auguring closer friendship between France and Italy.

Turin, 8 March—The manifesto of the Futurist painters is read by Boccioni at the *Politeama Chiarella*. The Futurist manifestoes are translated in Germany, France, Russia and America.

At St. Petersburg a Futurist group is born: David Burliuck publishes a manifesto in defence of the new art which is more or less a paraphrase of the one written by Boccioni and Carrà in Milan.

11 April—Boccioni, Balla, Carrà, Russolo and Severini sign the technical manifesto of Futurist painting.

Milan, 19 March—Boccioni, Carrà and Russolo exhibit pastels and drawings at the *Famiglia Artistica*.

Spadini leaves Florence and settles in Rome.

Florence—Through the enterprise of Soffici an exhibition is held at the *Ljceum* of works by

Monet, Pissarro, Degas, Cézanne, Van Gogh, Gauguin, Renoir.

8 May—*Comoedia* publishes the complete text of the manifesto of the Futurist painters.

Venice, July—Introduced in the catalogue by Marinetti, Boccioni exhibits 42 works (paintings, drawings, aquatints) at the Summer Exhibition of the *Ca' Pesaro*. This is his first one-man show as a Futurist.

At the Ninth International Exhibition of Art in Venice: one-man shows by Monticelli, Renoir (37), Courbet (19) and Klimt. Also engravings by Ensor and a lithograph by Munch.

1911

St. Petersburg—David Burliuck founds the association "Spokesman of Pictures" which exhibits works by Boccioni, Picasso, Matisse and Kandinsky.

Carrà in Paris: meets Apollinaire, Modigliani, Picasso. A Cubist room at the *Salon des Indépendants*. In the spring De Chirico, also in Paris, exhibits 4 pictures at the *Salon des Indépendants*. Meeting between Apollinaire, Boccioni and Severini.

Morandi paints his first landscapes.

Milan, May—Boccioni, with Carrà and Russolo, takes part in the first "Exhibition of Free Art" at the *Intima*; a second exhibition is held in the *Ricordi* Pavilion at which he shows *Retata* (The Netful), *Rissa in Galleria* (Quarrel in the Gallery) with the title *Baruffa* (Scuffle)—*La Città Sale* (The City Rises) with the title *Lavoro* (Work)—and *La Risata* (Laughter) which was attacked with razor blades. Article by Soffici in *La Voce* called "Free Art and Futurist Painting". Violent mutilation of the Futurist pictures shown at the *Ricordi* Pavilion.

Rome, 29 May—Lecture by Boccioni in the rooms of the International Artistic Association in the via Margutta: "The time when I was working on the three pictures (Plastic States of Mind) entitled (1) Good-byes, (2) Those who go, (3) Those who stay." An extremely stormy evening.

To the International Exhibition in Rome, France sends, among others, works by Bonnard, Signac, Monet, Renoir, Vuillard and Marquet.

October—The war with Turkey delays by some months the exhibition of Futurist painters in Paris for which Boccioni has written the preface to the catalogue.

1912

Gino Rossi exhibits in Paris at the *Salon d'Automne*. The opening of the exhibition of *Section d'Or* with Villon, Gleizes, Metzinger, Lhote, and the Futurist exhibition with Boccioni, Carrà, Russolo, Severini.

Paris, 6–24 February—Balla, Boccioni, Carrà, Russolo, Severini give a Futurist exhibition in the *Bernheim-Jeune* Gallery. Boccioni shows for the first time *La Strada entra nella Casa* (The Street goes into the House), *Forza di una Strada* (Forces of a Street) and his three *Stati d'Animo* (States of Mind). In March the

exhibition is transferred to the *Sackville* Gallery, London, in April to Berlin and in June to the *Salle Giraux*, Brussels. In Berlin Borchardt acquires several of the pictures and takes them around Europe. In Paris and Brussels Boccioni gives lectures in French. Apollinaire's comments on the exhibition in *Le Petit Bleu de Paris* of 9 February are still negative.

11 April—Technical manifesto of Futurist Sculpture, signed by Boccioni, "painter and sculptor".

At the Tenth Venice Biennale: among exhibitors, Carpi (1), Casorati (2), Tosi (2), Marussig (4). One-man show by F. Carena. In the new French pavilion, exhibition of works by L. Simon, Blanche, Ménard, La Touche.

Paris, October—Boccioni exhibits sculpture at the *Salon d'Automne*.

1913

Florence, 1 January—Publication of the first number of *Lacerba*, fortnightly review edited by Papini. Main contributors: Boccioni, Carrà, Soffici, Russolo, Palazzeschi. Published by Vallecchi.

Severini opens his first one-man show at the *Marlborough* Gallery in London.

Florence—Soffici's violent articles are transformed in *Lacerba* into theoretical clarifications.

Rome, February–March—Boccioni, Balla, Carrà, Soffici, Russolo and Severini exhibit Futurist paintings in the *Costanzi* Theatre. Among Boccioni's new pictures: *Costruzioni Orizzontali* (Horizontal Constructions), *Elasticità* (Elasticity), *Scomposizione di Figure a Tavola* (Splitting up of Figures at Table).

Florence—In March Carrà starts collaborating with *Lacerba* (No. 3) with an article "Plastic planes as spherical expansion in space" against Cubism.

An Italo-American, Giuseppe Stella, shows a selection of Futurist works in New York.

11 March—Manifesto, "The Art of Noises", signed by Russolo.

Rome—First International Exhibition of Secessionist Art with, among others, Bonnard, Pissarro, Matisse, Sisley, Renoir, Monet, Signac and Vuillard.

In Paris Alberto Savinio writes his play: *La Chanson de la Mi-Mort* (published by Apollinaire in *Soirées de Paris*) which gives De Chirico the idea for his tailors' dummies.

Paris, 20 June—Opening of the first exhibition of Boccioni's sculpture at the *La Boétie* Gallery, followed by a tour of London, Berlin, Brussels and Amsterdam.

29 June—Apollinaire publishes his manifesto: *L'Antitradition Futuriste*.

11 August—Carrà's manifesto, "The painting of sounds, noises and smells."

11 October—Futurist political programme of Marinetti, Boccioni, Carrà and Russolo.

Florence—From 30 November to 18 January, 1914, exhibition of Futurist work at the premises of *La Voce*, via Cavour, with works by Balla, Boccioni, Carrà, Russolo, Severini and Soffici.

Rome, 6 December—The *Galleria Futurista Permanente*, via del Tritone, is inaugurated

with Boccioni's "First Exhibition of Futurist Sculpture".

12 December—Futurist evening at the *Verdi* Theatre in Florence. The speakers are Marinetti, Soffici, Papini, Boccioni, Palazzeschi. The following, called Futurists *de passage*, join the Futurist movement: Rosai, Funi, Sironi.

A. Magnelli, who often visited the *Lacerba* group in Florence (Boccioni, Carrà, Soffici, Papini, Palazzeschi, Marinetti), moves to Paris and has a studio in the *Grande Chaumière*.

1914

Milan—Boccioni publishes "Futurist Painting and Sculpture" in the Futurist series, *Poesia*.

Rome—The Second Secessionist Exhibition shows works by Gino Rossi, Martini, Morandi; and among non-Italians Matisse (30), Cézanne (13).

Rome, February–March—Boccioni, Balla, Carrà, Russolo, Severini and Soffici exhibit 18 works at the *Galleria Futurista*. Among Boccioni's new paintings: *Dinamismo di un Cilindro* (Dynamism of a Cylinder), *Testa+ Luce + Ambiente* (Head + Light + Surroundings), *Costruzione Spiralica* (Spiral Construction), *Dinamismo di un Corpo Umano* (Dynamism of a Human Body), *Cavallo + Case + Cavaliere* (Horse + Houses + Horseman).

Florence, April—Monograph by Roberto Longhi entitled *Futurist Sculpture—Boccioni* published by *Libreria della Voce*.

Boccioni summons Sironi to Milan to help Marinetti in organizing the Futurist movement.

Paris—Picasso paints a *papier collé* called *Lacerba* as a gesture of friendship for the group of painters and writers gathered round the Florentine review.

Florence, April—Boccioni exhibits 10 works in sculpture and 46 drawings at the *Gonelli* Gallery; at the *Lacerba* exhibition he shows the first Italian abstract picture *Dimensioni Astratte* (Abstract Dimensions).

Rome—*Probitas*, offsetting Roman Secessionism, arranges an exhibition with works by Sartorio, De Carolis, Dell'Oca Bianca, Ferrazzi, Gaudenzi.

Florence—Rosai, introduced by Soffici, writes for *Lacerba* in Florentine and paints Futurist paintings.

Rome, April–May—International exhibition of free Futurist art by painters and sculptors at the *Galleria Futurista* organized by G. Sprovieri. Works by Bacchelli, U. Giannattasio, Balla, A. Martini, Morandi, E. Prampolini, O. Rosai, G. Rossi, M. Sironi, Zanini; and by Belgian, North-American and Russian artists including Archipenko.

Achille Funi and Sant'Elia found a para-Futurist movement called *Nuove Tendenze* (New Tendencies).

Florence—First International Exhibition of Black and White with works, among others, by Redon, Munch, Nolde, Daumier, Utamaro, belonging to the Richter Collection in Dresden. The following year this exhibition is held in Rome.

From an announcement in *Lacerba* (1 June;

No. 11): "*Libreria della Voce* has published volumes of reproductions of the works of Cézanne, Douanier Rousseau and Picasso; a volume dedicated to Degas is in active preparation."

London, 15 June—At the *Coliseum* a concert of *rumoristi* and an exhibition of Severini, Carrà, Soffici, Russolo and Balla.

Eleventh International Exhibition in Venice—retrospective exhibition of works by G. De Nittis. One-man shows of Zandomeneghi, Tito and Sartorio. A room is devoted to Italian Divisionists.

1915

Carrà writes on Giotto in *La Voce*: "We must go back to Giotto . . ."

Prampolini, having left the Rome Academy of Fine Arts, publishes his first manifesto "Absolute Construction of *Motorumore*".

Paris—Severini exhibits at the *Boutet* Gallery.

Rome—At the Third Secessionist Exhibition, one-man show of Casorati.

Publication of Carrà's *Guerra-Pittura*.

Magnelli, while in Paris, meets Picasso, Léger, Apollinaire, Juan Gris, Max Jacob, Archipenko, Kahnweiler. He does his first abstract compositions.

De Chirico, towards the end of the year, joins up as a soldier at Ferrara, where he stays until the winter of 1918-19. Carrà will arrive at Ferrara in January 1917.

Florence, 22 May—Last number of *Lacerba* (No. 31).

Florence—*Pittura Pura* by Kandinsky, published by *La Voce*.

1916

Boccioni's essay on Sironi as draughtsman.

Carrà leaves the Futurist movement, explaining his reasons in a letter: "My new trend was towards a necessary balance between art and tradition, between nature and art, a balance that would have been denied by Futurism."

Rome—First one-man show of Depero.

Carrà publishes in *La Voce* "Paolo Uccello, Constructor". He also publishes a monograph on Boccioni limited to 500 copies.

Boccioni falls from his horse and dies at Verona, aged thirty-three. Death of Sant'Elia on the Italian Front.

1917

Severini exhibits at the *Stieglitz* Gallery in New York.

Ferrara—Carrà arrives in January; meets De Chirico and De Pisis. The new Metaphysical painting takes shape. The first tailor's dummy, *La Solitudine* (Solitude), by Carrà.

Milan—Futurist exhibition at the *Cova*.

1918

Morandi launches his Metaphysical period with a series of *Still Lifes*.

Rome, 15 November—First number of *Valori Plastici*, an art review edited by M. Broglio. Chief contributors: Carrà, Morandi, De Chirico, Savinio, Cecchi, Melli, Bacchelli, Soffici, Zorn, Picasso, Braque, Archipenko. Casorati settles in Turin.

Giacomo Balla exhibits the abstract picture *Forme e Pensiero* (Forms and Thought) at the *Via Condotti* Gallery in Rome.

1919

Venice—Exhibition at *Ca' Pesaro* opened for the first time since the war. Works by Semeghini, Sibellato, Casorati, G. Rossi. This exhibition includes works by artists refused by the Biennale. Campigli, having originally gone to Paris as a journalist, stays there and devotes himself entirely to painting.

Rome—The monthly literary review, *La Ronda*, is started by the writers R. Bacchelli, A. Baldini, B. Barilli, V. Cardarelli, E. Cecchi, L. Montano, A. E. Saffi. Contributors among painters include A. Spadini and Carrà.

Carrà writes articles for *Valori Plastici*, becomes a critic for *Popolo d'Italia*, and publishes the book *La Pittura Metafisica*.

Exhibition of the *Valori Plastici* group at Hanover, Dresden and Munich.

1920

Modigliani dies in Paris.

At the Twelfth Venice Biennale non-Italian exhibitors include: Archipenko, Hobler, Van Gogh (9 canvases), Cézanne (28 paintings), Signac, Seurat.

Soffici takes a stand against "French-ism" in Italian art in favour of closer contact with local tradition.

Piero Marussig takes up residence in Milan.

Venice, 15 July—At the *Geri-Boralevi* Gallery an exhibition of the artists in disagreement with *Ca' Pesaro*: E. Notte, G. Rossi, L. Scopinich, Semeghini, Sibellato, Funi, G. Trentini, T. Wolf-Ferrari, Casorati, Cusin.

1921

Rome—At the Biennale works shown by Boccioni and Semeghini.

Paris—Severini, in a book called *Du Cubisme au Classicisme* (published by Povolozkj), explains his technical and aesthetic search after a return to the Italian Classical spirit.

Rome—De Pisis, resident in Rome since 1920, visits the Futurist painters of the second generation, Prampolini and Dottori, and re-establishes contact with De Chirico.

Carrà writes a monograph on André Derain published by *Valori Plastici*. He paints *L'Amante dell'Ingegnere* (The Engineer's Mistress) which could be called the last painting of his Metaphysical period. In the same year he paints *Pino sul Mare* (Pine Tree by the Sea).

Marinetti gives a lecture at the *Oeuvre* Theatre in Paris on "Tactile-ism"—stemming from some of the Futurist premises.

1922

Milan, September—Formation of the first group which was later to become the *Novecento Italiano*—consisting of seven painters: Anselmo Bucci, Leonardo Dudreville, Achille Funi, Emilio Malerba, Piero Marussig, Ubaldo Oppi, Mario Sironi.

Florence—Morandi exhibits at the *Primaverile Fiorentina* with the *Valori Plastici* group, introduced in the catalogue by De Chirico.

Paris—Licini exhibits regularly during his residence in Paris up till 1925 at the *Salon d'Automne* and the *Salon des Indépendants*.

Milan—Sironi collaborates as designer, clicker and, later, as art critic on the daily paper *Il Popolo d'Italia*. He also works on *Rivista Illustrata del Popolo d'Italia* and on the review *Natura*.

Prampolini, theorist of the second Futurist generation, writes a series of manifestoes among which the most noteworthy are: *Absolute Painting* (1922) which attacks Kandinsky's *Pure Painting*, *The Aesthetics of the Machine and Mechanical Introspection* (1922), *Mechanical Art* (1923), *Spiritual Architecture* (1924).

Venice—At the Thirteenth Biennale among the non-Italians: M. Denis, E. Bernard, P. Bonnard, Lieberman, Slevogt, Kokoschka (15 works), Ensor. Pica presents 12 paintings by Modigliani and, in an adjoining room, some examples of Negro art. Carrà exhibits 2 works.

1923

Gino Rossi, not yet forty, stops painting because of illness.

26 March—At the *Pesaro* Gallery in Milan, first exhibition of the seven *Novecento* painters.

Rome—At the Second Rome Biennale there are 70 works in sculpture by Degas. Other exhibitors include: Picasso, Léger, Laurens, Zadkine, Metzinger, Hofer, Kokoschka, Marc, Macke, Matisse, Pechstein, Gromaire, Permeke; Mancini, Dottori, De Chirico, Ferrazzi.

Venice, April—Thirteenth exhibition at *Ca' Pesaro*. Exhibitors include Semeghini and Saetti.

Rome—Giacomo Balla paints *Bal Tic Tac*, a vast abstract picture, now destroyed.

1924

Venice—At the Fourteenth Biennale the *Novecento* group exhibits, introduced in the catalogue by Margherita Sarfatti. The group is joined by Salietti, Tosi and Wildt, and all together form the organizing committee of the *Novecento Italiano*. Retrospective exhibition of Armando Spadini.

First publication of the fortnightly review, *Il Selvaggio*, edited by Mino Maccari.

Rome, October—In the green room of the National Theatre, the first one-man show of De Pisis.

Severini writes an article on Manet for *Valori Plastici*; Carrà writes on Fontanesi and Ranzoni.

1925

Paris—Prampolini prepares for the *Madeleine* Theatre décor for the *Pantomima Futurista*.

Zürich—Casorati and Oppi show works at the International Exhibition. Among those invited to exhibit were Matisse, Picasso, Utrillo.

Rome—At the Third Biennale: Carrà, with a one-man show introduced by Giuseppe Raimondi, De Chirico, De Grada, Funi, Sironi. Two Futurist rooms: Balla, Dottori, Depero. Among the non-Italians: Corot (28 paintings), Klimt, Stuck.

Venice—At Ca' Pesaro, an exhibition of Casorati and Gino Rossi.

Paris—First Surrealist Exhibition at the *Pierre* Gallery, with Arp, De Chirico, Max Ernst, Klee, Man Ray, Masson, Miro, Picasso, Pierre Roy.

1926

15 February—In the *Permanente* in Milan is held the first full-scale "Exhibition of the Italian *Novecento*" with 114 painters and sculptors participating. Among others: Medardo Rosso, De Chirico, Carrà, Morandi, Campigli, Martini, Licini, Guidi, Severini, E. Morelli, De Pisis, Casorati and the Futurists.

De Pisis, resident in Paris since March 1925, holds his first exhibition in Paris, introduced by De Chirico.

At the Fifteenth Venice Biennale: one-man shows by Carena and Soffici. In the Futurist room exhibitors include: Balla, Boccioni, Depero, Dottori, Prampolini, Russolo, Tato. Among the non-Italians: Bonnard (1), Degas (4), Denis (2), Derain (6), Dufy (2), Marquet (14), Matisse (1), Signac (6), Utrillo (9), Vlaminck (7), Vuillard (1), Permeke (17), Van Gogh (5), Böcklin (10), Giacometti (3), Otto Dix (1), Kokoschka (2). Black and white: Bonnard, Degas and 12 lithographs by Matisse.

Paris—Italian painters of the *Novecento* at the *Carminati* Gallery.

1927

Rome—Scipione exhibits at the *Bragaglia* Gallery.

Florence, February—Exhibition of the *Selvaggio* group.

In Hamburg and Amsterdam, exhibition of *Novecento Italiano*.

At Geneva and Zürich, exhibition of Italian works by Menzio, Campigli, Marussig, Modigliani, Ferrazzi, Funi, Carrà, Tosi.

The collected written works of Boccioni published in Foligno under the auspices of Marinetti.

1928

Rome—At the *Circolo*, exhibition of Scipione, Mafai, Ceracchini, Di Cocco.

Paris—First one-man show of Licini at the *Devambez* Gallery.

Paris—At the *Salon de l'Escalier* in the *Champs Elysées* Theatre, collective exhibition of a group of Italian artists living in Paris: Campigli, Severini, De Pisis, Menzio.

Venice—At the Sixteenth Biennale: two rooms for Matisse and Gauguin; one room dedicated to Sironi and the young Lombard painters—Ghiringhelli, Reggiani, De Rocchi, Lilloni, Carpanetti, Del Bon, Borra, Bogliardi. Among the foreigners: the Paris school.

1929

Turin, 12 January—The group of the "Six" Painters of Turin, sponsored by Edoardo Persico, exhibit in a room of the *Casa d'Arte Guglielm,i* in Piazza Castello 25. The six painters are: Jessie Boswell, Gigi Chessa, Nicola Galante, Carlo Levi, Francesco Menzio and Enrico Paulucci. Of the 53 works shown, about half find immediate purchasers.

Milan—One-man show of Carrà at the *Bardi* Gallery.

Genoa, April—Exhibition of the "Six" Painters of Turin at the *Circolo della Stampa*.

Milan—Magnelli exhibits at the Pesaro Gallery.

Turin, July—The "Six" exhibit 45 new pictures.

Nice—Exhibition of the *Novecento Italiano*.

Florence—The *Selvaggio* group exhibits, with Soffici, Rosai, Lega, and a group of independents including Ghiglia and Magnelli.

22 September—Manifesto of Futurist "Aero-painting" signed by Balla, Benedetta, Depero, Dottori, Fillia, Prampolini, Somenzi, Tato.

Milan—Second exhibition of the *Novecento Italiano* at the *Permanente*. Exhibitors include: Borra, Carrà, Tosi, Sironi, Vellani-Marchi, Campigli, Marussig, Rosai, Funi.

Milan, November—At the *Bardi* Gallery exhibition of the "Six", organized by Persico.

Edoardo Persico moved from Turin to Milan. One-man show of Pirandello at the *Vildrac* Gallery in Paris and the *Bukum* in Vienna.

Milan—With the full-scale exhibition at the *Pesaro* Gallery, Futurism is moving in the direction of Abstraction, especially Prampolini with his *Immagini Astratte* (Abstract Images), Marasco with *Equivalenze Geometriche* (Geometrical Equivalences), Munari and Fillia.

Paris—Campigli gives his first one-man show at the *Jeanne Bucher* Gallery.

1930

Turin, January—The "Six" exhibit again in Piazza Castello.

Milan, 25 January—Publication of *Omaggio a Modigliani*, edited by G. Sheiwiller.

Rome—At the *Arte Moderna* Gallery an exhibition of Gola's work, and *Poligono* devotes its September number to Gola in honour of the event.

Persico joins the editorial board of *Casabella*.

Paris—First International Exhibition of Abstract Art—*Galerie 23*.

Milan—At the *Bardi* Gallery one-man shows of Carrà and Soffici.

Rome—First exhibition of Japanese art.

Venice—At the Seventeenth Biennale, a room devoted to Modigliani (38 paintings, 20 drawings, 2 sculptures) sponsored by Lionello Venturi. Among other exhibitors: Morandi,

Carrà, Sironi, Birolli, Capogrossi, Scipione (*Cardinale Decano*), Mucchi, and the "Six" of Turin. Room of Italian Futurists. Room *Appels d'Italie*: Berard, E. Berman, Campigli, De Pisis, R. Paresce, Savinio, Severini, Survage, Tozzi.

Milan—The opening of the *Milione* Gallery with an exhibition of Rosai.

Milan, October—At the *Pesaro* Gallery a Futurist exhibition: Fillia, Prampolini, Oriani, Rosso, Pozzo, Sant'Elia, Munari.

Rome, November—Exhibition organized by P. M. Bardi at the *Roma* Gallery, via Veneto: Scipione and Mafai. People are beginning to talk about "The Roman School".

London, November—at the *Bloomsbury* Gallery an exhibition of: Levi, Menzio and Paulucci sponsored by Lionello Venturi.

Cesare Breveglieri wins a scholarship that enables him to go to Paris.

Milan—Carrà becomes art critic for *L'Ambrosiano*.

1931

Rome, January—Exhibition at the *Roma* Gallery: Levi, Menzio, Paulucci.

Milan, 5 January—At the *Milione* Gallery first exhibition of the works of Atanasio Soltati and Spazzapan.

Rome—At the *Palazzo delle Esposizioni*, First National Quadriennale of Art. Exhibitors include Tosi, Carena, Soffici, Carrà, Bartoli, Ferrazzi, Socrate, Casorati, Romanelli, Magnelli, Guttuso, Guidi, Funi, Semeghini, Mafai; the Futurists Balla, Benedetta, Dottori, Munari, Oriani, Tato, Fillia, Prampolini, Depero, Sant'Elia. Arturo Tosi received the first prize of the First Roman Quadriennale. Rooms dedicated to Medardo Rosso and Spadini.

Rome, February—First exhibition of "Aero-painting" in a palace in the Piazza di Spagna. Exhibitors: Balla, Prampolini, Dottori, Tato.

Milan—At the *Pesaro* Gallery, second exhibition of "Aero-painting": Fillia, Oriani, Prampolini, Tato.

Exhibition of *Novecento Italiano* at Buenos Aires and Montevideo.

Magnelli settles in Paris.

Paris, December—Chessa, Menzio, Levi and Paulucci exhibit 21 pictures at the *Jeune Europe* Gallery; Spazzapan shows drawings. Sponsored by Lionello Venturi.

1932

Paris, March—Exhibition of "Aero-painting" at the *Renaissance* Gallery.

The Museum of Modern Art in Moscow gives a special exhibition of all the Italian paintings in its possession, comprising paintings, drawings, aquatints, lithographs etc. by Segantini, Modigliani, Tosi, Salietti, Monti, Lega, Severini, Carrà, De Rocchi, De Chirico, Campigli, Funi, Guidi, Tozzi, Ferrazzi, Carena, Casorati, Rosai, Morandi and Galante.

Milan—the *Milione* launches its series of fortnightly bulletins which contribute to the establishment of the new art.

Zürich—Massimo Campigli exhibits with a group of artists of different nationalities in an exhibition entitled *Peintres Parisiens*.

Venice—At the Eighteenth Biennale foreign exhibitors include: Kokoschka, Derain; Retrospective exhibition of Monet. Exhibition of Italians living in Paris: De Chirico, De Pisis, Severini, Campigli, Fini, Garbari.

1933

November—Death of Gino Bonichi, known as Scipione.

Antwerp—Exhibition of contemporary Italian art.

Milan—At the *Milione*, exhibition of *Nuova Pittura Romana*: Cagli, Capogrossi, Cavalli.

Milan—Retrospective exhibition of Boccioni at the *Castello Sforzesco* to celebrate the fiftieth anniversary of his birth (organized by Prampolini).

Milan—First publication of the monthly review *Quadrante*, edited by M. Bontempelli and P. M. Bardi.

Milan—Fifth Triennale: a mural by Carrà, *Italia Romana* (Roman Italy), and decorations by A. Martini, *Mosè salvato dalle Acque* (Moses rescued from the Water). *Novecento* exhibition.

Milan—Renato Paresce, having lived in Paris since 1913, returns to Italy and gives a comprehensive exhibition of his last three years' work at the *Milione*.

Milan—First exhibition of abstract art in Italy at the *Milione*: one-man show of Atanasio Soldati (20 paintings in oils, 20 in tempera and 20 drawings).

Florence—Soldati, Ghiringhelli and Bogliardi send abstract paintings to the First International Exhibition.

Treviso—Retrospective exhibition of Gino Rossi at the *Palazzo Scotti*.

Milan, December—Exhibition at the *Milione* of Pietro Feroldi's collection of modern art.

Milan, December—"Manifesto of Mural Painting" by Sironi, Funi, Campigli, Carrà.

1934

Benedetto Croce publishes *La Critica e la Storia delle Arti Figurative. Questioni di Metodo* (Bari, Laterza).

Milan, 24 April—First one-man show of Kandinsky in Italy (45 watercolours and 30 drawings) and of Vordemberge-Gildewart at the *Milione*.

Venice—Nineteenth Biennale: International exhibition of nineteenth-century portrait painting. Other exhibitors include: Lilloni, Breveglieri, Capogrossi, Menzio, Campigli, De Pisis, Santomaso, Maccari. Retrospective exhibition of Manet.

Milan—Cantatore exhibits a group of drawings, mostly done in Paris two years before, at the *Milione*.

Bogliardi, Ghiringhelli, Reggiani and Soldati send Abstract works to the Exhibition of Contemporary Art at Geneva and Lausanne.

Milan—Exhibition of abstract art at the *Milione* with Bogliardi, Ghiringhelli, Reggiani who are signatories of the first manifesto of Italian Abstract Art. In the same gallery Luigi Veronesi exhibited with Joseph Albers.

1935

Paris—Magnelli returns definitively to abstract painting.

Rome—At the Second Quadriennale Room IX is officially dedicated to Italian Abstraction: Bogliardi, Ghiringhelli, Reggiani, Alberto Magnelli, Osvaldo Licini, Soldati, De Amicis. Other exhibitors include Scipione, Severini and Marino Marini. Rooms devoted to Mafai and Pirandello.

Milan—At the *Milione*, first one-man show in Italy of Osvaldo Licini.

Turin, March—First collective exhibition of Italian abstract art in the studio of Casorati and Paulucci: Bogliardi, De Amicis, D'Errico, Fontana, Ghiringhelli, Licini, Melotti, Reggiani, Soldati, Veronesi.

Milione publications produce the first Italian theoretical work on Abstraction called *Kn* by Carlo Belli.

1936

January—Death of Edoardo Persico.

Rome—one-man show of Soldati at the *Bragaglia* Gallery.

Birolli arrives in Paris.

Como—At the Exhibition of Modern Italian Art, exhibitors, other than the *Milione* group, include abstract painters: Mario Radice, Manlio Rho, Carla Badiali.

Venice—At the Twentieth Biennale, a selected exhibition of Degas. One-man shows of Severini, Casorati, Ferrazzi, Carrà. Retrospective exhibition of Gigi Chessa, one of the "Six" of Turin. Futurist section arranged by Marinetti, and a posthumous exhibition of Fillia.

Buenos Aires—The *Milione* and Como groups all send works to the First Exhibition of Abstract Art at the *Moody* Gallery.

Casablanca—The *Milione* group takes part in a Black and White Exhibition.

1937

Milan—Sixth Triennale: for which Munari does a large Abstract mosaic.

The Society of Independent Painters of Amsterdam organizes a large-scale exhibition in the Municipal Museum. Italian artists invited: Carra, Marussig, Tosi, Funi, Severini, Casorati, Prampolini, Sironi, Mario Tozzi, Carena, Oppo, Ferrazzi, Salietti, Vagnetti, G. Montanari, Tato, Dottori, Ambrosi and Benedetta Marinetti.

Following the example of Hitler's war against the Jews and "degenerate art", the periodical *Quadrivio* starts similar campaigns in Italy. In the December number G. Sottochiesa publishes an article called "Under the mask of Israel".

Paris—In the Spanish Pavilion of the Universal Exhibition Picasso shows *Guernica*.

1938

Milan—At the *Milione*, works of Magnelli and other representative Abstract and Surrealist painters: Arp, Domela, Kandinsky, Seligmann, Taeuber, Verzelay.

Publication of *Valori Primordiali* edited by Franco Ciliberti.

Milan, January—First appearance of *Vita Giovanile*, review of literature, politics and the arts which later becomes *Corrente di Vita Giovanile*. Founded by E. Treccani.

Venice—Twenty-first Biennale: Retrospective exhibition of Renoir. International exhibition of nineteenth-century landscape painting. Retrospective exhibition of Piero Marussig, who died in 1937. "Aero-painting" of Africa and Spain.

December—At the *Milione* the first one-man show of Cesare Breveglieri who gives the Milanese public the fruits of ten years' work.

1939

Rome—Third Quadriennale at the *Palazzo delle Esposizioni*. Rooms dedicated to Pirandello, Salietti, Bernasconi, Biagini, Gentilini, Semeghini, E. Gordigiani, Casciaro, Funi, Saetti, Giarrizzo, Ferrazzi, Capogrossi, Morandi.

Milan, March—At the *Permanente*, first exhibition of contemporary art organized by *Corrente* and confined to painters of the Milanese region: Manzù, Tosi, De Grada, A. Martini, P. Marussig, F. Messina, Mucchi, C. Monti, Cantatore, Tomea, Genni, Birolli, Bernasconi, Valenti, Badodi, Panciera, Migneco, F. Tallone, Cherchi, Lanaro, L. Bartolini, Cassinari, G. Mantica, L. Grosso.

Paris, April—Exhibition of Santomaso at the *Rive Gauche* Gallery.

Milan, December—At the *P. Grande* Gallery, second exhibition of contemporary art organized by *Corrente*, this time national in character: Brogini, Franchina, F. Tallone, Filippini, P. Martina, Prampolini, M. Reggiani, Santomaso, Cassinari, Fazzini, Guttoso, Tamburi, Mafai, Mirko, Afro, D. Caputo, Manzù, L. Montenari, F. Pirandello, Genni, Cantatore, Mucchi, Tomea, Cherchi, Salvadori, L. Fontana, Panciera, Badodi, Birolli, Migneco, Valenti.

This is the period in which the reactionary tendencies in painting are rewarded by the Cremona Prize, and the newer and more open tendencies by the Bergamo Prize.

1940

Publication of the Italian translation of Kandinsky's *Concerning Spirituality in Art*.

Milan—At the *Milione*, one-man show of Severini with 40 works.

Venice—At the Twenty-second Biennale, rooms dedicated to Carena, Tosi, Carrà, Romagnoli; one-man show of O. Tamburi; in the Futurist room, one-man show of T. Crali.

Milan—In June the review *Corrente* is suppressed, but *Corrente* publications about literature, criticism and art make a good start with booklets on Fontana, Birolli, Guttuso, Manzù and others.

Milan—In via Spiga the *Bottega di Corrente* is opened where exhibitions will be held of Birolli, Migneco, Cassinari, Badodi, Sassu and Valenti.

Up till 1945, while Italy is at war, there is little artistic activity worthy of note.

1941

Milan—At the *Brera*—retrospective exhibition of Scipione.

Milan—At the *Milione*, exhibition of V. Guidi with 40 paintings and 20 drawings and watercolours from 1921 to 1941.

Zürich, November—Exhibition of Italian art at the *Kunsthaus*: rooms dedicated to Carena, Carrà, Oppo.

1942

Cesare Brandi's study of Morandi is published.

Milan—Recapitulatory exhibition of Carrà, covering the years 1912 to 1941.

Bergamo, September—At the *Palazzo della Ragione*: the exhibition for the Fourth Bergamo Prize. Guttuso exhibits his *Crucifixion*. The first prize goes to Menzio for *Famiglia in Campagna* (Family in the Country).

Venice—Twenty-third Biennale—in a minor key because of the war. Rooms devoted to one-man shows: L. Bartolini, Casorati, De Chirico, De Pisis, U. Bernasconi, Frisia, Salietti, De Grada, Cadorin, E. Notte.

1943

Milan—Sironi takes up easel-painting again and the next year exhibits at the *Milione*.

Milan—At the *Spiga e Corrente* Gallery: Cassinari, Morlotti, Treccani. Drawings by Vedova.

1944

Rome—At National Gallery of Modern Art, exhibition of contemporary art, arranged by Palma Bucarelli.

From events that took place on the plains of Lombardy and in the bombing of Milan and Vicenza, Birolli finds material for his series of 86 drawings, at present in the Achille Cavellini Collection in Brescia. Entitled *Italia, 1944* they were published in 1952 (Giani, *Conchiglia* series).

1945

The manifesto "Beyond Guernica," signed by Ajmone, Bergolli, Morlotti, Paganin and others, is an indication of new European tendencies in the immediate post-war period.

1946

News of European tendencies in art pour into Italy, especially from Paris. Return of Lionello Venturi. Exhibition of "French Painting Today". Coloured reproductions of painters, from Manet to Picasso, circulate in Italy.

Milan—Exhibition of Modigliani, with catalogue edited by Lamberto Vitali.

October—Manifesto of the movement first known as "New Italian Artistic Secession" and afterwards as "New Artistic Front". With Birolli as instigator, the idea is taken up by Santomaso, Pizzinato and Vedova, is discussed in Rome and Milan, and takes concrete form in Venice. The participators are: Morlotti, Turcato, Vedova, Viani. Signatories to the manifesto: Birolli, Cassinari, Guttuso, Morlotti, Pizzinato, Santomaso, Vedova and the sculptors Leoncillo and Viani.

Birolli is in Brittany and Paris 1946-49.

Argan's essay on "Italian Painting and European Culture" is published in *Prosa*.

Milan—At the *15 Borgo Nuovo* Gallery, Meloni's one-man show draws the attention of the critics.

Rio San Paolo, Brazil—Exhibition of contemporary Italian art.

London, June—At the *Redfern* Gallery, exhibition of contemporary Italian painting. Preface of the catalogue written by Lionello Venturi.

1947

Milan, June—G. Marchiori presents the first exhibition of the "New Artistic Front" at the *Spiga* Gallery in which Corpora and Turcati, Fazzini and Franchina also exhibit. Cassinari withdraws his support.

Paris—Monograph on Magnelli with a preface by Jean Arp published on the occasion of his exhibition at the *Drouin* Gallery.

New York—Exhibition of "Twentieth-century Italian Art".

Milan—Vast international exhibition at the *Palazzo Reale* of "Abstract and Concrete Art" organized by the Swiss, Bill and Huber, and by the architect Bombelli. Among the Italians: Licini, Munari, Rho, Veronesi and other abstract painters of the post-war period.

Rome—Publication of the manifesto "Forma" against the 900 and neo-Cubism, signed by Consagra, Dorazio, Guerrini, Perilli, and Sanfilippo.

In the review *Domus* (No. 217), essay by Gillo Dorfles on Abstract and Concrete art.

First Exhibition of Abstract Art in Rome with works by Consagra, Dorazio, Guerrini, Sanfilippo and Turcato.

Brescia—Achille Cavellini starts systematically collecting the works of the new Italian and French painters: Birolli—on a large scale— Guttuso in his Cubist period, Santomaso, Cassinari, Vedova, Morlotti, Afro, Corpora, Moreni, Soldati, Turcato; Pignon, Estève, Gischia, Hartung, Manessier, Singier, Le Moal, Bazaine, Lapique, Lapoujade and others.

1948

Rome—At the Quadriennale, a historic exhibition of Futurism is organized.

Death of Cesare Breveglieri.

Venice, Twenty-fourth Biennale—New Secretary-General: Rodolfo Pallucchini. Rooms dedicated to "Three Italian Painters from 1910 to 1920": Carrà, De Chirico, Morandi. Exhibition of "New Artistic Front" presented by Marchiori: Turcato, Santomaso, Corpora, Pizzinato, Guttuso, Vedova, Birolli, Morlotti. One-man show of Picasso, retrospective show of Klee, and some Impressionists. One-man shows of Braque, Rouault, Chagall. Retrospective exhibition of Turner. Exhibition of Peggy Guggenheim's Collection. Retrospective exhibitions of G. Rossi, Breveglieri, Scipione, Badodi.

Soldati, with Dorfles, Monnet and Munari, founds the *MAC* (Movement of Concrete Art).

New York—Catherine Viviano begins to organize in her gallery exhibitions of Italian painters favouring the "abstract-concrete" idiom. The exhibitions go on tour through various cities of the United States. Some years later, marked success of Afro.

1949

New York—Exhibition of twentieth-century painting at the Museum of Modern Art at which the first Futurist period is represented.

Salzburg—Exhibition of Roman painters at the *Gurlitt* Gallery.

The Milanese group of abstract painters takes the name "Concrete Art" for its activities—a term already used by Kandinsky, Van Doesburg, Mondrian, Bill, and the Swiss and Argentine schools.

In the exhibition of "Concrete Art" at the *Libreria Salto* in Milan the following exhibit (among Italians): Veronesi, Mazzon, Garau, Berti, Brunetti, Monnini, Nativi, Munari, Dorfles, Monnet, Fontana, Dal Monte, Bordone.

Milan—At the *Naviglio* Gallery Fontana's exhibition called "Spatial Surroundings".

The custom of awarding prizes for pictures grows, together with corresponding exhibitions of the entries. Among others: The *Gulf of La Spezia* National Prize for Painting, the Suzzara Prize and the Fiorino Prize. Other prizes are awarded at Messina, Alessandria, Rome, Cortina, Taranto, Bari, Lissone, Naples, Sestri, Acitrezza, Monza and Desio.

1950

Leicester, August—Art Gallery: contemporary Italian exhibition.

Antibes, August: Grimaldi Museum: exhibition of Bruno Cassinari.

Lugano—International Exhibition of Black and White. Among the Italians awarded prizes: G. Morandi and L. Bartolini.

Bergamo, September—*Palazzo della Ragione*: International Exhibition of Drawing, organized by Nino Zucchelli. Foreign exhibitors include:

Picasso, Matisse, Derain, Dufy, Estève, Braque, Rouault, Grosz, Kokoschka, Chagall. Italians include: Morandi, Carrà, Campigli, Casorati, Soffici, Semeghini, Maccari, Guttuso, Birolli and others.

Paris, May—On the initiative of the "Friends of the Brera", Italian exhibition at the Museum of Modern Art: rooms dedicated to Modigliani, De Pisis, Casorati, Rosai, Tosi. The exhibition is taken to London and Zürich.

Boston, September—In the Institute of Contemporary Art, exhibition of Italian painting.

Zürich—At the *Kunsthaus*, exhibition of "Futurist and Metaphysical Painting": works by Balla, Baldessari, Boccioni, Carrà, Chiattone, Depero, Dottori, Funi, Giannattasio, Marasco, Prampolini, Rosai, Russolo, Sant'Elia, Severini, De Chirico, Morandi, Sironi, Soffici and Tato.

Paris—*Cahiers d'Art* devotes a whole number to Italian painting from 1900 to the present day, "Half a Century of Italian Art".

Venice—Twenty-fifth Biennale of Art: exhibition of the Fauves. Drawings by Seurat. Four masters of Cubism: Braque, Gris, Picasso and Léger. Painters of the Blaue Reiter movement and signatories to the first Futurist manifesto. One-man shows of Carrà, Bozzetti, Broglio, Lorenzo Viani, Semeghini, Severini, Magnelli. Other exhibitors: Villon, Bonnard, Matisse, Utrillo, Smith. Mexican Pavilion: Orozco, Rivera, Siquieros, Tamayo.

Florence, June—At the *Fiore*, exhibition of Archipenko, Boccioni, Chagall, De Chirico, Kandinsky, Klee, Picasso and Severini.

London, June—*Tate* Gallery: exhibition of "Contemporary Italian Art".

San Francisco, California, July—In the Palace of the Legion of Honour, exhibition of "Contemporary Italian Art".

Milan—Large-scale exhibition of Matisse at the *Arte Moderna* Gallery. Works from 1896 to the present day.

Venice—Publication of the first number of *La Biennale di Venezia*, a quarterly review.

1951

Munich, Mannheim, Hamburg, Bremen, Berlin—"Italianische Kunst der Gegenwart": illustrated catalogue with introduction by Ragghianti, Haftmann, Verner.

Palm Beach, U.S.A.—Exhibition of "Futurism and Later Italian Art" at the Society of the 4 Arts.

Paris—Exhibition of "Fifty Italian Painters of Today", promoted by the Centre of Italian Art at the *La Boétie* Gallery.

Milan, April–May—At the *Arte Moderna* Gallery, retrospective exhibition of A. Tosi to celebrate his eightieth year.

Ferrara—Large-scale exhibition of De Pisis in the *Castello Estense*, later transferred to the *Arte Moderna* Gallery, Milan.

Turin, October—First exhibition of "Painters of Today: France, Italy", exhibition of French and Italian painters.

São Paolo, Brazil, October–December—First Biennale of the Museum of Modern Art. Among contemporary Italian painters: Carrà, Morandi, Magnelli, Guidi, Campigli, De

Pisis, Spazzapan, L. Bartolini, Licini, Reggiani, Menzio, F. Pirandello, Paulucci, Cantatore, Birolli, Santomaso, Corpora, Gagli, Morlotti, Guttuso, Afro, Mandelli, P. Martina, Scialoja, Vedova, Moreni, Ajmone, Vacchi.

Rome, December—Sixth Quadriennale of Art. Among other things, retrospective exhibitions of Modigliani, Spadini, Viani, Martini, Gola, Gemito.

Cortina d'Ampezzo—Exhibition for the international prize, *Parigi*, won by Corpora and Music.

1952

Venice—Twenty-sixth Biennale of Art: rooms dedicated to Zandomeneghi, Corot, Soutine, Kokoschka, the Brücke group, Dufy, Léger, Flemish Expressionism, Permeke. Among the Italians, exhibitions of Casorati, Rosai, Marino Marini, Birolli, Cassinari, Guttuso, Saetti, Soldati.

Turin—Second exhibition of "Painters of Today: France, Italy".

Rome, June—L. Venturi publishes a book devoted to the *Eight Italian Painters*: Afro, Birolli, Corpora, Moreni, Morlotti, Santomaso, Turcato, Vedova.

Copenhagen, February—Exhibition of Arturo Tosi.

Vienna, February—At the Institute of Italian Culture, exhibition of "Concrete Art" presented by G. Dorfles. The exhibition goes later to Gratz and Salzburg.

Florence, May—At the *Arte Contemporanea* Gallery: "Joint exhibition of 4 Nuclearists: Crippa, Donati, Dova, Peverelli".

Milan, May—At the "Friends of France", first exhibition of the Nuclear movement: Baj, Colombo, Dangelo, Preda, Pascal, Holand, Tullier.

Florence, November—At the *Arte Contemporanea* Gallery: exhibition of Giacomo Balla presented by Prampolini.

1953

São Paolo, Brazil, December—Second Biennale, with a Futurist exhibition, as well as: Afro, Birolli, Clerici, Carnevali, Casorati, Cassinari, Fini, Geraldi, Maccari, Mafai, Manaresi, Morandi, Moreni, Morlotti, Paulucci, Rosai, Saetti, Santomaso, Sironi, Soldati, Spazzapan, Vedova and others.

Stockholm—Exhibition of contemporary Italian art.

Rome—*Palazzo delle Esposizioni*: "Art in the life of Southern Italy".

Zürich—At the *Kunsthaus*, exhibition of "Young Italian Painting". Works by: Afro, Birolli, Cagli, Cassinari, Corpora, Crippa, Dova, Guttuso, Moreni, Morlotti and others.

Rome, May—In eleven rooms of the *Arte Moderna* Gallery, large-scale "cyclic" exhibition of Picasso.

Milan, September—In the *Palazzo Reale*, a still larger version of the Picasso exhibition, including works from Russia and America, among them *Guernica*.

Florence—The Mattioli Collection on view in the *Palazzo Strozzi*.

1954

Rome—Exhibition of Scipione in the *Arte Moderna* Gallery: 50 paintings and 139 drawings. Catalogue arranged by Palma Bucarelli.

At the *Gemeentemuseum*'s, The Hague—From April to June, large-scale exhibition of Morandi, with catalogue arranged by Vitale Bloch.

Venice—Twenty-seventh Biennale of Art: exhibition of Klee; among Italian painters, rooms devoted to V. Guido, Savinio, Del Bon, Spazzapan, C. Levi, Santomaso, Prampolini, Melli, Paulucci, Dalla, Zorza, Capogrossi; retrospective show of Courbet; exhibition of Ernst, Mirò, Ben Nicholson, Munch, Ben Shahn. Belgium: Surrealism, Magritte. France: the Fauves (Derain, Matisse, Rouault, Vlaminck, Van Dongen), "Arte Fantastica", "Arte Astratta".

Milan and Rome increase their number of art galleries: the market is picking up.

Italo Valenti exhibits at Zürich and Basle.

1955

At the Biennale of San Paolo, Brazil, Magnelli wins first prize.

Antibes, August–September—Exhibition of paintings, collages and gouaches by Magnelli.

Rome, November—Seventh Quadriennale of Art: rooms devoted to an anthology of Italian painting and sculpture from 1910 to 1930. Works by: Balla, Boccioni, Carrà, Soffici, Rosai, Severini, De Chirico, Melli, Guidi, Tosi, Campigli, Casorati.

Pittsburgh, October–December—For the International Exhibition of Contemporary Painting at the Carnegie Institute, Afro is invited to sit on the hanging committee.

Milan, April—At the *Permanente*, recapitulatory exhibition of Bonnard.

Turin—At the exhibition of "Painters of Today: France, Italy" a vast retrospective show of Soldati.

1956

Rome—At the *Arte Moderna* Gallery: Recapitulatory exhibition of Gino Rossi, with catalogue arranged by Palma Bucarelli—112 paintings and 62 drawings.

In the first six months of the year: death of Arturo Tosi, Filippo de Pisis, Gianni Vagnetti, Enrico Prampolini.

Venice—Twenty-eighth Biennale of Art, retrospective exhibitions of Delacroix, Mondrian, Gris and Nolde. Among Italian painters: one-man shows of Afro, Cantatore, Carena, Cesetti, V. Ciardo, Corpora, De Chirico, A. Galvano, Mandelli, P. Martina, O. Martinelli, Meloni, Moreni, Morlotti, Pirandello, Reggiani, Tomea, Treccani, Vedova, Ziveri. Retrospective shows: Tosi, De Pisis, Vagnetti, A. Bucci. In the United States Pavilion: "American Painters and the City".

Publication of *Arte Spaziale*, with coloured reproductions (G. Giani).

Index